"Globalism and multiculturalism are growing steadily so it is really helpful to have some meaningful research results from this study of global cosmopolitans, the cohort who are exploring what it takes to manage multiple cultures as a life style not just as a tourist. This book explores through multiples cases the mindset and skill set of this group of people and illuminates, thereby, some of the important characteristics of being able to live in our interconnected world."

—Edgar H. Schein, *Professor Emeritus, MIT Sloan School and author of* Organizational Culture and Leadership, 5th Ed. *(2017)*

"Linda Brimm teaches us a new 'way of life' in this world of escalating complexity and change using 'stories.' Her stories are about the whole person and what it is like to be a person from a different culture, gender, religion, or personality type. Welcome to the modern-day global world of Jane Austen."

—Hirotaka Takeuchi, *Professor of Management Practice, Harvard Business School*

The Global Cosmopolitan Mindset

"At the heart of globalization are people rather than products or corporations. Globalization is changing how people behave, how they relate to each other, what they dream of and how they live and work. Linda Brimm is the foremost chronicler of the new global cosmopolitan reality which is shaping and re-creating the worlds of work and home. Her latest thinking provides a compelling and humane take on the new globalized world order."

—Stuart Crainer and Des Dearlove, *founders, Thinkers50*

"Linda Brimm has captured the essence of a new breed of Global Cosmopolitans that will provide key leadership in tomorrow's world. Many of her insights are drawn from her teaching and research at INSEAD which attracts these future leaders because of its global orientation and aspires to prepare them for effective and responsible leadership in tomorrow's organizations."

—Ilian Mihov, *INSEAD Dean and the Rausing Chaired Professor of Business and Economic Transformation*

"More and more people are living global lives, or aspire to do so. Based on a treasure trove of interviews with global cosmopolitans Linda Brimm's wonderful new book describes the challenges, identity dilemmas, and mindsets needed to work and thrive in this multinational and multicultural landscape."

—Herminia Ibarra, *The Charles Handy Professor of Organizational Behavior, London Business School*

"*The Global Cosmopolitan Mindset* provides a penetrating insight into the issues and dilemmas involved in the human side of global living and working. *The Global Cosmopolitan Mindset* by Linda Brimm is a must-read for leaders at all levels of society interested in leading a meaningful and successful global life."

—W. Chan Kim, *The BCG Professor of Strategy, INSEAD and* New York Times *bestselling author of* Blue Ocean Shift

"Linda Brimm's message spoke to thousands when, in her first book, she coined the now wildly popular term Global Cosmopolitans. Join her in her second book, *The Global Cosmopolitan Mindset*, for a fascinating journey into the skills necessary to succeed in today's multi-cultural world. If your mother is from Pakistan, your father from Peru and you've spent the last decades living in Abu Dhabi, Amsterdam, Anchorage and Amman this book is for you. While many have written about how to help people from different cultures collaborate, Linda explores what it means to have all those cultural differences right inside yourself."

—Erin Meyer, *Senior Affiliate Professor, INSEAD and author of* The Culture Map

Linda Brimm

The Global Cosmopolitan Mindset

Lessons from the New Global Leaders

palgrave
macmillan

Linda Brimm
INSEAD
Fontainebleau, France

ISBN 978-1-349-95344-8   ISBN 978-1-349-95345-5   (eBook)
https://doi.org/10.1057/978-1-349-95345-5

Library of Congress Control Number: 2017964572

Cover credit: hernza/iStock/Getty

Printed on acid-free paper

This Palgrave Macmillan imprint is published by Springer Nature
The registered company is Macmillan Publishers Ltd.
The registered company address is: The Campus, 4 Crinan Street, London, N1 9XW, United Kingdom

Preface

My journey continues...

I have been immersed in the world of Global Cosmopolitans of late. More specifically, I have been looking for a way to tell their story from the point of view of more seasoned travelers than I studied for my initial book on the subject, *Global Cosmopolitans: The Creative Edge of Difference*. The stories told by people with significant life and professional experience help us understand how they have developed their minds and their skills over time.

The Global Cosmopolitan Mindset: Lessons from the New Global Leaders gives the reader the opportunity to learn from anecdotes and stories shared by leaders of both organizations and change. By understanding how they have created their own career paths and built lives that they never could have imagined when they first started their journeys, many others can benefit.

Living globally sounds like some sort of peripatetic paradise. For some, it is. But it also raises many fundamental social and psychological issues. Where is home, if you were born in one country, live in another, and work worldwide? What is it like to spend your working life in one country and then return to where you grew up? What nationality should your children be? Does it matter?

These issues—the human side of global living—are the subjects of this book, which attempts to answer some increasingly relevant questions. What attitudes do people need to work successfully in an international landscape? What knowledge and skills do they acquire from the day-to-day reality of coming face-to-face with difference? How do they re-interpret their own values and traits? What is the nature of the challenges and opportunities they face as they develop on their global adventures?

The first part of the book presents the Global Cosmopolitan Mindset and Skillset. These two chapters introduce the lenses and some of the skills that Global Cosmopolitans use to navigate the challenges that they so often transform into personal and professional opportunities. Given their lifestyle and the nature of the challenges they face, they develop the very attitudes, knowledge, and skills that global leaders need.

The second part of the book gives the reader an opportunity to look in more depth at the nature of the challenges that they face as they compose their lives around the world. While these are similar to issues encountered by all human beings, including those who live local lives, there is no doubt that they are made more complex by global mobility.

The last part of the book gives the reader an opportunity to see how Global Cosmopolitans continue to compose chapters to their lives as they mature. There is no set pathway for people who live globally. While they understand the tension of finding a balance between being rooted and staying cosmopolitan, each new adventure is an opportunity to reflect on what gives meaning and value to their lives.

Every chapter could be a book on its own. I decided not to cover every possible subtopic, but to share stories that exemplified aspects of the issues, such as identity, that Global Cosmopolitans frequently raise. I have simply tried to give the reader a flavor of what people describe as relevant. Given that no two lives are ever the same, the stories do not provide formulas or solutions, but exemplify what people have a tendency to share.

The book should help the reader gain insight into how people develop lives over time, and how they benefit from their knowledge, attitudes, and skills. Whether you are considering starting a global move or wondering whether to continue your journey, their insights should be useful. If, on the other hand, you are trying to create or develop a global organization, this is the population that you need to learn from and work with. Global Cosmopolitans have been learning life skills and appropriate lessons that have contributed to their success. Their stories can also boost your success.

For global organizations looking for the most appropriate hire, I will not present a checklist of character traits that a person should have to work and lead across borders or cultures. Instead, I invite you to get to know this population and to understand what they have learned—and are continuing to learn—from their personal and professional experiences. The lessons from life are not universal, yet the potential for skills that can lead to success is always worth considering. While there are many ways to look at what it takes to be successful and many theories of leadership, this book turns the focus onto what can be learned from life and, in particular, a global life.

As I listened to Global Cosmopolitans and read the literature about learning and growth, it became clear to me that there was something magic about the combination of the need to learn—and to be flexible about what and how you learn—and the desire to understand the world from both a global and local point of view. These, together, are what I call the Global Cosmopolitan Mindset. It is the base upon which Global Cosmopolitans' learning about themselves and the world is built on. The little acts of creativity, which people often need to make such complicated lives work, complement the motivation to learn, to grow, and to develop global minds.

My own journey since I wrote *Global Cosmopolitans: The Creative Edge of Difference* has been filled with opportunities to learn about people living global lives, expanding my sample and expanding my ideas.

More and more people are living global lives. I meet them in my classroom—twenty- or thirty-somethings, possibly with parents from different cultures, who have already worked in two continents and speak multiple languages—and through my work with organizations and individuals. This is the new reality. Technology is also reshaping our world. With all of the questions currently raised about the impact of globalization, we now have an opportunity to address the inequities in our global village and to work toward more sustainable solutions.

At INSEAD, where I have been a Professor of Organizational Behavior, I have had the opportunity to work with and teach people from all over the world. Along with my own personal journey and a need for reflection, their stories were the basis of my desire to understand the impact of global living and globalization on the minds of people who are at the forefront of this experience. My work as a professor at INSEAD has given me the opportunity to travel and learn extensively throughout the world. For me, both teaching and writing are opportunities to learn, as well as to share what I have discovered along the way.

My work as a clinical psychologist in Paris has given me the opportunity to help people explore their inner worlds and great insight into how people put together their own very personal stories. Since many of my clients are living in Paris, but are not of French origin, they have contributed to my understanding of how the minds of Global Cosmopolitans work.

At the same time as I am learning about the lives of seasoned Global Cosmopolitans, I am following my own journey and acquiring a wonderful perspective on new beginnings.

Moving from Boston to Lourmarin, a small village in southern France, changed everything for me and for my family. While I had been raised to have a global perspective on life, my entire world changed when I actually started living a global life. Although I have not traveled as much as most of the people I interviewed for this book, we also lived in Jerusalem for three years, which changed my outlook on so many issues. There, even the maps were different and continued questioning the way of thinking that put America first. However, that did not stop me eventually establishing a second home in Wellfleet, Massachusetts.

I have to say, I am most at home when I have my family surrounding me, wherever we happen to be in the world. There is nothing like being a grandmother and having the opportunity to observe my own children parent their kids. A morning with one of my grandchildren not only gives me pleasure, but also provides me with deeper understanding of how the global mind develops. It was a fascinating journey watching my children mature with their Global Cosmopolitan minds; now I am enjoying watching the lives of their children unfold. Seeing my children raise their children has given me insights that I never had time to enjoy to their full extent as a parent. I promised that I would not write this book about them, but I could have.

I am also getting an insider's chance to appreciate how children and grandchildren learn when they speak multiple languages and meet people from very different cultural backgrounds on a daily basis. Observing their ease with difference and their initial strategies for connecting has been fascinating. Changing landscapes and languages is normal for them. They also know at some level what it means to have to leave—to be far away from the people that you love.

Chloé, my granddaughter, is a frequent traveler on the Eurostar train between London and Paris. At four, she is already trying to understand how she can love being in two cities at the same time. She has attachments and wants to have a home in both places. And she already understands that they would have different connections and people in them. We can already have interesting conversations about the differences between languages—and the frustrations of being more articulate in one than another. These are issues that Global Cosmopolitans work on their whole lives.

Julien is younger, just three at the time I am writing this, but he is learning three languages: French, Spanish, and English (or should I say American?). If he knows a word in one language, he is quick to find it in another. He understands, who can speak all three languages and who will speak to him in only one. Meanwhile, Luca, who will be one when this book is published, is already being exposed to three languages, but for the time being his beautiful smile his best way of communicating how happy he is to see someone.

Chloé and Julien know that family and friends live in different countries. They can identify places around the globe where they already know people or where they have been. Video technology allows them to feel connected with people living everywhere. They can see that movies, TV shows, or songs can be seen or heard in multiple languages.

Their experience is not exceptional, but part of a new normal in many metropolitan communities. While we cannot predict what this will mean for them in the future, there are more and more children growing up with sophisticated concepts of culture, language, difference, and beyond.

Change is just a part of life, but it is a given for Global Cosmopolitans, and the changes in my family have opened new doors for me. They give me great stories, push my thinking, and, yes, challenge me on a very personal level. Just listening to my grown children attempt to plan global continuity for their children has opened my eyes to the possibilities of global living. Languages, schools, friends, Skype, iPads… have changed their lives.

Learning through the sharing of stories

As you can well imagine, I learn from the stories people tell. While my colleagues might look at other ways to uncover the 'truth,' I believe that stories capture important narrative truths about life experiences. Collectively, they reveal patterns or questions that need answers.

Conversations about living globally are part of my everyday life. Colleagues, over coffee or lunch, have plenty of stories to share.

Past students and co-workers continue to send me anecdotes about the development of their lives.

While some of the chapters of this book could be filled with facts and figures, I have chosen to help the reader understand the issues through brief anecdotes or stores. Each chapter is not a definite statement about the relevance of the issues it covers but an opportunity to understand what questions are frequently raised and in what manner.

I want to emphasize that people do not need to lead a global life to have a creative mind, an inquisitive mind, or a global mind. While many of my friends have stayed in one place, they are as interested as ever in the world around them. While they might not have experienced some of the major choices that come with global living in such an intense way, their desire to learn and their global perspectives are what has cemented our continued friendships over time.

The political and economic atmosphere has had a huge impact on the telling of the stories in this book. While I was writing it, serious questions were raised about the impact of globalization. Major policy changes have already affected the lives of people building their lives and careers globally. Local versus global perspectives can seem polarized. However, if we can only use *both* lenses, we have the opportunity to use globalization for the greater good. This, above all, is the beauty and the power of the Global Cosmopolitan Mindset.

Paris, France   Linda Brimm

Contents

1

Introduction: Welcome to the Age of the Global Cosmopolitan

Will Elise's[1] life ever look normal, whatever that might mean? Does she even want it to be?

She is currently the Managing Director of a consulting company in the UK. She has set up and managed hotels all over the world, but her global experience started at birth, since her father was Norwegian and her mother was Indian. She appreciated her cross-cultural childhood and what she learned along the way. Educated in Europe and the US, she chose to work in the hotel industry, which allowed her to continue her global adventure, and gained a reputation for excellence that gave her exciting projects. Her last luxury hotel in Asia was perfect in many ways, since she knew it was a great place to live, to work and to raise her two children.

Elise fell in love again with an Englishman, and they decided to get married and move to England. Now, she is in the midst of another chapter in her life.

Elise does not focus on what is, but on what can be. For her, life as an opportunity to learn and to grow and to contribute to a better world, which has helped her navigate the many challenges and opportunities she has experienced. She exemplifies the Global Cosmopolitan Mindset in both her openness to and consciousness of diversity across cultures and markets.

Over the years, Elise has offered me the opportunity to look at the complex process of composing a life in circumstances that keep changing and a global context that keeps shifting. She is one of a new breed of individuals that I described in my previous book, *Global Cosmopolitans: The Creative Edge of Difference.*[2] Global Cosmopolitans are the rapidly expanding population of highly educated, multilingual people who have lived, worked, and studied for extensive periods in different cultures. Extremely talented, they have grown up

© The Author(s) 2018
L. Brimm, *The Global Cosmopolitan Mindset,*
https://doi.org/10.1057/978-1-349-95345-5_1

in an ever-changing political/economic context and technological reality that has significantly impacted their worldview and skill set. Their backgrounds and their life histories make them particularly suited to working and leading in the global economy. And today, they are not only growing up but also maturing into global leaders with a distinctive mindset that others can learn from.

Global Cosmopolitans are the talented population of highly educated, multilingual people who have lived, worked, and studied for extensive periods in different cultures.

The seeds for this book, *The Global Cosmopolitan Mindset: Lessons from the New Global Leaders*, were sown by people from all over the world who engaged me in similar conversations to those I have had with Elise over the years and told me about their developmental journeys as Global Cosmopolitans.

Whether I was in Buenos Aires or Hong Kong, people were describing the varied but similar experiences of living and working globally. The world of Global Cosmopolitans was immense, yet the distance among the individuals seemed to disappear. Beyond differences based on multiple factors in an individual's personal history and career story, people talked about navigating similar challenges and opportunities, and discovering and creating new life chapters for personal and professional growth over time. Their stories gave me a greater understanding of the complexity of the topic, the concept of Global Cosmopolitans was validated, and my earlier messages were reinforced.

This book expands the circle. It deepens and improves the understanding of what it is like to lead a global life. Whether you are a so-called Millennial[3] or mid-life newcomer to Global Cosmopolitanism, an existing Global Cosmopolitan reflecting on what next, or part of an organization trying to develop its responses to an internationally mobile workforce, this guidebook to global living and working offers essential insights.

The stories that I am using to describe the characteristics and skills of the new global leaders are based on individuals already living in and con-tributing to the creation of this new global reality. Their experiences illustrate the challenges they have encountered and the opportunities they have pursued, as well as the possibilities they have explored as they added new chapters to their lives. In finding the words to describe the life skills that people have learned from living, studying, and working abroad, and in sharing this aspect of their learning curve, I hope I can encourage organizations going global to provide experiences that will prepare their employees to become better leaders in the future. I hope too that I can help individuals develop themselves into leaders with a truly global mindset.

The Global Cosmopolitan Mindset: Lessons from the New Global Leaders proves that globalization is not simply about economics, politics, free trade, or international brands, but about people combining a growth mindset with a global mindset and a creative mindset, choosing to compose a life outside of conventional scripts, and experiencing global citizenship first hand.

What can Global Cosmopolitans teach us about personal development and professional effectiveness? How do their stories provide a map for navigating the challenges and opportunities of a global life? How do people leading change at work continue to drive change in their already very interesting lives? Answering these questions means looking beyond the résumé that typically serves to define an individual's worth and identity. Most people who seek explanations of Global Cosmopolitans' strengths and dynamic resilience are drawn to the outer journeys, such as the development of cultural and linguistic knowledge. But the real learning lies in the invisible inner journey and the uncommon obstacles found along the way.

Three core truths emerge as underpinning the Global Cosmopolitan experience: First the fact that Global Cosmopolitans are an ever-expanding group to be reckoned with; second that developing a Global Cosmopolitan Mindset is essential to survive and thrive in this brave new world; and third that learning from life experiences, both personal and professional, is mandatory for maximization of potential.

Truth 1: The Rise of the Global Cosmopolitan Continues

'Being a Global Cosmopolitan, it's not a question, it's just a part of who we are,'
A Dutch consultant who grew up in a family that lived around the world and is currently working in Australia.

Millions of people are now living truly global lives.[4] These are the people I have labeled 'Global Cosmopolitans.' And they form one of the fastest growing clubs in the world. Every club has its rules, but the rules for membership of this particular club are changing. No longer identified with an elitist background, its members are united by the common bond of global experience that has significantly changed their lives.

They might be young professionals beginning their global journey with few responsibilities to hold them back. They might be joining the Global Cosmopolitan Club mid-career, uprooting families, and making a dramatic change in their personal and professional lives. Or they might be returnees, going back to their country of origin but taking their Global Cosmopolitan Mindset with them and applying it with a local perspective.

It is not unusual in many major world business cities to have colleagues or friends with multiple passports and fluency in more than one language. The number of such people is going to increase rapidly as we become ever more mobile: Residing, marrying, and having children in multiple countries over the course of our lives. Despite the rise of nationalism in many parts of the world, today nearly 90 countries allow some form of dual or multiple citizenships than ever before. This is just one indicator that Global Cosmopolitans are on the rise. And, as these people move through their lifecycle and have families, new generations are growing up as Global Cosmopolitans from birth.

But what does living a global life really involve, and what are the implications for individuals, families, and organizations? Are the next generations ready to write new life chapters across different cultural backdrops and ready to create organizations that deal with the new global reality? What are the challenges for CEOs seeking leadership for new models of cross-border organizations and looking to build a workforce that can think and act both globally and locally? Are organizations overlooking potential employees from diverse cultural backgrounds as potential candidates for global training and leadership? How can we prepare people to be the rising stars of our globalized world? How can we benefit from their experience and skill base to create organizations that sustain society?

Today's global, economic, and political landscape is in a state of constant flux. It is against this backdrop that the rise of Global Cosmopolitans and their contribution to the modern world can best be understood.

Truth 2: A Global Cosmopolitan Mindset Is Essential for Twenty-First Century Success

'What is it that makes me feel so comfortable, sitting in this group of people who have lived and worked all over the world? What is it about the way we think and the ways we use our minds that is different and makes me feel so much a part of this group?' An American entrepreneur in Hong Kong, discussing the concept and feeling of being at home with other Global Cosmopolitans.

This book provides a framework for understanding the mindset of Global Cosmopolitans. Given the additional complexity of their lives and the resilience that they need to deal with multiple levels of change, how do their minds work? What is it about the way they think that contributes to their identity as Global Cosmopolitans and, increasingly, as global leaders.

The Global Cosmopolitan Mindset evolved out of an attempt to articulate answers to these questions and to define what such diverse individuals have in common. I concluded that the Global Cosmopolitan Mindset (or GCM) is a hybrid of a Growth Mindset, a Global Mindset, and a Creative Mindset: A combination that helps us understand the motivation, skills, and potential of a new breed of global leaders who will help organizations face the ever-evolving complexities of the twenty-first century.

> Global Cosmopolitan Mindset =
> Growth Mindset + Global Mindset + Creative Mindset

Each of these three elements is crucial and challenging. Usually, people begin by describing the opportunity that living a global life offers to grow and develop over time. By definition, this Growth Mindset represents a challenge. Working in a new country is as much about an opportunity to learn as it is about the opportunity to apply the skills and knowledge developed previously.

A Global Mindset is defined by the belief that both local and global orientations are needed to make sense of the world. For many people, their understanding of life and work, their attitude to building networks, and their perspective on finding solutions can be based locally. Global Cosmopolitans, on the other hand, can understand a local orientation—and often have to build bridges to it—but are globally minded.

Finding solutions for the challenges that Global Cosmopolitans face—from the mundane to the complex—often requires what I refer to as a Creativity Mindset. While not without its own difficulties, living in one place can provide familiar structures that help people build and sustain lives. Moving away from these known structures means creating new ways of living and an inventive approach to meeting life's needs.

The equation above will be developed in the first part of the book to provide a framework for understanding what people are learning as they face life challenges and plot interesting global trajectories. Some people with a Global Cosmopolitan Mindset have had lives where global moves were central, while others will identify with the mindset through understanding, experiencing, and acting in the world from a limited number of locations.

Presenting descriptions of Global Cosmopolitans in a variety of settings all around the world has given rise to lively discussions. Gathered together, people who identified in some way as Global Cosmopolitans explained to me how they felt that they were different, and that they often lived in a space in between cultures—and not necessarily the culture they currently lived or worked in. They found it easy to share what they had learned from their global journeys with other Global Cosmopolitans without much explaining, because they had a similar outlook.

Their stories illustrate the attitudes, knowledge, and skills they have developed as a result of their experiences and define a mindset that we all can learn from. Globalization is here to stay. Developing a GCM is essential to survive and thrive in this brave new world.

Truth 3: Learning from Life Is Mandatory for Maximizing Potential

'*This voyage has helped me learn about who I am. It is a process. I am not finished and would not want to be, since a key aspect of who I am is always learning and always growing.*' A managing director who started life in Canada commenting on what defines him.

As we have already seen, an important element of the Global Cosmopolitan Mindset is a Growth Mindset: The belief that it is possible to develop as a person and to improve skills through learning. Listening to Global Cosmopolitan stories over the years, I have been fascinated by the power of the learning experience and the personal resilience that it fosters. When I first wrote about Global Cosmopolitans, I highlighted certain commonalities around the challenges that they faced and the patterns of skills that they developed as a result. Expanding the range of my work to explore different ages and life stages, from Millennials to those facing retirement and beyond, has underscored the importance of continuing to learn from, and reflect on, experience over time.

While each individual has a story, there are certain patterns to the possibilities for learning on a global life journey. Individuals who remain local and prefer to develop their influence from a home base can also be on an exciting learning curve, but what tends to differentiate Global Cosmopolitans is the impact of their experience on their mindset, particularly on the skills that the complexity of their lives requires.

In general, we learn who we are through the challenges we face. Through a process that is often invisible, we convert the obstacles that stand on our path through life into learning opportunities to find our strengths and change our perceptions of what we are capable of in the future. Because Global Cosmopolitans encounter more challenges than most of us, they also tend to learn more.

The backdrop of a global life is one of exceptional complexity and change, and Global Cosmopolitans often perceive change as an opportunity. Given the multiplicity of changes that they encounter, reflecting on what they need, how they handle major dilemmas, and how they preserve a sense of motivation and excitement about what life has to offer and what they can learn over time becomes increasingly important.

I have attempted to identify a cluster of common challenges that provides a window into the world of this group. These challenges include identity development and being different—and of managing difference for other people.

Ultimately, the lessons that Global Cosmopolitans learn from their ever-shifting experiences contribute not only to their personal development but also to their effectiveness in professional environments, where they are often driving change. While it is not desirable to be formulaic about how to develop a strong personal life, we can all learn from the way Global Cosmopolitans are framing challenges and opportunities. This group offers us all hope that we can forge exciting and meaningful lives and build organizations that are able to meet the needs of an increasingly global and volatile context.

The Importance of Stories[5]

Global Cosmopolitans find that they frequently need to explain who they really are, where they are from, where they have been, what they have learned from the complexity of their lives, what they can do, and what they can learn to do. With experience, they can become highly articulate and create meaningful dialogue with key players in their lives. The most skillful storytellers have learned how to use their self-reflection in a motivating and instructive manner.

The stories of strengths, skills, and attitudes that Global Cosmopolitans use to describe themselves are analogous to those that the best leaders tell. Leadership experts have identified stories as one of the tools that characterize—or facilitate the development of—outstanding managers and entrepreneurs. The process of storytelling also models the importance of a lifetime of learning about who you are and who you can be.[6]

A Geography of Ideas About Globalization

Geographical location does not matter for some people. They rely on news, especially via the Internet, to form their opinions about the world without ever stepping out of their familiar geographical and relational environments. However, for others, there is a growing acceptance that geography can impact people's perspectives on the meaning of globalization and how it might (or might not) affect their lives. Even within the same country, people living in the same economic conditions and listening to the same news can value or reject globalization, depending on where they live.

Living and working with people from very different geographical regions can open the door to different ways of understanding globalization. People who have lived in multiple parts of the world and in varied cultural contexts have experienced the impact of language and culture on how they understand the world and explain it to others. Discussions with Global Cosmopolitans are enriched by their understanding of regional politics and cultural or regional identification on the potential for developing networks, projects and leadership.

They understand that we can no longer predict who someone is and how he or she will react based on assumptions about their identity groups or perceived cultural background alone. They recognize that putting people in categories such as 'Asian' or 'European' can easily miss the long history of differences among people from different nations, and listening to the subtleties of difference within perceived identity groups becomes a very useful skill.

A Life Span Perspective

My first book focused on the younger cohort of Global Cosmopolitans, many of whom were starting out on their global journey with open minds, few ties, and a strong sense of adventure. But since I started studying the phenomenon of Global Cosmopolitans, life span perspectives have shifted.

Life expectancy is increasing. Not everyone wants or is able to retire from their professional responsibilities, and writing new chapters of their lives will become increasingly significant for people as they move through the life cycles. While we always need to meet the more basic human needs, such as health and financial security, rather than focusing on self-actualization, we are now faced with deciding where to go and what to do next at an age when the choices of previous generations were limited. The fortunate ones will have the health, resources, and motivation to find new directions. Recognition of this reality and finding new ways to define new stages is both daunting and exciting.

The issue of what changes over time as we compose our lives offers a fascinating lens through which to examine how people address major questions and decision points. Using a life-development perspective, this book highlights the movement over time from learning to articulate, develop, and share decision-making skills to understanding how they can be used to create new projects, whether career- or life-related. In particular, this whole-life approach offers a fresh angle on the skills that people need to work globally. The stories in this book reveal the existence of a group of people taking a new kind of responsibility for what is possible and making it happen. This circle is rapidly expanding, and societies, organizations, and individuals are starting to break out of traditional viewpoints of what a life should look like. When the mindsets open up, so do the possibilities.

In *The Global Cosmopolitan Mindset*, I have tried to capture stories that show how people maintain holding onto a sense of who they are, while also allowing room for who they can be as a result of certain choices and experiences. Their decisions often turn out to be based on different ways of seeing themselves in relation to people, career, and environment at different stages in their lives. Life-stage realities include: committing to relationships, children, success, or aging parents; confronting ill health; and needing a greater sense of purpose or meaning. There are inevitably bumps along the road that people need to address. How they do this can have significant implications for their lives. What might have been a distant concern at one stage can become a painful or joyful reality at another.

What becomes apparent, through having people tell their stories, is that career identity, while ever important, is only one aspect of a person. People interviewed at different life stages increasingly emphasize the importance of the whole person when looking at trying to enjoy a relatively successful life.

Some questions are particular to different ages. For instance, do Millennials—and eventually Generation Z—want to join the Global Cosmopolitan Club? What is different about today's worldwide population of young people and the perspectives that they have about their voyage through life, compared to their parents and grandparents? Are they looking at global options in the same way as previous generations?

Joining the Global Cosmopolitan Club mid-career raises other questions around opportunities, challenges, professional choices, and the potential impact on families. And those who choose to remain in one place for an extended period of time, or to return home, must question whether this means losing club 'membership' or indeed the skills and the mindset that went with being a Global Cosmopolitan. Will they now be a 'local cosmopolitan,' or can they still have a global outlook?

Certain Characteristics Hold True Across the Life Stages and Generations

As the world continues to change, and the controversies and conflicts around those changes continue to evolve, every generation will have its perspective on being a Global Cosmopolitan.[7] However, along the age continuum, certain characteristics of Global Cosmopolitans hold true:

- They consider change as normal, positive, and a source of opportunity;
- As outsiders to any one set of fixed cultural rules, they rely on creative thinking and adaptation to confront new situations;
- They are able to reinvent themselves and experiment with new identities as they move into new settings;
- They become experts at the subtle and emotional aspects of transition;
- They easily learn and use new ways of thinking; and
- They have learned how to take risks that lead to self-efficacy.

Lessons from the New Global Leaders

This book builds on the concept of Global Cosmopolitans and follows their experiences over time. It is designed to help readers understand this complex, fast-growing, and influential group as they compose their lives in a changing world. It offers the reader an opportunity to understand how Global Cosmopolitans learn from their both personal and professional experiences, and how this contributes to their ability to lead in the emerging global environment with reflective knowledge—using their difference to make a difference.

Full of personal stories from around the world (but with names and certain details changed to protect identities), the book explains how Global Cosmopolitans develop the skills and knowledge that make them so effective over time. It highlights the breadth and depth of their inner complexity. It provides a concrete way to uncover the hidden value of the Global Cosmopolitan experience so that organizations, families, friends, and Global Cosmopolitans themselves can make the most of it.

If you are starting your own business or leading a large organization, get to know this population, since they can lead the changes necessary to respond to the needs and opportunities of the ever-changing global economy.

Part I, *Learning from a Global Life*, develops the notion of mindsets and introduces some of the ways people learn from challenges and opportunities that can be both transformational and developmental. It also provides an introduction to developing some of the attitudes, knowledge, and skills that contribute to an exciting voyage through life.

Part II, *Composing a Global Life: Navigating the Challenges and Benefits Along the Way*, explores how to cope with the challenges and make the most of opportunities of building a global life over time through different aspects of identity and personal development. Choosing to compose a life outside of conventional scripts, as Global Cosmopolitans must do, includes defining and redefining:

- Identity and the 'Professional Me,' including how professional decisions impact on personal identity and relationships;
- Creating and maintaining a relational world, with an emphasis on relationships, couples, and raising the next generation;
- Home, including the issues of defining home and how these definitions affect a decision to return to a place called home or to create a new home; and
- Managing major transition and complex change.

Important questions about personal meaning and having an impact are threaded throughout this section, reflecting how they become central to a feeling of success over time.

Part III, *Creating New Chapters in an Already Interesting Life*, examines how Global Cosmopolitans continue to add to an already interesting portfolio of experiences, and gives the reader a first-hand insight into how people are redesigning their lives for a new world. Through stories of development and change, the reader gets a glimpse of what it is like to continue developing a global life over time, and how people use the expertise developed throughout their global journey to manage change, lead organizations, or create their own ventures.

The people that I have gotten to know through my research are most likely considered the elite by some, although this is not how many of them see themselves. Many of them come from humble immigrant backgrounds and have had to work very hard to get where they are today. They have accomplished much and have been well rewarded. Yet, I have never felt an arrogance of power in our conversations. I have noted that those in powerful positions feel a certain responsibility to make a difference and an incredible optimism about what they can do. Their stories illustrate how the global journey evolves and changes over time, and each time we meet them, we will learn a little bit more about the complexity of living a global life. Given their life and work experience, they have a great deal to teach us about the new ways to address some of the complicated challenges of today.

Part I

Learning from a Global Life

Most Global Cosmopolitans can tell stories about their life and work that reveal how they think and act, and how their outlook has developed over time. With apologies to Shakespeare, some are born with a Global Cosmopolitan Mindset, some achieve it through learning, and some have it thrust upon them. However they reach it, whether by being born into a global family or by growing up as Millennials in a globalizing world, whether by switching to a global career early or by choosing to start a new global chapter in later life, many will say that they began their global journeys with the appropriate attitudes in place. These attitudes, of openness and willingness to learn, gave them the motivation and know-how to approach the initial challenges of complex change and to learn and grow along the way. Some will say they do not recognize their old selves, because they have changed so much in response to the challenges they have faced.

The challenges and opportunities encountered on a global journey through life can be both transformational and developmental. Understanding the Global Cosmopolitan Mindset—and the attitudes, knowledge, and skills people develop as they learn from a global life—provides key insights into what contributes to an exciting and successful personal and professional voyage.

2

The Global Cosmopolitan Mindset (GCM)

A Mindset Is Not a Set Mind

After two, three, or more moves and multiple life stages, any individual's outlook on life may change and develop. What is particular to Global Cosmopolitans is that the moves are between countries and cultures, which add many layers of complexity. Listening to Global Cosmopolitans tell their stories and describe what they have learned over the years has given me a certain perspective on how they use their minds.

The idea of a 'mindset' can evoke an image of rigidity, but this is certainly not the case. American psychologist, Carol Dweck, has described two extreme types of mindset, fixed and growth.[1] People with a fixed mindset believe that they must play the hand they have been dealt and that, if they fail, it is because they have reached the limit of their abilities. By contrast, those with a growth mindset believe that they can improve their abilities and outcomes through their own efforts.

While it is important to emphasize that each individual's mind develops differently and under different circumstances, looking at what Global Cosmopolitans say about the factors that underpin their successful navigation of complex and unique lives can be very informative.

The Global Cosmopolitan Mindset is certainly not fixed. From my many years of interviewing and teaching this group, I find that what characterizes them is a combination of learning and growth, a global perspective, and creativity. Given that change and complexity are constants in

© The Author(s) 2018
L. Brimm, *The Global Cosmopolitan Mindset*,
https://doi.org/10.1057/978-1-349-95345-5_2

their lives, their stories reinforce my perspective for Global Cosmopolitans their growth and development are clear drivers in their lives. But these drivers are influenced by a journey that exposes them to multiple outlooks and perspectives, and so leads to the development of a global mindset as well, enabling the Global Cosmopolitan to apply several perspectives to any given situation. As Global Cosmopolitans go through their careers and life stages, they also demonstrate an expanding ability to think creatively, as they face new and complex challenges. Thus, the Global Cosmopolitan Mindset is—of necessity—a hybrid of growth, global, and creative mindsets.

> Global Cosmopolitan Mindset =
> growth mindset + global mindset + creative mindset

Survival and success on a global voyage through life depend on a capacity to develop the attitudes, beliefs, and skills that mark the difference between a fixed mindset and a Global Cosmopolitan Mindset. A positive attitude toward growth, a global outlook, and creativity become essential attributes. These traits enable Global Cosmopolitans to use their creative edge and their difference in all its varieties to find new ways of building a life and contributing to their work environments.

Learning with a Growth Mindset

Global Cosmopolitans describe a fundamental desire to learn and grow over time. When they tell their personal and professional stories, the words they use to describe their mindset are very open-ended, but based primarily on notions of learning and growth as sustaining their life course. The attitude that their lifestyle is an adventure that allows for learning and growth is the basis for their continued motivation and achievement. This attitude contributes to their ability to function and flourish in a life of constantly changing circumstances.

Carol Dweck has aptly described people with a growth mindset as seeing that intelligence can be developed, having a desire to learn, embracing challenges, persisting in the face of setbacks, seeing effort as the path to mastery, learning from criticism, and finding lessons and inspiration in the success of others. All of this, she says, gives them a greater sense of free will, and as a result, they reach ever-higher levels of achievement. Other experts describe links between a growth mindset and creativity, critical thinking, and relationships.

A growth mindset is defined by understanding that intelligence can be developed, having a desire to learn, embracing challenges, persisting in the face of setbacks, seeing effort as the path to mastery, learning from criticism, and finding lessons and inspiration in the success of others.

Having a more rigid mindset with clear rules about 'right and wrong,' 'good and bad' can help people to feel secure in knowing who they are and what they stand for. This helps them make decisions based on what they believe to be true, but according to Dweck—and to Global Cosmopolitans themselves—it can limit their ability to grow.

Experienced Global Cosmopolitans often describe the importance of attitudes that allow them to learn from difference on multiple levels, including the importance of openness and being humble. Confrontation with difference can help clarify what frames the Global Cosmopolitan's understanding of the world and reactions to it. Having the attitude that their global life is an opportunity to learn and to grow helps substantially in new situations where they face a new situation and have to deal with the complications of difference.

But cultivating this attitude is not always easy. Growing up in one culture—and being successful in that culture—can make it difficult to put aside what one has learned about how things should be done to make room for alternative ways of approaching life and its challenges. For instance, success as a student does not naturally translate to a growth mindset, because being successful in one academic system can prevent people from taking the risks that might help them see other ways of learning. The arrogance of perceived knowing can be severely limiting. Some people never really learn how to step out of their comfort zone and work hard at understanding a new situation, while others describe how the opportunity to study or work abroad gave them a chance to understand those from different cultures and get a better perspective on their own culture. Serge is no exception. When I first met him, he had already been living in London for fifteen years. The giant step he had taken when he left Russia had marked the beginning of a new life for him.

Serge describes himself as someone who did well in school and was driven to learn and explore new possibilities. He was an outstanding student in Moscow. His background was deeply Russian and his family did not encourage him to travel. He was proud of his background and initially never questioned what he was learning about the role of Russia in the world. But as he matured, he became more aware of the political and economic environment that he lived in.

He decided to leave Russia in his early 20s and work in investment banking in the US, a first step into another world. He admits to having traveled abroad initially with a certain arrogance and a feeling of unreflective pride in his background.

A couple of years later, he made the decision to step out of his comfort zone and work in Germany. Although technically very successful, he found working on teams with others challenging. His formulaic thinking, which had served him so well in school and even in his initial career steps, did not work when he needed to gain respect and understanding. Letting go of the notion of rules and starting to observe, listen, and learn was a major turning point for him.

Living abroad gave him the opportunity to listen to and learn from people who came from very different cultural backgrounds. His desire to learn kicked in and he began to understand how different perspectives enriched his understanding.

He continued his journey by moving to London and fell in love with and married a woman from Greece. Doing an MBA in London with people from all over the world contributed to the development of his Global Cosmopolitan Mindset. Now, he loves living in London and raising his children in an international atmosphere.

He remembers realizing that there was no return to his old, Russia-centric mindset. This left him concerned about the impact of the change on his relationships at home. Old friends and family were important to him, and he knew that he could not impose – or even communicate – the change that had taken place when he went back to Russia to see them. His way of thinking and consequent possibilities for work would never be the same. The stimulus for learning and growth and a global perspective had changed his life.

He is thankful to his wife and children, who – he is convinced – helped him stay in close contact with his family. He is also grateful to one of his good friends from back home, who also ended up living in London after his own global journey.

Serge's story demonstrates how Global Cosmopolitans develop through difference—but only if they have a growth mindset and are willing to learn. As Serge went through the life stages from studying to working and to moving countries and starting a family, his willingness to continue learning—and to act on that learning—was the key to his success. While interpersonal relationships are not his strong suit, he knows how to benefit from coaching when he gets stuck. This helps him to see that there is even more he can learn on his global journey.

It is the motivation to learn and create beyond what is already known that helps Global Cosmopolitans to maintain momentum, continue on their global journeys, and develop new ways of thinking as they go through different stages in their lives. Given the additional complexity of living globally and having to make life choices that sometimes require difficult trade-offs, the belief that a global life presents an opportunity to learn and to grow becomes fundamental to their success.

Global Cosmopolitans with a growth mindset are also flexible. The unexpected is often seen as an opportunity to learn and grow. Without flexibility, that opportunity for learning and or self-improvement might be lost. Hence Global Cosmopolitans acquire, develop, and reinforce certain skills that allow them to benefit from changing their point of view, while at the same time making important life and work decisions. We will explore this skillset in more detail in Chapter 3.

A Global Mindset: Seeing the World from Multiple Perspectives

Meera grew up between the UK and India. Her parents wanted their children to live in both cultures and benefit from their biculturalism. They emphasized the importance of education and that learning could open doors to possibilities and growth experiences in life. Conversations around the dinner table involved examining the differences between an English and Indian perspective. She learned very early on that people had different points of view depending on their life experiences and their education.

When Meera was 16, she decided to go to Spain for a year. She decided that stepping out of her comfort zone would help her see if she had the ability to survive and flourish in another culture, just as her parents had done when they moved to the UK.

She had a wonderful year and discovered that she could thrive outside the safety of home. And she learned much more besides. Suddenly another language and another culture helped her see a new dimension of the geopolitical arguments that she loved at home.

That was years and years ago. Her exposure to different perspectives and at the same time the ability to connect the dots of the various challenges that the world is facing laid the groundwork for her entrepreneurial achievements. Armed with her deep multicultural understanding and her strong motivation to learn and achieve, she is never without a new business idea that could have global implications.

Like Serge, Meera took the plunge, but while she already had a global background, she was not sure that she was ready to undertake a global journey herself. Thanks to her growth mindset, she knew that the only way she could learn about her own capacity to face the challenges and complexity of a global life was to test herself by setting off on her own.

The number of people who have lived and worked in different countries is growing. Many newly minted MBAs started their global journey years ago, while other professionals are embarking on their global adventure much later in their lives and careers. All of them, at whatever life stage, are actively choosing to develop and utilize the second key factor in the Global Cosmopolitan Mindset, the global mindset.[2]

Some people, like Meera, say their global mindset started to develop at an early age, whether because of extensive international moves, life in a bicultural home, a family history shaped by global issues, or an attitude developed as a result of discussions around the dinner table. Others say that they developed their global mindset as result of later life experience, possibly starting with a choice to study or work abroad.

So, what is this elusive concept of a global mindset? It is hard to pinpoint or codify since it is often seen as a state of mind, an attitude, or a way of knowing that is developed over the years. There are varying definitions, which reflect slightly different perspectives and different research agendas.

For some, it is simply the cognitive ability to conceptualize complex geopolitical and cultural forces as they impact business. For others, a global mindset is a set of attitudes that predispose certain people to cope constructively with competing priorities (e.g., global versus local priorities) rather than emphasizing one dimension at the expense of others. Another key concept of a global mindset centers on the ability to accept and work with cultural diversity.

These different approaches share a common factor, however. That is, they present a global mindset as characterized by the ability to see and understand the world from multiple perspectives. I would add that the capacity to learn exemplified in the growth mindset we saw earlier in this chapter contributes to the capacity to develop a global mindset.

A global mindset is defined by the ability to see and understand the world from multiple perspectives. The development of a global mindset is enhanced by a general desire to learn.

How does a global mindset make people more effective in life and in work? When asked for examples, Global Cosmopolitans often cite their ability to understand and manage cultural diversity and the complex challenges of an ever-changing environment. Less obviously, they talk about knowing who to trust in their networks and demonstrating cognitive flexibility when they attempt to reconcile local and cosmopolitan perspectives. Indeed, their stories frequently reflect the tensions of managing a global perspective in their local work environments. Take Simon, who works for a family business in the UK with a global reach…

Simon is a member of the second generation. He and his siblings had the privilege of global experience, education, and professional development, which contributed to giving him a global mindset. When he decided to return to work in his family business, he was staggered by the resistance to new ideas that he encountered – not only from other family members but also from very competent managers from very different cultural backgrounds.

Similarly, Rajiv returned to India after many years abroad to work for a major global business that was still rooted in the family that started it.

Rajiv believed that the way to move forward was characterized by a respect for global interconnectedness and the values of cultural diversity. He also knew and respected the importance the company leaders placed on cohesion with the values of the family and their cultural background. He wanted to create a diverse global team and was met with huge resistance on the part of the senior managers, who were adamant about local leadership. His biggest challenge was getting them to understand that global influence was not going to threaten the local control of the organization, but would only increase its market value and global power.

In certain countries and organizations, there is no doubt that Global Cosmopolitans encounter the frustration of visible or invisible limits imposed on people from different cultures. No matter how well they understand the local perspective, they may have to make professional moves that impact their entire families if they want to reach senior positions or make a real impact.[3]

Conversely, it is important to note that some people are capable of living and working in another country without paying much attention to what they can learn from the new culture and context. They take a step out of their home base and return without developing a truly global mindset, finding that they are more interested in working locally or less interested in gaining new perspectives. Others will work on developing worldwide markets without leaving the comfort of their home environment. And even though young people are increasingly encouraged to gain global experience, learning about other countries for many of them starts with TV and movies and then switches to the Internet. They may think that they know a lot about other cultures as a result, but it does not necessarily equate with gaining a global perspective. While these groups may reach a certain level of success in new global situations, they may never develop the mindset that marks the true Global Cosmopolitan.

However, those who choose to be Global Cosmopolitans talk about how their preconceived notions were challenged by their life experience. The reason many of them find their adventure so fascinating is that they are learning about people from all over the world and can see how their own global perspectives are developing.

While their attitudes are grounded in background, experience, and education, Global Cosmopolitans describe how their frames of reference for many things have changed as a result of their global journeys. They often depict themselves as having the capacity to simultaneously hold multiple perspectives in their heads.

They acknowledge this global mindset in many aspects of their lives, starting with how they see themselves, their identity. They understand the impact of their cultural background—or backgrounds in many cases—and how that has contributed to their identity as Global Cosmopolitans. From this vantage point, they are keenly aware of the ways in which culture affects how people define themselves, how they behave, and how they might or might not understand people that are different.

> *Early in his career, François, a French engineer, was given the opportunity to work for his company in Asia on the construction of a bridge. He assumed that the task would be relatively simple, given his education at a top engineering school and the reputation of his organization. What he did not anticipate was the challenge of building a team that would work together effectively and dealing with a political environment that did not trust outsiders. In fact, another international company had recently tried to build a different bridge, and left before the project started.*
>
> *François saw this experience as a major turning point in his life. His relational toolkit for doing this type of work was practically empty. He had always been surrounded by like-minded people, including family, friends, and colleagues. He had never worked with people who had different agendas and minds that worked differently. Yet he knew that he needed and wanted to build this bridge, so he worked hard at understanding the different players and building metaphorical bridges with the people on his team. His attitude and the lessons he learned became key building blocks for a successful global career.*

Global Cosmopolitans like François are keenly aware of cultural difference and recognize the need to develop a range of skills (which we will explore further in Chapter 3), including the ability to observe and to listen to similarity as well as difference, and to create appropriate dialogue that helps find a balance between respecting difference and finding shared ways to work together.

Their viewpoint on globalization is based on their understanding of different perspectives and the interdependence of the people of the world. They understand and have experienced how changes in one context can have major impacts on another. This has major consequences for their beliefs not just around how global business needs to develop, but also around geopolitical and environmental issues. Some label their concerns and efforts to make a difference, 'global compassion.' For Global Cosmopolitans, social justice and human rights, peacemaking and conflict resolution, and working for a sustainable future all have global implications. When an action needs to be taken, their global mindset gives them an understanding of the crucial interplay among different perspectives, and as a consequence, they are ready to develop and embrace complex solutions.

The Added Edge of a Creativity Mindset

Marie always remembers being different. She was very smart and quickly became a target of bullying because of her need to be right. Her parents came from two different countries, Italy and the US, yet she was mostly schooled in Paris – except right after her parents got divorced, when she went to school in Milan and then New York. Academically and linguistically, each move was easy and, although her parents did not get along, she felt loved by both of them and their families. Her biggest challenge was being accepted by other children. Although not a natural athlete, she realized her best strategy would be participation in sports, which could help her find friends. She found her place when she realized she could be an outstanding skier.

With that childhood experience long behind her, she has learned many social skills, which make her social integration much easier. She defines herself as a Global Cosmopolitan, who knows that the key to her professional success is her ability to think outside of the box. If someone feels stuck at work trying to find a solution, she helps them see alternative perspectives. She loves that she is often labeled at work as the person who finds a creative way to see things. Finding different routes to her goals became a skill that she developed when she started to feel different. She is convinced that it has led to her ability to find new ways of addressing and solving complex problems.

Global Cosmopolitans might or might not describe themselves as creative. Yet, when they tell their stories of adapting to changes in place, work, and relationships, and how they are able to flourish in new settings, they are really describing the importance of having a creative mindset.[4]

A creative mindset is characterized by attitudes and behaviors that include curiosity, the ability to suspend judgment, tolerance of ambiguity, childlike wonder, and a persisting belief in one's ability to find creative solutions. Even if these factors are part of someone's initial self-description, Global Cosmopolitans demonstrate that evolving and expanding a creative mindset can also be a natural part of self-development.

> **A creative mindset** is defined by attitudes and behaviors that include curiosity, the ability to suspend judgment, tolerance of ambiguity, childlike wonder, and a persisting belief in one's ability to find creative solutions.

Numerous studies have looked at the development of creativity (3). 'Creative conceptual expansion' is a term used in cognitive psychology that relates creativity to the ability to combine one concept with one or more others that are seemingly unrelated. One example is the idea of putting a camera into a mobile phone: two functions seemingly entirely separate, but now a feature that we take for granted.

As I have asserted in my previous work, an international life is a fertile breeding ground for the development of a creative mindset. A closed, monocultural life can confine the individual to a restricted set of concepts and attitudes. In the multicultural global journey, there is a level of complexity even to the ordinary tasks of life that requires new or slightly modified solutions.

Over time, Global Cosmopolitans become sensitive to who they are, their perceived needs, and new ways of functioning. They tend to look for new ways to address their needs, the needs of others, and what needs to be done both in professional contexts and for the greater good. What they realize is that they often have to create opportunities to meet these needs and challenges. This recognition contributes to their ability to continue successfully on a global journey. The solutions they find inevitably require a creative approach, as there are no maps or guides to building a global life. Even when they see others in similar situations, Global Cosmopolitans consistently say that they have to find their own solution, one that fits their own particular needs.

Being proactive and able to communicate creative solutions to career and professional challenges is a primary skill for Global Cosmopolitans. It enables them to bring their creative edge of difference into all kinds of problem-solving, as we will see in Chapter 3.

The Global Cosmopolitan Mindset and Leadership

Over the years, studies of leadership have highlighted the importance of learning. Warren Bennis, for example, wrote very persuasively about how the basis for leadership is learning—and importantly learning based on experience.[5] To survive and thrive in a complex and constantly shifting business environment, a leader's ability to learn is crucial. In addition, that learning must be continual—leaders must always be ready to absorb new lessons, otherwise they will stagnate and fail.

Global Cosmopolitans understand that they need to learn how to lead in a new culture. They know how to stay motivated and resilient enough to face the disadvantages of complex and dramatic change—and how to capitalize on the advantages. The motivation to learn and then learn how to lead organizations becomes central to their voyage.

A growing number of researchers and leaders describe how having a global mindset is an essential aspect of successful leadership. They concur with my view that individuals with a global mindset are less likely to simplify the global realities of today's business, but rather acknowledge and address the full extent of the complexity and ambiguity involved.

Leading change in the current context calls for new solutions to global challenges. Global Cosmopolitans have the experience of living this changing reality, and a recent definition of the global mindset from the *Financial Times Lexicon* reinforces its importance to global leaders and their organizations.

We would define global mindset as one that combines an openness to and awareness of diversity across cultures and markets with a propensity and ability to see common patterns across countries and markets.

In a company with a global mindset, people view cultural and geographic diversity as opportunities to exploit and are prepared to adopt successful practices and good ideas wherever they come from.

The twin forces of ideological change and technology revolution are making globalization one of the most important issues facing companies today. As such, cultivating a global mindset is a prerequisite to becoming a global company. Companies exhibiting global mindsets include GE, P&G, Nestlé, Unilever, and Colgate.[6]

While much of my work expands on this definition, as discussed earlier in this chapter, I believe that the creative mindset is a critical component of the global mindset. This is an aspect of what many researchers have identified as cognitive complexity which I believe is a key component of the Global Cosmopolitan Mindset and the modern leader. World economic and political pressures have given a new urgency to the search for different perspectives on how to build global organizations and work globally. The Global Cosmopolitan Mindset confers critical leadership skills in this changing reality, including an ability to adapt, to see change as normal, and to be able to work in a constantly changing environment.[7]

Yet leadership does not always take place in a global context. And cognitive complexity is also what enables the Global Cosmopolitan to think locally. In reality, most Global Cosmopolitans have developed the skills of bridging a local mindset and a global mindset. They keep up to date with both global and local situations. They read newspapers from home, spend time there, and send their children to schools that reflect their roots. Yet they also keep in touch with other local perspectives linked to their past and present experience.

On a personal level, these new leaders of the world often have to find a balance between a global perspective and their own need to know where their values come from. Understanding that your life purpose is attached to making a difference in a place called home calls for being in touch with the local realities.

Kham is very clear about being globally minded and locally very grounded. He has a deep commitment to his country of origin, Myanmar, and his source of meaning and purpose are grounded there. Kham moved back to Myanmar after working in the US and realized how hard it was to be understood and treated enough like a local to be trusted and respected. He is keenly aware of the political dynamics in Myanmar, and while he would like to be an active player in the political situation, he knows that this means finding a way to build trust and respect.

Like many Global Cosmopolitans who reach a stage or age where the importance of meaning in their lives becomes paramount, Kham arrived at a point where he wanted to take his global perspective and leadership skills and put them to use in benefiting his country of origin. But once global, it is often hard to return to the way things are done at home. Kham's global voyage has changed him and has changed his perspective on how to bring about change back home. It has also given him the mindset to find creative solutions to the challenges his country faces, as long as he is given the opportunity to put his skills into action.

Organizations of all kinds need to recognize the potential embodied in Global Cosmopolitans, or they will quickly lose the best ideas and the best talent. Spotting where the new talent is emerging, giving developmental opportunities, and then giving appropriate recognition will be key. In other words, understanding the role of a Global Cosmopolitan Mindset in developing leaders—both local and global—will be paramount.

When Global Cosmopolitans acknowledge their leadership advantage, they tend to describe what they have learned about themselves and how their minds work, and what skills they have developed in working under complex, challenging, and ever-changing conditions. They talk about how they have developed their social skills and their sensitivity to people from different cultures and backgrounds. Even before becoming leaders, they have usually developed a mindset that is already accustomed to addressing the issues that twenty-first-century organizations are facing.

Living globally adds a level of complexity and necessitates decision-making that often involves competing forces and needs. Learning how to act in this context also helps Global Cosmopolitans develop the psychological strength necessary to lead global organizations and builds on their attitudes toward growth, a global perspective, and creativity. In today's world, the Global Cosmopolitan Mindset and the leadership mindset are rapidly converging.

It is with this combination of 'mindset descriptions,' that Global Cosmopolitans encounter the challenges and opportunities of their lives. The skills they learn from navigating life challenges help them develop the confidence and ability to create new life chapters that contribute to their well-being and their ability to contribute to a greater good, be it in their work, in their relationships or to the larger global community.

3

The Global Cosmopolitan Skillset

'A life lived on the move has greatly affected me in ways I am still trying to understand. I believe that for Global Cosmopolitans, the complexity of the world becomes reflected within ourselves and we must learn to be adaptable to both deal with and harness this potential.' A Swiss consultant and entrepreneur currently living between Peru, Brazil, and Switzerland.

We all go on a journey through life with key turning points, which may include going to school, graduating from college, starting a career, committing to a relationship, having children, and getting promoted. Global Cosmopolitans are no different. However, they face the same events and challenges as everyone else against a backdrop of uncommon complexity and change. In order to navigate their journey, which is a global journey as well as a life journey, they gain knowledge and abilities that set them apart. Thanks to their distinctive mindset, through their many and diverse experiences, they also develop a distinctive skillset.

> Global Cosmopolitan Mindset + Experience
> = Global Cosmopolitan Skillset

CVs can reflect where someone has worked and what languages they speak, but often miss the deeper linguistic, cultural, and regional skills or understanding that have been developed from professional and life experiences. And it is the deeper skill base and understanding that sets the Global Cosmopolitan apart. The Global Cosmopolitan Skillset reflects

L. Brimm, *The Global Cosmopolitan Mindset*,
https://doi.org/10.1057/978-1-349-95345-5_3

both the curiosity to get to know people from different backgrounds and the ability to understand them—which are two qualities that contribute to enjoyment and success. Research into neuroscience is beginning to validate the idea that operating in different languages and cultures increases cognitive complexity,[1] which is also known to generate creative solutions to challenging problems.

Experience is an exceptional teacher. A resume may describe Global Cosmopolitans' outward journey, but the challenges they have faced frame the silent inner journey that is the root of their strength and dynamic resilience. Understanding the lessons and skills learned from life can give Global Cosmopolitans both confidence and the ability to succeed through future challenges and opportunities. This chapter will attempt to articulate the development of attitudes and skills over time that can make all of the difference.

Generally speaking, with each new move, Global Cosmopolitans need to learn to interpret and respond to their surroundings, to find meaning in what they do, and are often expected to imagine possibilities when other people are stuck. At work, they are often in a position to shake up perceptions and to question assumptions.

The ability of Global Cosmopolitans to learn from that experience is crucial. Those I interviewed said they started with a positive attitude toward the complex challenge of learning from their global lives. Over time, they built the knowledge, attitudes, and skills necessary for navigating both their personal and professional journeys. Given the different levels of complexity in their lives, they also had to learn how to make difficult and complex decisions, an ability that became increasingly important with age and increased responsibility, especially when working in global organizations.

Tied to learning is the ability to understand oneself and to be articulate about presenting oneself. Changing countries and professional contexts often means needing to tell and re-tell your story, as the context of life changes and the story keeps evolving. Self-knowledge, what works, what does not, and where the potential for growth could be are crucial aspects of that story.

The Power of Change

Learning how to embrace complex change can come from dealing with a number of significant experiences. Having a Global Cosmopolitan Mindset often contributes a positive attitude, agility in overcoming certain phases of a change, and an ability to see new possibilities.

To begin with, one of the aspects of leading global lives is the fundamental challenge of transition and change, which is loss. Experience teaches even the most sophisticated adults that certain aspects of loss are inevitable. On a very individual level, individuals learn about their own tolerance and how to overcome challenges. Many Global Cosmopolitans describe the initial stages of a transition to opportunities for growth and development, while accepting that with every move, there can be:

- The loss of power to get things done;
- The loss of the ability to relate to people and motivate them;
- The loss of control, security, and feeling anchored;
- Responsibility for the losses the family is experiencing because of the move;
- The loss of knowing the most mundane things, such as where to go shopping or find a doctor;
- The loss associated with command of the language and cultural meaning; and
- Many more losses: knowing how to do things, familiarity, feeling competent, important relationships, or even knowing who you are among others.

People frequently describe learning who they are through the challenges faced in life. In the best of circumstances, we convert challenges along developmental pathways into learning opportunities to find strengths and to change our perceptions of what we are capable of in the future. In the next section of the book, I have attempted to identify a cluster of common challenges that provides a window into the world of Global Cosmopolitans. Their ability to see opportunity in difficult times and to take risks with confidence parallels the work they have done to construct their own identities in the face of uncommon complexity and constant change.

To Global Cosmopolitans themselves, many of the skills they acquire feel normal, since they are developed as intrinsic elements of their global journey. Unless articulated and given value, these skills can remain invisible to the person who possesses them and to the rest of the world. But the strengths developed by a Global Cosmopolitan lifestyle can, if identified and used correctly, provide a significant competitive advantage in any marketplace, since the people running today's organizations need to be comfortable with change and have the right expertise to manage the process. Organizations often fail to recognize these skills, yet they are of immense value in a globalizing world.

In Global Cosmopolitans, The Creative Edge Of Difference, I shared certain insights about skills.[2] As I talked to more mature Global Cosmopolitans, they reinforced my previous descriptions and gave me examples of other skills that had become clearer as they continued on a global journey. While it is impossible to list everything that they learned, I hope at least to show how important the capacity and the ability to learn from experience can be.

The Most Important Skill of All Is the Ability to Learn from Experience

Many people embark on a global life with enough ready-made knowledge and skills to be effective, but the opportunity to develop further is immense. Looking at life lessons and the stories that support them can help Global Cosmopolitans identify what they are learning from their experiences. Some of those lessons are easy to describe and talk about, while others are less visible and connected to the development of a core sense of identity and well-being. While it is impossible to list everything that can be learned from a global life, there are some commonalties that are worth noting. Taking the time to examine and articulate what has been learned leads to an even deeper learning.

When she was in her 30s, Judith reflected on how her global journey began, the life lessons she had learned so far, and the skills that she developed with each new phase.

> *I went to 7 different schools in 12 years, in 4 different countries. Change became second nature, and I learned to detach myself easily from my last environment and relationships each time I moved on. Besides, I always saw change as positive and something to look forward to.*
>
> *After university, I spent three months backpacking and developed a 'let it go' attitude when faced with situations out of my control. But after I returned, I was sick for several months, which taught me to be more careful of my health, and now I take regular exercise and eat healthily. I would even choose yoga over an extra hour of study!*
>
> *I had worked for four different companies in seven years, and because I am so used to change, I felt like moving on every two years or so. I was highly flexible, and had used this skill to adapt quickly to a new environment, but I began to wonder about the disadvantages. I realized how much my own needs were changing. I was becoming less committed to work and to people, which was leaving me feeling too detached and too lonely. Recognizing that I needed a sense of commitment and belonging made all of the difference for me.*

Learning has always been a big part of my life; it motivates me and makes me feel alive. Changing environment for me is and was another opportunity to learn about a new culture and people. At the same time, I didn't have one hobby or pastime; I kept acquiring new ones. I had been learning Mandarin, Spanish, jujitsu, windsurfing, Pilates, and wakeboarding, among other things. It sounds like a lot! But having so many different interests helped me to connect with people more easily. I can almost always find a common interest when I meet someone new.

I realized I had to learn new skills, skills that allowed me to become more engaged at work, in my relationships, and in life. I had to learn how to fight my old reaction to boredom – just move. I also had to learn how to take risks to become more engaged on an intimate level in my relationships and to look for ways to stay more engaged with work.

Judith not only shows how a positive attitude toward learning and development can make the journey more rewarding, but also demonstrates the value of examining the skills she has developed and seeing both their positive and negative sides.

Over time, the Global Cosmopolitan Skillset becomes increasingly clarified and personalized. Seasoned Global Cosmopolitans, those who are further along in their lives and careers, can recognize the attributes that helped them become—and continue to be—successful.

Sebastian is in his 60s. He has spent most of his life based in the UK, but his grandmother was French and he went to the French Lycée in London. Living in a bicultural family, he learned a lot about valuing and dealing with difference. Combining the skills he started developing as a child with his financial wizardry and an entrepreneurial know-how, Sebastian has been extremely successful. He has built multicultural teams and bridges with partners from diverse cultural backgrounds. Now he is using these strengths to launch another new venture.

Now, at 62, I can take some risks. I have one more start-up in me, and, while the easy option would be to work in consulting, I know I need the freedom – and something slightly risky.

Skills acquired earlier in life serve the more seasoned Global Cosmopolitans well. For many, the focus expands to include other aspects of life apart from career. Some put the emphasis on key relationships, while others take to mentoring, helping younger Global Cosmopolitans to gain the necessary skills for working in and leading competitive and global organizations. Still others create organizations in the private or public sector that are sustainable, can compete on the global market, and at the same time contribute to a greater global good.

Joe has been on the global road for over 20 years. For the last few years, he has been living in and working in Dubai, but knows he is about to be assigned elsewhere. He was actually born in Birmingham, England, surrounded by people who were conservative, avoided difference, and did not like things to change. But he had an opportunity to take a job that would allow him to earn significantly more if he went to live and work in Asia. He and his wife and two children moved to Malaysia, and so began an incredible global journey.

Joe knows he will never go back to being the person he was. While improving his financial and social situation has been rewarding in itself, he has also benefited from a sense of personal development and expanded professional possibilities. As his experience thrust him into working with people who were very different, his openness to learning from others became one of his significant traits. He has seen how it has worked for him.

He describes a combination of humility, a willingness to learn more about what he does not know, and respect for others that gives him totally different perspectives on how to solve problems. Also, and more importantly, he knows how cultures vary in the ways that they communicate and live universal values.

The Key Components of the Global Cosmopolitan Skillset

With an open attitude to learning, Global Cosmopolitans acquire a number of attributes and skills that combine into a tool kit that they continue to apply and develop over time.

Cognitive Flexibility

Cognitive flexibility[3] allows people to switch their thinking, for instance when faced with a new set of rules—or when they need to alter their previous beliefs, thoughts, or habits to address a new situation. They develop the ability to consider multiple aspects at once, whether two sides of a specific object or many facets of a complex situation.

Cognitive flexibility enables Global Cosmopolitans to develop the mental ability and the strategies that will help them to face new and unexpected conditions in their environment, and confers the ability to see new patterns and new solutions. They understand that truth is not an absolute; it changes depending on the cultural context. This capacity to understand how differently people can understand—and then behave—is crucial to working globally.

Cognitive flexibility contributes to a Global Cosmopolitan's ability to adapt by helping them to adjust their perception of change. By seeing that change can be an opportunity, rather than a problem, Global Cosmopolitans become more open to learning and personal development.

Adaptive Capacity

Global Cosmopolitans have often been through major transitions that others might see as a devastating blow to their sense of identity and capability. I often hear stories of how Global Cosmopolitans have gained a better understanding of their own sources of dynamic resilience, or turned a crisis into an opportunity.

Eric moved to the US from Kazakhstan when he was very young. His parents were very well educated, but they did not speak English and were only able to secure jobs on minimum wage (at best) during his early childhood. While he was a very successful student, Eric felt rejected by his peers and could not see a way forward, so he started pulling away from school.

Eric was lucky enough to get work as a golf caddy at a club in a wealthy neighborhood. He was able to earn some pocket money, but more importantly, he found a sponsor at the club who ended up guiding him into a rigorous scholarship program, where he excelled. He learned how to seek help and how to work very, very hard. It was not easy, since he felt so different, and his high school background was very weak.

Excelling at math and needing financial security, it was no surprise that he chose to go into finance. From there, the ride has been easy for him. He reaches for new possibilities and believes that, with intelligence, hard work, and the right support, challenges are just new opportunities.

Given the importance of learning how to adapt when changing cultures and languages, Global Cosmopolitans, particularly those who started their journey very young, become experts at adapting to new environments. But this process can become so seamless that they might rely on their capacity to adapt and ignore their possibilities for differentiating. There is a danger that they will fail to see and articulate what they have learned. Thus a key skill is to recognize the extent of their own adaptive capacity and find a way to share and benefit from their different voice.

This is where Global Cosmopolitans have to find the right balance in order to enjoy continued international success. Those who grew up in a bicultural or multicultural household often describe understanding different ways of being or bridging across differences from a very early age.

When they are young, it might feel as if the differences are in conflict, but as they grow older, there is less of an either/or attitude. With maturity, there are fewer stories of learning how to balance adaptation and differentiation, and more about using the creative edge of difference.

By the time Global Cosmopolitans are 40 or 50 and have significant successful experience, they have a much better sense of their adaptive techniques and how to either alter them or work with them. Awareness and confidence have helped them gain a better sense of who they are and what can change with new career demands. They have often seen the dangers of adapting without retaining awareness.

Knowing, Not Knowing, and Knowing How to Find Out

Global Cosmopolitans understand how destabilizing it can be when situations in the world change, and how uncomfortable it can feel not to know or understand the context they find themselves in.

If people stay in the same or a similar environment, there is a tendency to take an understanding of the local context for granted. Moving to a radically different environment can cause a fundamental shift, reawakening the need to understand the context quite dramatically. This experience can push people into a new phase of learning, as they try to discover and comprehend what is happening.

Global Cosmopolitans are skilled in assessing what they know in a new situation, what they thought they knew but no longer do, and what they want to find out. This capacity is invaluable not only for personal development, but also for helping others cope with uncertainly.

For example, returning to a place where you lived or worked before, there are often many changes that one has to be able to see or to learn about. At times, it can call for a new way of functioning.

When George first worked in France, he learned the language in part because his colleagues only spoke French to him. Thirty years later, moving to France in a senior position in an international organization, sounded perfect. While his French served him well, he had to recognize certain changes that made a difference in his relationships with his colleagues and subordinates. To start with, many could speak English and speak it well. Also, attitudes toward job security and mobility had shifted. He found many of his employees wanting to talk about new and different ways of doing things. Turning a page on the 'good old days,' when he thought he understood the unwritten rules had shifted and helped him understand how to manage in this familiar, but new environment.

Reinvention

Global Cosmopolitans are often described as not only flexible but also capable of reinvention. They can find themselves in situations where their old identity is stripped away completely—and reinventing themselves is the only option, whether because of changes in geography, career, or relationships. This expertise in reinvention contributes to a can-do attitude to driving change. This in turn can impact on the people being led or mentored by Global Cosmopolitans, resulting in a collective determination to 'think outside of the box.'

HR managers often say, 'When I have a person who wants to be a global manager, I like to see that they can adjust their goals or how they will get there.' Awareness of their inner learning journey and their sources of resilience can be helpful when Global Cosmopolitans are assessing whether to say yes or no to another change, and whether they are ready to reinvent their lives once more. One of my research subjects, a Romanian general manager living in the USA, made the following observation.

> I have a history of reinventing myself when I move countries and work environments. I am a pro at knowing who I need to be to feel grounded and what can change. It gives me an opportunity to see myself evolve and stretches my sense of what I think that I can do. This way, I don't get bored.

Cross-Border Collaboration

From working on virtual, international teams to developing worldwide markets, Global Cosmopolitans gain experience and skills in handling many of the complex issues of working across borders.[4] One of these is the ability to manage multiple relational networks that span the world. They learn how to work with and maintain relationships with a variety of people in different time zones and cultures. They have learned when someone needs a personal email or call to nourish the relationship. These networks often leave them a phone call, email, or Skype session away from people who can help them develop solutions to complex problems, and this ability will expand as new technologies promote ever-faster and more efficient ways of maintaining networks and relationships.

But experience of being on the ground in other contexts has also taught Global Cosmopolitans what they can or cannot see when working virtually, and thus they also possess the key skill of knowing when they have to be there in person, or change how the team operates to strengthen working relationships.

Their cross-border skills, whether described as dealing with difference, boundary spanning, or navigating the space between cultures, can become second nature. Global Cosmopolitans can often describe how they have transferred what they learned from one experience to a new and challenging cultural setting. Over the years, they become more able to admit when they do not understand and need help, which is often key to succeeding.

> *Nathalie had a great deal of trust for her teams in Asia. She had spent her formative professional years in Korea, Japan, and Vietnam, but was now back home in Seattle. Given her mixed racial background as a Japanese American, she understood and could identify many underlying issues that her teams would not raise openly. She had friends and relatives in Asia that she felt very close to. While maintaining her global network was not easy, she knew when and how she needed to initiate direct contact, either with a call or arranging to get together. When she sensed an issue that was not being talked about – one of her strengths, she knew who to all and how to initiate a discussion that would help her understand and deal with unstated and important issues.*

Relational Understanding, Competence, and Respect for Difference

Global Cosmopolitans need relational awareness and competence to forge successful relationships with diverse sets of people. They must learn to grasp invisible rules and norms in order to integrate and build relationships across cultures. Bridging, navigating between worlds, and boundary spanning are frequently used to describe the skill base developed.

Global Cosmopolitans grow thanks to the relationships that they develop wherever they travel. The qualities and skills that they acquire in the face of the inevitable connections and disconnections of a global life become a much needed relational toolbox. These tools are built on the ability to show humility and empathy and to develop powers of observation and the ability to recognize and work with difference.

Humility is one of the first lessons that Global Cosmopolitans need to learn. It is closely associated with empathy and the need for respect. Whether they grew up in relatively closed societies, which encouraged them to be like everyone else in the community, or they were raised to be different, whether they have traveled globally or not, many Global Cosmopolitans have painful or happy childhood memories of growing up different. Learning humility and empathy at an early age has helped them to continue on their global journey.

Elise was only eight when she first visited a refugee camp with her father. She describes glimpsing a world of people who were fenced in with nothing to do. She looked at the children her age and wanted to take them all home. Empathy has – and will always be – her strength. Her capacity to identify the ties that bind all people is one of her outstanding skills.

Humility and empathy might feel like survival tactics initially, but they can be lifelong lessons and skills to be built on. For many people, early-career forays into very different cultures started out as failures because of arrogance and lack of sensitivity to local norms.

Liam describes a key turning point when a professor told him to get out there in the world and learn about life, and at the ripe old age of 21, he did just that.

For Liam, this step was much bigger than he imagined at the time. He did not even understand the extent of his arrogance until he was confronted with a completely different reality. While his world had been limited to his relatively elite environment in the UK, he saw the multiplicity of opportunities in learning about the world and learning about himself. The greatest gift of his first experience, working in Africa, was becoming humble.

'From the first month of working in a small village in Africa, I learned the limits of my knowledge and my ability to get something done,' he says. 'Success for me was marked by becoming humble and respectful of people who were very different. I also learned that this skill would help me for years when faced with new and complex projects in countries that I did not really know or understand.'

Tom had a similar experience working for the US Peace Corps in his early 20s. An American, this was his first step out of his world as well. Suddenly he had a project that he believed into develop and initially panicked when he realized that he had no idea how to do it or where to get help.

Some Global Cosmopolitans say they learned their relational skills through doing, while others describe learning from their own experience of being different, taking note of what helped and hindered them, or what they wished that they had understood at the time. Everyone, of course, needs to find ways to learn how to live with difference. Working globally simply accelerates that process.

The ability to adapt to a new situation is not limited to learning a new culture and working with difference. Global Cosmopolitans, particularly those who started their adventure as children, will often adapt to new cultures but also to new relationships and new contexts seamlessly. They can appear very astute when it comes to understanding what others need in a new context, and they can show their cultural intelligence when it comes to changing contexts, whether corporate, cultural, or personal. This is because they have developed contextual intelligence, which contributes to their sensitivity to how much—and in what ways—context matters.

Over time, these tools give Global Cosmopolitans the extraordinary confidence and flexibility they show in their interactions with others. Their confidence comes wrapped in any number of personal and professional challenges that they have faced over multiple life stages. Each challenge gives them an opportunity to learn about themselves; each lesson reinforces their ability to handle change and complexity and thus expand their flexibility.

Management of multiple relational networks across the world is another skill acquired through experience by Global Cosmopolitans. Most of them maintain relationships with a variety of people in different time zones and cultures. These networks often leave them only a phone call away from people who can provide ideas for solutions to complex global problems.

'Kaleidoscopic' and 'Peripheral' Vision

During their lives, most people develop a filter through which they understand the world around them. As we saw in Chapter 2, Global Cosmopolitans develop a multifaceted view of the world. Through experience, this becomes more than a mindset and turns into an ability to see the world a certain way. Over the years, the lenses of the Global Cosmopolitan have been described to me in different ways. Two metaphors that arise frequently are 'peripheral' and 'kaleidoscopic' vision.

For the Global Cosmopolitan, peripheral vision is the ability to view people, organizations, and issues from a wider angle. This allows them to see situations from different viewpoints and incorporate the broader context into their understanding. This strength allows them to expand their awareness beyond the narrow vision that most people have. They can focus on the periphery of the picture and give new meaning to the foreground.

Diverse teams that function well reveal peripheral vision in action. Finding a 'new normal' for how to collaborate involves sharing ways to maximize different perspectives. Seeing that the group can find better solutions using different perspectives can set the tone for a person's ability to build on that experience at work. As one Global Cosmopolitan HR director of a multinational company told me:

I am frequently in a position of deciding about a global transfer. If the assignment involves dealing with complex issues with unclear solutions, I listen for he ability to use different ways to understand problems and the ability to see different solutions and I hire people that have that capacity.

An experienced international consultant shared with me how he tries to get people to see how their goals for their organization are shaped by their backgrounds and roles.

He often asks senior managers to share their different visions for the organization in question, which allows for the possibility of discussing their different backgrounds and roles. He has seen how sharing a diversity of perspectives helps clients understand the limits of a single vision, glimpse the possibilities of another and, even better, arrive together at a whole new vision. This type of intervention is very natural for him, given the many cultures that he has lived in, the multiple perspectives he has developed, and the peripheral vision that has resulted from his experiences.

Kaleidoscopic vision is the result of observing how a small change can fundamentally alter many aspects of the issue at hand. People who have learned to use their kaleidoscope to view change as opportunity not only see the possibility of new vistas opening up, but also realize that another twist of the kaleidoscope can reveal new aspects or forms of change that might have seemed lost. This technique can be useful when approaching a major move, where certain aspects of lifestyle or career will be significantly different. Global Cosmopolitans use their kaleidoscopic vision to look at how they can rotate different aspects of their experiences to arrange and rearrange their roles, relationships, or perspectives on their career in new ways.

Global Cosmopolitans often relish change because their kaleidoscopic vision enables them to see further opportunities for significant improvement created by a small initial change. Liam, for example, is extremely happy living in Dubai. However, he knows that he has some major life changes coming up that could dramatically alter the direction of his global journey. He also recognizes that he has the capacity to adapt and make the new situation work.

Liam knows that, when his children go to the UK for boarding school in the next couple of years, his vision of what his family will look like will shift.

Having moved back and forth already from London to Dubai, he knows that the move will not only raise questions about where he and his wife should live but will also call for changes in how to relate to his children and his parents. Open to possibilities and used to finding ways to meet his basic need to have a great career balanced by close connections with family, he is already thinking about what he must do in order to have a positive view of his new life.

Understanding how one twist of the kaleidoscope can change everything is extremely useful in many situations, particularly when addressing change in people's lives or organizations. It can also be useful when looking for more creative ways to understand problems and solutions at work. One Global Cosmopolitan put it this way:

> *I am known as Mr 'What if'. I am always commenting in one way or another, 'What if we change just this, how will the rest of our proposal look?' As a child I was always moving one or two or five key Lego blocks, looking for something different. I have been moving around the world, enjoying the changes that give me a different perspective on life and yes, at work, I am always saying, 'What if...'*

'Inside-Out' and 'Outside-In' Vision

Another benefit of holding multiple perspectives at the same time is that the Global Cosmopolitan can be simultaneously an insider and an outsider. This leads to the ability to fully engage in a given context, while retaining the capacity to step back and observe the situation in a dispassionate manner.

An insider/outsider perspective affords a self-check on getting too involved but also carries risks. Along with the analytic benefits that come from a dual perspective, Global Cosmopolitans are also aware of the costs of moving between the two. The strength that can emerge from confronting this challenge gives them a powerful ability to bring about change. Hence, Global Cosmopolitans have long been valued in the workplace for their ability to interpret—literally and figuratively—the needs of both home and foreign operations. They know who to talk to and how to get answers. They know the fine points of doing business. They are the people who get things done, no matter where they are in the world.

The skill of seeing from both the inside and the outside is becoming more significant as organizations recognize the important roles that 'boundary spanners' can play in global operations. Global Cosmopolitans are eminently qualified for this role, because they can see the nuances of the different perspectives.

The insider/outsider capability is also evident in the way that Global Cosmopolitans can simultaneously take a global and a local perspective. There is nothing like leaving home to give you a new angle on where you have come from and the limitations of your previous outlook, but at the same time, Global Cosmopolitans are also in a good position to see how local efforts can contribute to a greater global good.

This experience can also give rise to a greater understanding of globalization and its positive or negative impacts. Understanding how interconnected the world is has led many Global Cosmopolitans to take action that will help sustain our planet, whether through projects at work, in their community, or out in the world.

Risk-Taking

One skill that Global Cosmopolitans often acquire along their journey is the ability to take the risks that lead to self-efficacy. They are often willing to take another risk, even after they have just gone through a successful change—or are struggling to recover from an unsuccessful change. Knowing they have the skills to cope and to overcome their fear, they have the self-confidence to take further risks.

People describe and handle the notion of fear differently. Global Cosmopolitans can overcome fear through their general sense of optimism or their tendency to see the glass as half full, which allows them to look at change through the lens of possibility, rather than challenge.

Martin describes himself as having no fear, but he also knows that he has gathered many skills along the way. He first noticed this characteristic when he was growing up in Norway and believes that it has served him well living internationally. His father died when Martin was still a child. He describes being very protected as a result, but his entrance into the military changed everything. This was a totally new culture for him. He was confronted with difference within his own culture. He was young, just 18, but had to lead men his age or older and he knew (and they knew) that they came from different worlds. He had to prove his worth, attempt to understand and respect where they came from, and lead them. It was an upward climb, and that story of success has propelled him ever since. Subsequently, he left his very comfortable situation in Norway to live in various cultures and then to lead in organizations where he could make a difference.

Martin talked to me about being a risk-taker. He has been one all his life. This attitude helped him go out and create a very global life and then make a decision to create a home in the UK for himself and his family. However, not all Global Cosmopolitans use this lens to describe themselves, even though they may appear consummate risk-takers from the outside.

Sana says that what gives her life direction and meaning is linked to living a life of adventure, which includes doing meaningful work. The security of this knowledge, which that she shares with her partner, allows her to move and work on projects that others might describe as risk-taking. She does not. She also works *with entrepreneurs most of the time, apparently taking many more risks. She is willing to try to develop new projects and approaches to solving complex sustainability problems. Again, however, as long as she is not risking what grounds her, she does not feel like she is taking risks.*

Complex Decision-Making and Managing Complex Change

Given their lives of uncommon complexity and change, combined with their professional experiences working with global organizations, two key and crucial skills emerge when engaging more senior Global Cosmopolitans. One is the ability to make complex decisions and the other is to manage in circumstances of complex change. Many do not see a complex crisis as a disaster, but as an opportunity. They have found that the ability to understand and solve complex puzzles has been a driver of personal and professional success. The capacity to learn contributes to their self-confidence when facing new challenges, particularly when the stories they tell genuinely recognize mistakes made and lessons learned. Some of these anecdotes turn into the stories that leaders tell when they want to encourage their employees or when they want to communicate the importance of lifelong learning—as you will see in later sections of this book.

The Two-Edged Swords of the Global Cosmopolitan Skillset

Earlier, we saw how Judith recognized that some of her skills could also be problematic. She wondered if she might have formed more lasting relationships if she had not moved so often in her early life, and feared that her need for frequent change affected her commitment both to her work and to the people in her life. This is an example of what I call the 'two-edged swords' of mobility.

Two-edged swords of mobility develop as an adaptation to a challenge. The strength can be highly visible, but it can overshadow the need to develop abilities in the opposite direction. People often reach backward to move forward, relying on what is easy, what works, and what gives them both the confidence and the knowledge that they can change. In the case of Global Cosmopolitans, change may feel normal but can also be a trigger. It sets off repetitions of earlier patterns of adaptation. The more the adaptation works, the stronger and more confident people feel. They feel so confident, in fact, that the strength becomes central to their identity.

At work, the very strengths that make Global Cosmopolitans experts at constant change can potentially create hurdles for their professional development. Moving up the career ladder can call for mentoring, teamwork, and other capacities that sometimes conflict with cherished adaptive strategies such as autonomy, a frequently cited two-edged sword. Judith developed her enthusiasm for change at an early stage in her life, but as she got older and more experienced, she started to recognize the other side of the coin. She once told me:

> *My strength and my weakness is my autonomy in new situations. I can usually handle new situations very well, but I do not know when and how to get help.*

Seamless adaptation, which characterizes many Global Cosmopolitans, particularly those who started their voyage when they were young, is another two-edged sword, and often an impediment to articulating what they have learned. Awareness of this often very intuitive process is key over the long haul, since people can gradually lose a sense of self or what is really important. They need to identify the two-edged nature of their virtues in order to confront the downsides, just as Judith has recognized:

> *I am starting to think about my future, and what is the core of myself. I know I like to take risks, look for challenges, and live up to my personal values. I know too that I can adapt to change easily. But I also know that I don't stay in one place long. As a consequence, my professional network is thinly dispersed, and I don't feel like an expert at anything. I'm maturing as a person, learning how to make better decisions for my career, and now I know exactly what to look for next, and what to avoid.*

A Personal Toolkit

The Global Cosmopolitan Skillset varies considerably from person to person. Each individual uses the knowledge, attitudes, and skills they have developed to create a personal toolkit for self-efficacy. One generalization that can be made, however, is that the vast majority of Global

Cosmopolitans learn to be articulate about the levels of development of their minds, knowledge, attitudes, and skills that place them apart.

Seasoned Global Cosmopolitans easily describe the attributes that have helped them become—and continue to be—successful. Their skills have become increasingly clarified and personalized, but may have been developed over a very long period of time. While some of these skills can endure for the rest of their lives, when people are adding new chapters to their stories, they need to be open to developing new abilities to make the change successful. In other words, the personal toolkit keeps on expanding as the decades go by.

Part II

Composing a Global Life: Navigating the Challenges and Benefits Along the Way

Introduction

I am on a continuous journey to understand how the places and people I have been exposed to have changed me so that I might live with a better sense of who I am and see the potential for where I can continue to create and make a difference in the lives of others. As a serial entrepreneur, I have been so busy that I have not taken the time out to understand who I am. I just sold my business and after a mindfulness retreat, I have organized working with a coach for some personal exploration before I start my next venture in social entrepreneurship.

Global Cosmopolitans depart from conventional life scripts, and this is both a challenge and an opportunity. Many turn the first page by making a move overseas without realizing where it will lead. Going off-script can be very seductive, yet it has complex consequences. And there are no simple formulas for addressing them. So Global Cosmopolitans must learn some new techniques and create alternatives that help make a life off-script work.

Many factors affect the way people think and act when navigating the challenges and opportunities of a global life over time. There are frequent opportunities to question the sustainability of a global life, even when the wind is in your sails and life is filled with adventure, or you are experiencing a moment of calm. The global voyage can last a lifetime, so the answers to these questions at one stage in your life can be challenged or reframed at another.

Complex challenges at different life stages can force Global Cosmopolitans to explore the issues and emotions associated with resolving the needs that arise in new situations. Life-stage challenges can change the balance of perception of needs, the experience of emotion, and indeed the whole constellation of your existence. The adventures of a global lifestyle might have been very seductive at one time, but some challenges bring your goals and current lifestyle into question. While economic and political turbulence can cause major layoffs and shifts that readily initiate conversations about change, many tipping points in people's careers are prompted by questions that start to feel like they need new answers.

In my previous book, *Global Cosmopolitans: The Creative Edge of Difference*, I focused on people in their 20s and 30s, in the initial phases of building an adult life. They were often trying to figure out who they were and what they could achieve. But most of those I have interviewed for this book are in their 40s, 50s, and 60s. They have a much stronger sense of who they are, but they are revisiting the questions they asked their younger selves about what they needed to compose their future lives.

Awareness and acceptance of changing needs or commitments require a certain level of personal reflection, maturity, and confidence. The Global Cosmopolitans who shared their stories with me 10–15 years ago have new stories to tell. Many start with changes that characterize perceptions of maturity or share an invitation to see the evolving self.

The Challenges and Opportunities of Global Living

We saw in the previous chapters that Global Cosmopolitans start with, or develop, a distinctive Global Cosmopolitan Mindset that contributes to the way they see the challenges and opportunities of a global life, and develop an equally distinctive skill set that evolves as they learn from experience. Global Cosmopolitans are composing their lives and attempting to drive the next stage in a stimulating and almost certainly challenging direction.

The chapters in this section focus on the composition of a life story over time. Certain challenges can feel complex, and making decisions about them is not easy. Global Cosmopolitans might have to dig deep into their resources of resilience to decide what to do next. Other challenges can be relatively easy to transform into opportunities. While each of the chapters highlights different aspects of these challenges encountered along the way, they are all part of a bigger, longer story that involves complex decision-making.

The different threads that compose a life are woven closely together, which makes it difficult to separate them and look at the nature of dilemmas that are both challenges and opportunities. Each chapter in this section separates certain challenges to clarify and illustrate their importance in the lives of Global Cosmopolitans, raising lifelong questions such as:

- How do I forge meaningful personal and professional identities over time?
- How do I create and maintain a world of relationships?
- How do we become and continue to be a resilient and vital couple?
- How do we raise the next generation of Global Cosmopolitans?
- Where is home and how do I define it?
- How do I manage major transitions and change in my life?

The stories of Global Cosmopolitans can help us understand the complexities of working across the world and describe the nature of some of the dilemmas as they evolve over time. No two stories are alike, yet it is possible to see patterns in the way people acknowledge their key dilemmas. Their stories often illustrate how certain trigger events, feelings, questions, and opportunities lead to turning points that result in an unpicking and reweaving of multiple threads of complexity.

Composing a life involves confronting the triggers of change at various times. Issues that you have put on the backburner might move to the front at later stages in life. Attitudes about children knowing people in their families or having connection to cultural values can raise the stakes when you are deciding whether or not to return home. The choices at age 35 can seem very different than the choices at 50. When parents age or have health scares…or even die, questions can arise again about going home. New concerns and questions emerge for people facing their 60's and 70's, not the least of which is in respect to the notion of where is home.

The process of reassessment of where is home can start in many ways, but a potential move can provoke a new perspective. It can be an opportunity to develop an Asian market that would necessitate another global move for the family, a family business that calls you home, or a commitment to a decision that your children should be educated in your 'home' country after they reach a certain age. How do you weigh the importance of attachment to place for yourself and your children? Does it make a difference when you are living in a country where you cannot become a citizen, and when you are perfectly happy with the other aspects of your life in the present?

Do I Stay or Do I Go?

Decisions to join the 'Global Cosmopolitan Club' are often based on a short-term vision, which might be motivated by a sense of adventure as well as the pursuit of professional success. The initial excitement about an international assignment can come from the sense that it is a voyage, allowing someone explore not only the world but also his or her own potential to learn from the opportunities along the way.

The decision to set off can be life changing for some and just another experience for others. Some people say that what they thought would be a short-term move has evolved into a significant chapter, or chapters, of their life. Some say that they will continue on their global voyage as long as they can, while others talk about the need to create a home where they are, or that they want to go home.

Do I stay or do I go? This is a question Global Cosmopolitans face frequently. Do they make another move? Should they stay put? Is it time to settle down and create a home? Deciding what type of membership of the Global Cosmopolitan Club you want and need is complicated, and there are as many answers as there are individuals facing the choices.

4

Who Am I? Identity and the Global Cosmopolitan

Who am I? Who am I becoming? Do I like what I see? Our identity story—the story we tell ourselves and others—can be experienced as solid ('This is who I am') or fluid. As we go through the different stages of our lives, multiple factors can influence how the identity story develops. Your identity is not your CV; it is a complex mixture of the personal, the professional, the social/cultural, and relational. The Global Cosmopolitan voyage can make that identity story even more complex.

Certain assumptions that guide the ideas in this book are particularly relevant when looking at the development of identity. One is that personal identity can be defined as the qualities, beliefs, personality, looks, and/or expressions that make up a person. Identity is a combination of different parts of a person's history, a distillation of past and present stories blended with a sense of future possibilities.

Another assumption is that our personal identity story reflects growth and development over a lifetime, and what seems important at one stage in that personal narrative can feel very different at another. While the process of constructing a personal narrative is particularly salient in adolescence and emerging adulthood, development of the narrative can evolve significantly over time. The stories people tell reinforce a strong belief that identity develops over the entire life cycle. While people describe aspects of their identity as their core, a sense of self that travels with them, their descriptions of their identity, and the skills that they develop reveal that the picture of who one is and who one can be constantly evolved.

© The Author(s) 2018
L. Brimm, *The Global Cosmopolitan Mindset*,
https://doi.org/10.1057/978-1-349-95345-5_4

We create stories about ourselves that are often rooted in the life challenges we encounter, how we resolve them, and what we learn from them. We tell these stories to ourselves and to other people and then use them as a lens for interpreting our life experience. How we tell a story that is both consistent with our background yet can be understood in our current context, and how we feel about the story that we are telling or that is being told to others are key.

Because the creation of an identity story is an essentially personal endeavor, it is difficult to define what should be included in the story, what is central or more peripheral, and how much change affects both the core and the periphery of the story. Cultural, relational, and familial factors impact on the creation of an identity story, as can past and current contextual climates.

The identity story influences the decisions people make about the dilemmas they face. Their perceptions of how to manage their professional lives, relationships, purpose and meaning, home, and re-entry can evolve considerably and reflect different standards of how they want and need to lead their life. Whether it is, as one person said, waking up one morning and suddenly understanding the meaning of life, a phone call about an emergency far from home, a child being born, or even a promotion to CEO, dilemmas and opportunities reappear at different times in life and raise questions that need to be addressed. What people decide to do, or not to do, can have an impact on their sense of their own identity and the future story that they tell about themselves.

Some of the classic ways that individuals present themselves as part of their identity story are as relevant for Global Cosmopolitans as for anyone else. But Global Cosmopolitans add levels of complexity when facing a major challenge or change that can disrupt the flow and consistency of the story. Global Cosmopolitans have to author and understand who they are, what they can change, and what must remain the same, as they develop their personal identity stories.

Global Cosmopolitans find that it helps to be able to articulate aspects of their identity and how their identity has developed through their stories of creating a life over time. They often talk about the importance of feeling rooted in a core sense of self, as well as how the changes that have made a difference over time. They also talk about an internal barometer that tells them when there is too much or not enough change, so that they feel at ease with themselves. Even the sometimes humdrum realities of life at different stages on a global journey can be associated with important questions about identity.

Recognizing the Changes Within

"I used to think that I could only exist if everything was constantly changing, but now I can see that while I might like variety in the work that I do to avoid getting bored I can only manage extensive change in my life when I am in touch with a sense of continuity about who I am, what I am good at and what I stand for."
Reflections shared by a senior executive who had to downsize his company.

Successful Global Cosmopolitans need to be aware that personal needs can shift in their importance or in how they are met. People who remain in one cultural environment still have to readjust to changing personal needs, but Global Cosmopolitans may have the more complex challenge of meeting these same needs while trying to integrate into a new culture or planning a new move.

As people mature, they are often clearer about who they are and how their needs might be evolving. Their perspectives on what they need to know in order to make yet another life or career decision can be in a state of flux. Many of the people I interviewed were very career driven, but decisions to move for career reasons can be deeply embedded in relationships that are most likely evolving as well. Seasoned travelers often know how they need to gather sufficient information to make the next move and often know who and how to ask for it.

Transitions often require a re-establishment of self to meet basic psychological needs. In particular, understanding the contradictory nature of certain needs can help explain the underlying issues and emotions that develop during transition. Learning the fine art of resolving these apparent paradoxes can lead to significant personal awareness and strength and contribute to the development of strategies to use when the next turn in the road appears. It can also provide a measure of what has changed and what has remained the same.

For instance, balancing the need to belong with the need to differentiate oneself shifts with a new setting. Motivation to live this change with potentially different strategies can be exciting for some and difficult for others.

Another example is the need for continuity versus the need for change. Managing this contradiction involves finding a fine balance between the urge for growth and development, and the desire for personal integrity. How much you change your sense of your core—and your core values over time—is a question that many people struggle with and a potential source of stress. Some adjust and seem to constrict the sense of who they are in ways that are not painful. Others may feel a loss of the sense of who they are, which needs to be addressed.

Closely linked to this is the tension between the need to move on and the need to settle down and stay. It is a contradiction that is particularly felt by those who feel that 'global' is part of their identity.

Is 'Global' Part of Who I Am?

Can you believe it? I'm married now and that changes everything. Ten years ago, I loved being on my own. In retrospect, I was not ready for commitments because I didn't have enough self-confidence, and I was still worried about ending up in an unhappy marriage or divorce like my parents. A couple of years ago, I started to feel lonely. I had lost my sense of purpose and meaning. I did not want a scripted lifestyle, but I didn't like the life that I was leading any more. There were too many nights spent in hotels alone, too many flights and nobody that I really wanted to call when I finally got home. I could see that my good friends were married and seemed quite happy. I was open and fell in love. Both of us travel a lot. I do not know what will happen when we have children, but now I have a relationship to go home to. I am actually a committed and responsible person, unlike the guy that went to business school. I love seeing you at this alumni reunion, but today, I'm actually missing home. I never thought that I would say that.

As with all aspects of identity, the importance of being global—its meaning and its part in the story—differs considerably from one person to another. Some people feel that having a Global Cosmopolitan Mindset is central to who they are. Others mention it only when asked. Sometimes, it only emerges as an issue when change implies a loss of how people are seen or how they see themselves in relation to their global life.

Managing these challenges and changes is a key skill in composing a life of meaning and purpose. A major change on the horizon can mean focusing on what to do, but it can also raise questions such as 'Who am I now, and how will this change impact my story of who I am or can be?' It can even be difficult to integrate new successes into an identity story.

Examining what Global Cosmopolitans say about composing an identity as they develop and learn while navigating the challenges and opportunities of global living can be revealing. Putting identity stories into the context of life stages helps understand how coming from a Global Cosmopolitan family, choosing to take up the global journey after studying, taking the first steps later in one's career, or taking risks as an older adult all have their own implications for identity development.

Born Global

My grandparents fled China and my parents were born in the US, but I was always curious about the history of my family. While there were many secrets that it took me years to discover, they also told many stories that made me want to see the world, and in particular, their world.

Many people say that their global journey started when they decided to move abroad, but actual starting points can be attached with invisible threads to family history, family moves during childhood, or having parents of different nationalities. These early experiences continue to make an impact on the choices Global Cosmopolitans make.

For some Global Cosmopolitans, global identity issues have their origin in the family stories that make up their family histories. The impacts vary with the stories. While many Global Cosmopolitans see themselves as pioneers of global living compared to their family and friends, others see the roots of their global story in the decisions of their parents.

My parents are from different countries and met after they settled in Canada. They were Global Cosmopolitans and that has made all the difference to my life.

The majority of stories of childhood experiences I heard when researching this book were from people who had lived in different cultures because of their parents' personal or professional choices. Emigrating as a child and studying abroad for a significant period of time at an age when their identity is developing can have a strong impact on how people define who they are and where they belong.

My parents left Pakistan so that I could be English and have an opportunity for a better life. While I am forever grateful to them, I am now sitting in Lahore, but continuing to look at the issues of being different and the need to belong. I am an entrepreneur, so how do I deal with my own issues of having grown up British with Pakistani immigrant parents?

Much of the theory about identity development is based on the work of the psychologist and psychoanalyst Erik Erikson (1902–1994), who emphasized two important developmental stages in the narrative theory of the self, one in adolescence, where identity development begins in earnest, and one in emerging adulthood.[1] People who have traveled with their parents during adolescence often share stories of the impact that crucial period had on the development of their identity story, particularly their global identity.

As these so-called third-culture kids[2] approach adulthood, they have constructed their identity stories in multiple voices, within multiple cultural contexts, and can often seem very sophisticated, yet their internal struggle for self-definition might be a bumpier ride. Being adaptable or too chameleon-like can lead to a certain level of identity confusion.

> *Lisa had started life as a 'third culture kid' as her Korean parents moved around the world. It was hard at the beginning of each move. The feeling of loss was painful. Yet, as she developed her own adult pathway, she could see the many positive attributes she had developed that kick-started her own professional development as a Global Cosmopolitan.*
>
> *While working on her MBA, she stopped and took a look at what all of this meant to her and what she wanted to do next. She recognized that her adaptability had been both friend and foe. She could move into almost any new situation and adapt. However, as a fast learner she found she quickly became bored and had a strong desire to change countries and move on.*
>
> *She also realized that she had believed for years that she had wanderlust, that she was a global nomad. But reframing made her understand that she was a Global Cosmopolitan: many facets of her identity reflected her global mind and experience. Now, she no longer wanted to keep changing countries. At the age of 30, the tradeoffs of being on her own and never feeling settled needed attention. She was ready to look at how to develop as a professional and develop the many identity traits that would help her find more satisfying work.*

Each individual has a different experience and reaction to aspects of their global journey. When the core of a story about global living is threatened or feels too distant from the story being told, young adults must resolve what needs to be done so that their personal resources and resilience are not challenged too far. One of the issues that often needs resolution is the impact of being global on their identity and in creating contradictory needs of the kind we saw earlier in this chapter.

> *My parents are from warring countries. I had to find a third one, a neutral place without so much conflict, which is why I live in the UK. I have German and French parents. While they met and married in Germany, they fought about where to live until my Mom finally won and they moved to Paris. It took be many years to find my own identity, free of their issues.*

But our identity is more than DNA. As one young woman put it:

In spite of speaking three languages, learned in three different countries before I was 18, I just wanted to settle down and have a normal life. My sister had a completely different attitude. Her choices reflected her desire to follow my parents' example. Ironically, she was the rebellious child. She hated being told what to do. But now, she has chosen a global life like our parents. For me, it feels right to be the one deciding what I want to do and how much being global will be how I see myself. My perspective on life is still very global and it will always be that way.

Being a member of a visible minority is a challenge that many children face as third-culture kids or as immigrants. Learning how to deal with difference or the assumptions made because of that difference can be further complicated by lack of adult awareness or support. Many children feel as if they have to fight to establish themselves, even in schools where everyone is different and attention is paid to bullying. On the journey toward self-acceptance, many find that the global journey contributes to personal understanding as a result of stepping out of the environment where they were raised.

Michael, an Asian American, found that being super smart gave him certain privileges in his very white, Midwestern, middle-class American community. It was only when he was at university that he started thinking about the impact of his difference on his sense of who he was or could be. In his effort to integrate, he had not wanted to know about that part of his identity. While his parents had left China to be academics in the US, he knew very little about their stories and his Chinese roots. He did know that they emphasized his weekend education in Chinese and that their close community of friends were Chinese. His curiosity about his family story was the initial motivator toward leading a global life. He also realized that part of his difference had been being a child of parents who had a very global perspective.

Dan's parents were poor immigrants, having left China for economic reasons. He felt like he grew up in a war zone in America, where different ethnic groups fought on a regular basis, and his parents were just struggling to survive. Many of his friends ended up taking drugs and never completing high school. He was hard working and lucky, and escaped by winning scholarships. He is now very successful professionally, but says that the loss of feeling rooted somewhere and being identified with a place and the people in that place still haunts him. He cannot go home to his old group of friends and his success often places him with people that have not suffered from class and racial difference. He knows that he comes to trust slowly in relationships, so while he loves living in different cultures, he is seriously considering settling down in order to develop relationships that will help him feel more grounded and like he belongs someplace. Accepting his background has helped him accept himself, which makes building trust a lot easier.

Owning the Identity Journey[3]

Looking back, many Global Cosmopolitans recount that the work they did after their MBA or other postgraduate degree had a profound effect on their identities. For many, this is where their ownership of their global journey began.

Roger's father emigrated from Iraq to London before he was born, and he grew up feeling very English, having been a product of the country's best educational system. He had difficulty identifying with his father for many years, yet as he matured, he was able to see their close resemblance. They both saw the world from a very global perspective, and yes, they were both very entrepreneurial. Speaking Arabic, he decided to work in Dubai after university graduation. For years, he had never imagined working in that part of the world, yet he saw what an exciting place it could be. After a few years of working, he decided to get an MBA. With his confidence and experience, he was now ready to open his own company, and the best place for him to do it was Dubai.

People of Asian origin who have settled around the world tell similar stories of reconnecting with their family history and looking at aspects of identity cutoff at early development stages. They often look to global and professional opportunities in Asia. Even if they stay there for only a limited period of time, they develop the ability to connect with their history and the sources of their identity story.

Victor grew up in Australia. In spite of having a very successful life as a consultant there, he wanted to understand his Chinese background more. In his 20s, he took advantage of an opportunity to work on a sustainability project in China. It changed his life. His life plan shifted. He felt that he had a greater purpose and sensed a connection to his Chinese roots. Australia would always be home, but his world and worldview expanded in ways that he had never imagined. This was only the beginning of his global journey.

Changes in the World Can Reroute the Global Journey

When they describe the 'young professional' period of their lives, Global Cosmopolitans often talk about how the political and economic environment of the time affected them, their journey, and their identity. They recognize that they were given opportunities by upheavals that opened unforeseen doors. Their ability to take calculated risks at this crucial moment made all the difference. For example, having the opportunity to work in what was still the USSR in the early 1990s changed everything for Vijay:

> *I know that I would never have had the kind of opportunities to develop my ability to get things done in a vastly different environment, which in turn has developed in me a sense of myself that is confident and sees risks as opportunities. I am a different person than I ever could have imagined. Now I live with the consequences, and from this perspective, almost 30 years on, they are very positive.*

For other graduates, burgeoning economies like the UAE have provided professional opportunities that they could not have imagined. For some Middle Easterners, working in Abu Dhabi or Dubai has allowed them to remain close to home and to their cultural background, a possibility that they never anticipated earlier in their lives. For others, mainly Westerners, it has meant learning about the region and developing a global perspective.

Meanwhile in many Western cultures, there have been seismic shifts in attitudes to issues such as sexual identity. In previous generations, people with sexual identity concerns often felt they had to leave home to accept aspects of their identity and have other people accept them. Their journeys were often motivated by a need to run away rather than running toward a global life. Now, their stories tell of people moving to contexts that are more accepting so that they can focus on developing other aspects of their identity.

Personal Timelines: Critical Decisions that Impact Going Global

When Global Cosmopolitans tell retrospective stories, they frequently describe decisions that gave direction to their voyage, or critical moments in their emerging adulthood that shaped their future. They see both the process of decision-making and the decisions that they made as key factors in the development of their global identity story.

When people describe their developmental timelines, the significance of global moves is often quite obvious. Participation in exchange programs, the opportunity to study or work in another country, or the choice of where to pursue university studies can have a significant impact on identity and global choices in the years to come. Many people describe the importance of this first step and how it contributed to their curiosity about the world and learning about their own difference.

Another common turning point in the formation of identity comes with graduation. Choosing what to do after university is often the first big independent decision people make, especially as it can mean living alone for the first time.

When I left Cambridge University, I was given great advice. Go out and learn about yourself and the world. I did just that, and it changed my life forever. When I left business school, I felt like we were being told to see ourselves with the label MBA, and this left me feeling limited and set in stone. The good news is that I have kept following the first piece of advice, the most influential message in my life.

People who start their global journey with volunteer work in very different and often difficult situations, such as by joining the US Peace Corps, begin to see that their culture and their abilities are not the only ways to get things done. Professional responsibility in a totally new cultural context can be daunting when people are young and inexperienced and away from their usual sources of support.

I was sent to teach them, and they taught me. At 22, I was sent to a very poor village to help on an important water development project. I had a Masters in engineering and my work experience consisted of working in a local garage, rebuilding motorcycles. There I was, being told that I was in charge, but I had no clue what to do. I felt helpless and desperately wanted to go home, but I knew that I could not let them down, or myself. Success came when I learned how to listen and learn from them and gain their trust and respect. This experience gave me lifelong lessons that I carry with me now wherever I go.

Developmental Moments Continue Over a Lifetime

Developmental moments or trigger events can suddenly bring identity questions and the management of personal needs to the fore. While some trigger events are transformative life experiences, others involve developing a perspective over time. New perspectives on identity can be prompted by a great opportunity, or a decision about children and their schooling. Questions that reappear often relate to keeping a sense of core identity. How much change is too much change? Who am I and who am I becoming?

The issue of passports can provoke heated arguments. Most of us take passports and visas for granted, but many of the Global Cosmopolitans that I have talked to understand that having the appropriate papers for travel, residence, or work, and as a marker of identity, can raise issues for both themselves and others. Losing or gaining a passport can have significant meaning.

Karen went to the US at age 17 to complete her undergraduate and graduate studies and had her early work experience there. While very rooted in her culture of origin, Karen had achieved a reasonable balance between recognizing and appreciating where she came from and finding herself at home in the US, where she was busy trying to find her way as a young professional. She took the opportunity to contribute to projects worldwide, and saw that she could have a significant impact on her firm and sector.

It was not always easy. She missed her family and she traveled extensively, which was exciting, tiring, and on occasions very lonely. She had battled to get the appropriate papers to live and work in the US and her goal was to settle there. However, the laws and atmosphere had changed significantly since she first arrived. While she could find interesting work in many places in the world, what would she do with the part of her identity that felt American? What would she do with her feelings of belonging if that choice was no longer available? She knew that she would surmount this challenge. She had plenty of resilience, but it left her feeling fragile and sensitized to rejection. Even if she got her papers, she would have to address the question of whether she wanted to belong to a country that did not want people from her background?

Some Global Cosmopolitans describe a process of change in their identity, attitudes, and skills over time that is the result of dramatic changes in the context of their lives. They sometimes take a life-changing risk just because it looks like an alternative pathway to financial success.

Matt, an Englishman who has been working abroad for 20 years, told me how respectful he has become when around people who are very different. He has made rapid strides in his global career, thanks to the attitudes that he developed and the skills he learned from his journey. It started on his first assignment in Indonesia.

> I grew up in a very conservative neighborhood, where anything and anyone different was rejected. I was a product of that background, but I wanted to earn a good salary for my family. When the opportunity arose, I took my wife and children on an adventure that would change our lives forever, and moved to a distant country.
>
> We started out buying only English food, but little by little we started opening up to the opportunity before us. Since then, everything has changed. We have lived and worked in multiple cultural contexts. While there have been times of trial for my family and me, we have all benefited. I never imagined the life that we have had, nor my professional success.
>
> My ability to build bridges across difference is now my calling card. But this was only the beginning. I feel like my identity has expanded far beyond the label of being a Global Cosmopolitan, and it's all to the good.

Global Cosmopolitans seem to become clearer about the sources of their competence and confidence as they mature. However difficult the turning points, this combination, along with a certain resilient dynamism, makes it easier to follow the road less traveled. While a person who never leaves home will also mature from life experience, the isolation and the drama of a global life can create a need to understand the sources of personal power that contribute to a sense of well-being and an ability to make a difference.

The Impact of Change on Identity Development

The strengths that Global Cosmopolitans develop through living and working globally can become central to their evolving identity story. As they tell their stories, they describe changes in both self-perception and the perception of others that have led to fundamental identity shifts.

Part of what appears to open the door to change when people start on their global voyage is accepting the apparent loss of competence. Initial experiences of trying to live and work in another culture can bring out feelings of failure to live up to the story that is being created. People can feel like a failure when they are unable to get the most basic things to work in a new environment; some will want to exit fast and return to feeling like a competent human being. Yet, successfully riding this cycle of change can develop the lifelong strengths and skills needed for living in a world of change. For example, many Global Cosmopolitans relate that they start to love the sense of not knowing and then finding their way through a maze of difference to new solutions.

> *While I did not label it as such, I always was a risk-taker, frequently making choices that were not necessarily what my parents, particularly my father, wanted me to make. Luckily, I was a good student and was able to win scholarships and basically make my own decisions. Those decisions took me far away from the security of my family and friends.*
>
> *I met my wife in London, but she is French and can only pursue her career in France. That was fine with me, since I have a mobile career. We have two beautiful children who are young and lively and I have enjoyed being around enough to help raise them.*
>
> *However, the more we settled into our lives here, the more I started to feel a panic – will I ever feel at home here? Will I ever speak the language well enough to connect on an intimate level with the few people I have time to meet? Instead of making the necessary changes that could have helped me feel connected and included, I found that I was avoiding people and in many ways, actively making it not work. I was losing a sense of who I was, and it was dangerous.*
>
> *I realized that at 45, I felt the loss of what I had growing up. I could not see how to get past that loss so that I could move on with my life Luckily, I broke my silence and started to get some therapeutic help and found some colleagues that were also going through similar challenges of re-establishing themselves in another culture and language.*

A technique I have used with people when they try to describe who they are, beyond the roles they might play in life, is getting them to draw concentric circles, with core descriptors in the middle and less central descriptors on the outside. A discussion can ensue about what changes and what remains the same, what is core to feeling that they are living their identity story and what is not. This is a way to get people thinking about who they are, who they want to be, and what they believe they can change and what they cannot. It can then help to look at the outside influences that have made a difference in the development of their identity over time.

With significant life and work experience, Global Cosmopolitans often describe themselves, at least in part, as having some attributes learned or at least reinforced by their global experience.

I am a humble man, who treats everyone with a certain respect.
I solve complex problems.
I am local and global, and I use this perspective every day.

This can then lead to a conversation about how they are doing in the roles they are playing in life and whether their self-description matches who they are—and who they want to become in the course of time.

A Life Mosaic

Definitions of identity, home, a sense of meaning or purpose, and the role of relationships and work are intertwined for most people. Given that a change in relationships, work, or location can bring with it changes in all other aspects of life, Global Cosmopolitans need to be able to put these pieces together in such a way that the whole makes sense.

I have already described how the idea of a kaleidoscope can be helpful to the Global Cosmopolitan. For many, the image of a kaleidoscope articulates the process they go through when reflecting on major transitions in their lives. But changes can also be seen as pieces of a mosaic that constantly shift position as the Global Cosmopolitan composes a life over time. The pieces can be redistributed, creating different designs that look different from different perspectives—and as in a kaleidoscope, some might disappear from view for a while and reappear later. The life mosaic is a metaphor that enables many Global Cosmopolitans to describe a sense of self that travels over time and through change.

> *I know that if we move to Dubai, I will not be as close to my family and friends, but the plan is to move to London in five years, and I have already worked on how to have regular trips there with my company, while I am living in Dubai.*

When using the image of the mosaic, many Global Cosmopolitans talk about the impact that conflicts between messages from their home culture and their current lifestyle have on their self-acceptance. These can be exaggerated by different cultural norms and the distance required for being a good enough son or daughter, as they deal with aging parents, as well as time management issues caused by extensive travel for work. Maintaining and differentiating the self is an ongoing life challenge.

An Identity Check

Evolving designs of the life mosaic suggest that internal monitoring is a necessary skill for Global Cosmopolitans, for whom complex decision-making is part of everyday life. Doing an identity check becomes part of addressing the next step or steps on a global journey.

A useful measure for reflection purposes is whether the balance has shifted in relation to the paradoxical needs discussed earlier in this chapter which often underlie an individual's sense of well-being: belonging and being different, continuity and change, moving on, and staying put. Other examples are independence versus dependence and connection versus disconnection. Living with internal ambiguities requires frequent rebalancing.

Black and white perspectives are rarely found in a global mindset. The gray zone becomes a place of internal dialogue and finding a new balance. Learning how to live with ambivalence and the lack of clear answers about how to relate to fundamental needs can make it easier to address what needs to change: an internal reshuffle or an external shift. It also helps people recognize that a move or a change in life stage can shift the sense of internal balance.

While a youthful need to prove their independence launches many Global Cosmopolitans on their international journey, moves provoked by a feeling of loneliness are common later in life.

I have lived on three continents and in 16 countries over the last 10 years. I have the perfect job, I love what I am doing and could do it for the rest of my life. My stories entertain all of my friends, but the truth is, I am very, very lonely. This lifestyle is not sustainable unless I make the time to create a loving relationship that will feel like home to me. I have never learned how to be very dependent, but I am ready to give it a try.

The Importance of Purpose and Meaning

Global Cosmopolitans often recount that having a sense of 'purpose' or 'meaning' is an important aspect of feeling positive about their global journeys. While definitions of both purpose and meaning can be very personal, people often describe making decisions based on seeing the purpose of the next move in relation to their overall life plan. Similarly, seasoned travelers frequently describe changes or moves that give their lives more meaning or are more consistent with their values.

One of the major threats that people describe at various points as they try to compose and recompose a life is the *loss of* purpose or meaning. When purpose and meaning are aligned with what we are doing, it is easy to ignore their importance. But when there is misalignment, it can feel as though a central narrative of our identity story has been disrupted.

What do I want to get out of my life now? Which values define who I am today? The role of purpose and meaning in our personal definition can shift over time. At certain points, it can feel central to the core of an identity story; at others, it can be placed safely in one of the outer concentric circles of our identity story.

How we understand and construct an understanding of purpose and meaning in our life has traditionally been defined by our cultures. Global Cosmopolitans, particularly those who feel defined by several cultures, often find themselves questioning which values guide them. A sense of misalignment can be triggered by a personal loss, a landmark birthday, an anniversary, a promotion, an accident, or an illness. All of these can make us question who we are and our role in life. Less dramatically, simple lack of motivation can raise similar questions. There is no need for clinical depression or the desire for a completely different life to feel this way. It can just be a matter of misalignment of motivational factors or knowing that we are not having an impact in a way that matters to us. When everything seems to be unwinding, it is often difficult to pinpoint what the actual trigger is.

Life started in Colombia for Sofia and her husband, but both of them wanted to settle down in the UK.

After her MBA, Sofia loved living in Europe. In her first stop, France, she built on her previous business experience working for French multinationals. It was difficult gaining the respect of the French, but she rose to the challenge. She continued on her highflier track in the UK, where she gave birth to her two children.

She loved living in Europe, travelling, using her global skills, and seeing herself become a Global Cosmopolitan. It was a label that she happily integrated into her sense of self, her identity story.

Being labelled as global by HR, did not mean that her organization understood what that meant – either for her or the organization. Right after her son was born, they offered her the promotion she deserved, but it was in Australia. Sofia wanted to be in headquarters and wanted to establish her base in the UK. She felt completely misunderstood, and could see that her future would be limited if she stayed with her current organization. She and her husband had already purchased a house and her daughter was enrolled in a great school.

Meanwhile, Sofia's marriage was falling apart and she questioned whether they could make it as a couple. They had arranged excellent childcare, but it soon became clear that her son had serious learning challenges. Could she give up all her investments in living and working in the UK and go back to Colombia, where she knew that she would be seen for her competence and potential? She started questioning her life on every level. She wondered how to unravel the essence of her life's purpose and what she wanted to do about it.

She organized a trip home to explore the possibilities. It was clear that she could work there. It would not be easy, since commuting would be a nightmare, but she could arrange support from her family and good schooling and childcare. It was hard to say what the tipping point was. It was a confluence of factors that helped her decide to go to Bogotá. Her husband agreed to a divorce and to visit the children regularly in Colombia. She found a unique therapy for her son and it appeared to work very well.

While her new position allowed her to develop her work status and skills, she was very concerned about losing her Global Cosmopolitan status. Promises were made of experience on a global scale and eventually a possibility of returning to Europe. The decision was made.

How Will *You* Measure Your Life?

Mature Global Cosmopolitans frequently raise the question of how to define what they value and what gives their life meaning. What are the profound beliefs that are central to their story? Is it being a good son or daughter? A high achiever? Or a caring person? People who have changed countries are often faced with a clash between the loss of a cultural mandate and the imperative of a new agenda.

Andre had just taken on the directorship of a major institution in Hong Kong. In his late fifties, it was the opportunity of a lifetime. Then, in the midst of a strategic process at work, he found out that his sister, who was still living in his hometown in Europe, was very ill. All his life, he had measured himself in relation to his caring role for his family and the important people in his life. How could he call himself a good brother, if he did not go home? Yet, at this moment, he felt that he had to choose to see through the first steps of his professional commitment.

Until now, his role at home, in his family, had kept him rooted in the rich soil that nourished him. He had always been a good son and family member. He had also been the good son by being so successful in his career. But for the moment these two aspects of who he needed to be were in conflict.

Living in different cultural contexts far away from home, he had come to depend on his professional identity for acceptance and respect as he traveled the world. He valued his global reputation and had never imagined the profound impact it would have on him to not be there for his sister.

Suddenly, he was worried about who he really was. What was really important to him?

The threads of identity are complex and intertwined. Whoever we are, our identity story is carefully woven through shifting commitments, relationships, and perspectives. The challenge of nurturing a sense of self is only heightened for the Global Cosmopolitan, who must weave an intricate multicultural pattern into the rich tapestry of life.

5

The Professional Me

The 'professional me' has been central to the stories of global journeys that I have listened to. The people interviewed for this book were very career driven, yet understood that a decision to move for career reasons can be deeply embedded in personal relationships that are most likely evolving as well.

At different stages of their lives, Global Cosmopolitans find themselves questioning whether they have the energy to devote to a change of country, organization, or position, particularly if they have made a commitment to investing their time elsewhere. A new location, a new house, a different school for the children, a greater distance from aging parents—these are all factors that can influence the Global Cosmopolitan's professional choices.

While it might seem as if Global Cosmopolitans lead fascinating lives, in which anything is possible, the reality is that people have to like who they are and who they are becoming. Career decision points, especially those involving another relocation, highlight the implications of prioritizing career and professional development over personal relationships and responsibilities.

Careful investment in understanding and addressing the concrete impacts of a move on these relationships is central to making successful decisions.

In addition, there is the major consideration about how the decision will affect the long-term career story: professional identity, potential, competence, knowledge, and developmental opportunities.

I have found that seasoned travelers talk easily about what they add to their professional environment. They describe how they have developed and

© The Author(s) 2018
L. Brimm, *The Global Cosmopolitan Mindset*,
https://doi.org/10.1057/978-1-349-95345-5_5

learned from their lives, and how their confidence and competence help them take a more accurate look at themselves. This knowledge, as well as a sense of purpose and meaning, fits into their global identity story, which becomes increasingly articulate over time. The ability to understand how they evolve professionally, and how that affects relationships at work and in the other spheres of life, becomes crucial.

Developing and Benefiting from the Global Cosmopolitan Mindset and Skillset

The Global Cosmopolitan Mindset is often fundamental to how people define and differentiate themselves in a professional environment. The global journey hones the multiple skills introduced in Chapter 3, including: making complex decisions; developing positive relationships across multiple layers of difference; having multiple lenses for approaching a challenge; and knowing how to manage oneself in a constantly changing environment. Those Global Cosmopolitans who continue on their world journey find these 'second-nature' skills invaluable in their work. They are often used to describe both how they function and who they are.

For many, the perception of working globally as an ever-evolving adventure that allows growth and development is key and contributes to a 'professional me' that they are proud of. They look for opportunities that enable them to benefit from and continue to develop a Global Cosmopolitan Mindset. Personal growth, a global perspective, and creativity become central to their professional experience.

Building Bridges Across Difference

Global Cosmopolitans understand the importance of bringing their unique and experienced voices to working with others. They come to assume that colleagues will have different perspectives and ideas, and that it is important for teams to benefit from these differences. They have significant experience of finding the best way to work across multiple layers of difference and of building bridges of communication whenever possible. Learning how to participate proactively and help others do the same becomes part of their relational skillset. One executive managing a midsize company in Dubai told me:

We are all working for the same company, but our nationalities are very diverse. That is my new normal. I love it. I have learned how to lean into potential cultural differences or interests when necessary, but I have also been able to build teams that operate effectively by emphasizing what excellence at work means in our organization. Our corporate culture is strong, so people are hired and trained to work in that culture.

Global Cosmopolitans become sensitive to the ways in which an office in Japan, for example, has different modes of functioning than the office in Australia. They learn how to identify and work with the impact of the local culture and understand how it affects the way colleagues work together in a different context. It goes without saying that working across cultural borders—either face to face or on virtual teams—also becomes part of daily life. Knowing when and how to have team meetings or whether direct reports need personalized treatment becomes clearer. Understanding when you have to get on a plane and just be there becomes instinctive.

Experience with very different populations can contribute to excellent negotiation skills.

Everyone at work knows that I have a great deal of expertise in negotiating in Asia. I grew up negotiating for my immigrant parents in Sweden. I learned how to find as many win-win situations as possible. My experience and success as a top-notch negotiator have been well recognized.

The personal experience of managing difference, sometimes starting in early childhood, means that Global Cosmopolitans can be sensitive to these issues in others and among teams. This attention and sensitivity to global and local influences is just one aspect of what they notice or know to look out for. If given the opportunity, they can help the head office build appropriate bridges between different parts of the organization.

Feeling at Home with People from Different Cultural Backgrounds

Another aspect of Global Cosmopolitans' professional identity is their ability to feel at home in various cultures. This helps them to be happy in their global lifestyle and contributes to their success at work. While they know that they are different—and that they have a global perspective—they can also enjoy experiencing being local.

Georges was born in France but has lived in a number of countries. He has been very successful and attributes his success to his ability to really listen to the people he meets along the way. He goes to a new country, develops a client base, and subsequently engages in serious negotiations as part of his work in private equity. He has cultivated the skill of deep listening.

However, he uses only one language to do all of this: 'I have lived in many places in the world for significant periods of time. I am married to someone from another culture. We are raising our children here in Singapore. While I identify as a Global Cosmopolitan, I have never been able to learn languages other than English. I have developed skills that have allowed me to develop deep cultural understanding, both where I live and where my work takes me.'

Georges has developed the art of observing people outside their work environment, engaging people on topics unrelated to business. Since he often has to spend weeks away from his family, he uses his spare time to learn about local politics, food, and cultural activities.

Understanding and Redirecting Your Motivation

Given that any big endeavor takes a lot of time and energy and usually requires trade-offs in other aspects of life, knowing enough about what motivates you, how to find ways of using that motivation, and the skillsets needed to further and benefit from that motivation all develop over time. João knows:

I am much more motivated during certain stages of developing a business than others. When I am creating, I am highly motivated and I motivate others, but I need teamwork during other developmental phases.

People who have experienced a certain success often believe that the very characteristics that they have developed on their global journey are as motivating as turning a profit. For some, the complexity of challenges can be a driver in itself and they actively seek out problems. Others need to solve complex puzzles regularly; otherwise, they get bored and lose their momentum. As Richard, a senior executive from Australia, puts it,

The one thing that is clear through all of my experience is that I like to understand. That is my biggest motivator. Having gone through all of the challenges and changes, having gone through the insecurity puts you in a good spot to go through new learning cycles. It particularly works if you pay attention to where you want to go and what you want to do.

Aaron added:

I feel much more motivated now that I am in charge of my organization. I love advising others and helping people understand what is interesting and exciting about their projects.

All three—João, Richard and Aaron—have built successful careers paying attention to the role of passion and drive over time.

Radical Professional Shifts and Their Personal Consequences

People naturally raise questions about making a radical shift in their professional lives. Their stories about potential change are generally embedded in stories about the relationships that give their life meaning beyond their professional context. They frequently talk about children needing a different environment, family members aging or dying, or getting seriously sick themselves and needing to take time off.

It is important to remember that some changes, such as taking time off from professional life, can mean that the entire family loses its right to residency. Alternatively, a move to another country can completely change the whole-family dynamic. Decisions like these cannot be taken lightly or in isolation, without dealing with the potential consequences. Conversely, seeing and believing that your expertise can be applied to other possibilities allows a certain freedom of movement.

Stan recognized the attributes that meant he could be labelled a Global Cosmopolitan. He was born in Hungary but grew up in Canada, where he attended university, then medical school, and started working.

It was clear that Stan was very proud of being a doctor and the work that he had accomplished as a doctor. But, he had at least another nine lives that he wanted to lead. So, although being a doctor was central to his identity, he took advantage of a chance to do a graduate degree in management.

Stan would probably say that, while his more personal ways of describing himself defy categorization, adopting new 'labels' has facilitated his ability to make major changes in his life. He has openly welcomed being a father. As a child, he wanted to describe himself in many ways, not the least of which was to be a writer. His ability to integrate also allows him to assume new roles with ease and enthusiasm.

Mid-career Entry—An Important Demographic

When you are in your 40s, and a professional opportunity to enhance your international profile appears, it can be the best possible career move. Life can feel too complicated or rooted for some people to move, and they might find it difficult to leave the head office, but for others, the draw of learning and having a different life experience, as well as the potential for new professional opportunities, is very seductive.

Steve worked for a large American organization that had been sending people abroad for many years. In his mid-40s, he had made it known that he was interested in living outside of the US for a while.

When the opportunity arose, Steve and his wife, Sharon, jumped at the chance of living in Europe with their two young children. The assistance the family received made all the difference in their adjustment. Steve had regional responsibilities, which meant that he had significant travel obligations, while Sharon and the children had to adjust to a new setting, new language, and of course finding new friends.

While they had never lived outside of the US, they had traveled extensively and loved the sense of adventure and the opportunity to learn about another culture. It was not easy for Sharon, who was taking a break from her career to raise the children. Steve's travel meant that she was on her own quite a bit, but she made friends easily among other women in the expat community.

While the strength of the organizational culture made communication quite easy, Steve loved working directly with people from different cultures. He was confident in his ability to manage people, which made it easier for him to tackle some of the differences that he encountered. When it was time to go back home, the family was not ready for their adventure to stop, so they signed up for an extension to Steve's contract.

Moving to a new country, even if the language is the same, can be much harder than envisioned.

When her partner Tom, had a great career offer from his company that meant moving from New York to London, Mimi decided she could continue working from her new home in London, with occasional trips back to NYC to touch base with her colleagues, when necessary. She started to understand that being away from her head office in New York and her network at a crucial time in her career, might limit her future opportunities.

While it was possible to work at home in London, Mimi was lonely and missed the day-to-day contact with her colleagues and friends. She admitted that she could not have realized ahead of time how much she would miss the broader context of her life. Tom was frequently working in the evenings, or was tired from working long hours. In New York. Mimi knew who to call when she wanted to go out.

It was difficult for Mimi to admit that the move to London was not working out for her, since she saw herself as someone who liked adventure. She and Tom were able to talk about their situation and agreed to leave after two years instead of three. Mimi, determined not to let this move be a failure, decided to take courses at a local university, which allowed her to open new areas of interest and at the same time, meet new people.

Learning how to manage this type of global change for the mid-career cohort is crucial. Companies are more creative than they used to be in finding formulae that make it work, but they also know that moving a whole family means making sure that the move—or potentially moves—will go smoothly. It is a big investment, but global mobility will only continue to increase. CEOs will have to work on identifying the best and the brightest for such assignments and look at new ways of recruiting and retaining them.

Role and Career Changes Often Feel Like Identity Shifts

Certain roles in life become integrated into identity stories. Some are personal, such as, 'I'm a father, while others are professional, such as 'I'm an investment banker/entrepreneur/CEO.' Certain roles are closely associated with identity descriptions, such as 'I'm responsible/committed/a change leader.' Altering role description can change the story one tells about oneself or that others tell about the individuals concerned.

Even with the benefit of experience, maturity, and increased competence and confidence, a career decision can still involve a change in status, and a global move can raise serious identity questions. A decision to move is like a turn of the kaleidoscope; it redistributes the hierarchy of the pieces in our personal mosaic.

I've been living abroad for 15 years and I've just been offered the perfect re-entry position in the US. I've been saying that this is exactly what I want for years, and now I have it. It should feel like it's opening all the doors that I want to open, but right now, I'm experiencing closing doors. Is this the end of my global career and will the expertise that I developed get lost in the immediacy of local pressures?

While I've loved what I've been doing, how much of that was linked to living and working in different cultures? The learning, the difference and the adventure have always given the added edge that made my work exciting, but also made me feel exciting and special. Will I still be part of the global picture or will I be thrown into some of the dynamics that I've been avoiding at headquarters? I've always valued my independence, and being in charge of important global projects has been a perfect match. While it's time for me to take a much more senior position, I'm concerned that I'll lose two important keys to my motivation: my ability to be in charge of what I'm working on and my global mindset.

The freedom some people experience and their identity as Global Cosmopolitans often becomes a central theme of their story. Re-entry, even after many years of success, can raise fears of losing cachet or independence—and necessitate a reframing of professional goals.

Professional and Financial Success—A Mink-Lined Trap

For certain Global Cosmopolitans, professional success has also been financially rewarding. While money might not have been an important part of their earlier life story, once they are used to having it, it can become essential. Perks, such as paid school fees and affordable domestic help, have facilitated family life for many people. They acknowledge how comfortable all this can become but sometimes feel they have to weigh comfort against other life goals.

For Stuart, a major promotion that meant significantly more financial security and a leap into a very cosmopolitan lifestyle had many benefits. Yet, over the years, he started to feel trapped in Hong Kong, a city that did not feel like home. He could see the strain it put on his wife and children, including one child who appeared to have learning disabilities. He was traveling all the time, and wondering why he kept running so fast. A move back to Europe would be better for them, and an excellent offer came his way.

While this new situation would be ideal, it came with increased responsibility and significant international travel. Going home for him also meant accepting that he belonged to the community of Global Cosmopolitans and he wondered whether this was the person that he wanted to be with his old friends and family.

Home Is Where I Work?

For some people, global organizations provide a 'home,' as they move from one office to another. For employees of these organizations who identify with the corporate culture and the way things are done, working in a new culture or a different region can mean both the exposure to difference and the comfort of a home base.

A professional environment that people call home can also be the source of ideas for starting a business. This can have major implications, particularly if the relevant professional networks are based in a different location. While some people hang on to a dream of starting their own business, this might not be practical or even feasible after years of traveling. Certain sectors and professional networks can keep people feeling enmeshed in a culture that is different from what they wanted or expected.

> *Max is from South Africa. He comes from a family of entrepreneurs. After a number of years in investment banking, he was ready to start his own investment fund. The factors were complex, since he adored South Africa and the life he had there. However, it was not the right place for starting his fund. He had gone to university in both the UK and the US and had worked in both London and New York, as well as South Africa. He knew that he was overdue for settling down with his family – and creating his own business would mean a commitment to one place for an extended period of time. Accepting that he would not be living close to his family and friends in South Africa, he considered moving to the same city as his older sister. While his sister was very busy with her own business projects and family, Max decided that her presence made all the difference and decided to base his fund in London.*

Place Matters

As they advance through life, Global Cosmopolitans become increasingly conscious of the importance of place. Experience and change help them to learn what brings out certain attitudes and skills, and they will look at the context of their lives and their work to see if there is enough alignment to bring out their best sides and possibilities for development. One successful entrepreneur who had transplanted himself to Silicon Valley told me:

> *I like to be where the action is. I love to live in a vibrant economy where I can see possibilities and, of course, I like to be with people that are like-minded. I have the opportunity at this stage in my life to help people that are trying to create companies.*

I love mentoring, and that is so easy to do here. Helping others to be successful and investing in their projects is a perfect combination for me. The best part is, I do not need a fancy office or clothes to impress people.

However, there are inevitably times in a Global Cosmopolitan's life when they feel as if they are in the wrong place. Being different can become a burden rather than an advantage. It can become tiresome to represent a particular culture or even a very different professional background. There are also lifestyle differences that can impinge on feeling welcome or at home. For people concerned about how they will be treated because of their sexual identity, context can make a huge difference. Being valued for who they are and what they can contribute professionally is key and the bottom line for judging where to work. Obviously, the issues for this group can be complicated by the cultural attitudes that people come to work with. This will impact the choices of many, particularly when they are considering a long-term commitment to global living. Others have country-specific issues, rooted in stories that may be difficult to understand.

Chen said that he was able to work comfortably in China, but he did not believe that he could live his marriage with his European husband comfortably if he went home to China. His parents have made it clear that they want his relationship kept a secret, which he respects, but it has meant that he has directed his career toward opportunities where he could be open about his marriage.

Being Entrepreneurial in Multiple Ways

Many Global Cosmopolitans identify themselves as 'entrepreneurial.' And being an entrepreneur on a global scale certainly comes with both challenges and opportunities. Some of the people I interviewed had been entrepreneurs before they left home and would happily move to create an organization, if that is what it took. Over time, the reality of certain ventures means longer-term investments in building local networks and living in places that do not feel like home. Confronting this reality can be a turning point for people who see themselves as at their best when creating their own businesses.

Certain entrepreneurs follow an idea or move to an area where they think they have a good chance to be successful or at least have an adventure. But they soon realize how entrenched they have become in building their own organizations. Some find that they can be victims of their own success.

Working hard to build an organization, time can fly by, and extracting themselves from possibilities, networks, or a family that loves where they are, can contribute to them creating homes in unexpected places.

Although some people do not identify with being an entrepreneur, they end up creating companies because they can or need to do it.

> *Victor is working with other others to create and develop a sustainability consulting company. Having a sense of purpose has been the momentum for his taking the risk to leave strategy consulting, which gave him much more security. His team works in key locations around the world, and he is developing the office in Hong Kong.*

While some Global Cosmopolitans describe themselves as risk-takers and entrepreneurs, most describe themselves as having an 'entrepreneurial spirit' that allows them to be innovative at work and comfortable with entrepreneurs. I noticed this particularly in people working for organizations that are finding new solutions to global challenges, where Global Cosmopolitans can put their multiple skills to good use.

> *Sana is working with a start-up in Singapore. In describing her contribution to the company's sustainability projects in the region, she says: 'I can go to Myanmar and set up at least 25 meetings over the course of a couple days with people representing different aspects of the scope of our work who understand how to find and implement solutions. I am not an entrepreneur in the sense that I do not need to start my own organization, nor do I want to take that kind of risk. But I am very entrepreneurial in my attitude to organizing a working process. I know when to adapt to a situation in a new culture and when to initiate. I also know when and how to build trust with people in another culture, helping them feel comfortable with both who I am and what I can bring to the situation. It is not always easy, since at times, I feel like they appreciate that I look like them and at other times they have expectations that people with the knowledge and power to make a difference are probably the Westerners on my team.'*

Professional Networks are Crucial

Global Cosmopolitans frequently talk about their worldwide professional networks. Maintaining these relationships across time zones and long distances can be complex. Moving to a new environment also means building local networks and often—for those who have regional responsibilities—across multiple cultures.

People who never leave home can maintain close contact with their professional and school networks, old friends, and extended family with relative ease. Global Cosmopolitans need to build their own web of connections. It is important to find people who share similar challenges and who can provide both understanding and the ability to challenge one's thinking—often other Global Cosmopolitans.

Presenting my work to the Young Presidents' Organization (YPO) in Singapore gave me the opportunity to understand some of the benefits people derive from being part of a professional club. Many of the audience members were not native Singaporeans and found the network particularly helpful when grappling with professional and personal issues. They had established a system of small support groups that discussed topics such as budgeting, doing business in Indonesia, dealing with stress, or decision-making. The idea was to have leaderless groups with very clear boundaries around what could be discussed. This helped people build a sense of trust and mutual respect, as they shared and learned from others who had faced similar challenges to their own.

A large number of highly successful entrepreneurs can be found in Silicon Valley. Many of them started their global journey elsewhere, but have made California at least one of their homes. Two transplants who had come from the same MBA program in Europe—one from India and the other from Spain—decided that it would be beneficial to create a group that would be similar to the YPO, but centered around the business school they had attended.

While not a solution for everyone, this is a model worth considering. The two Global Cosmopolitans concerned have developed a network of people from different cultures, backgrounds, and age groups who understand enough of each other's professional and personal situations to build a trusting and dynamic system of support in Silicon Valley. The group has helped each individual go beyond what they know already—so much so, that they have helped other alumni groups get started in the Bay Area and elsewhere in the USA.

What is interesting is that this is not a group of outsiders to the Silicon Valley culture. Although they might have been born in other countries, they are successful and well-integrated business people who live comfortably and for the most part feel they belong to the community they live in. Yet they also value what they can learn and develop as a result of working together.

Global Cosmopolitans can also use their professional networks to help them make the next step in their journey.

Matias is a Chilean living in Dubai and preparing his return to Chile. While he loves his company, he has already realized that working for it anywhere in South America would not be of interest. He tried a sabbatical year a few years back to explore his options and realized that the ideal solution was to start his own business. A true networker, Matias actively managed his network back home, which he knows will ease his professional re-entry to Chile. Since he had already started a couple of successful new ventures, he was excited about the possibilities.

Non-professional Networks Matter Too

Another type of network is the social identity group, such as sports clubs, hobby circles, philanthropic projects, parent organizations, and other activities that revolve around special interests. For many Global Cosmopolitans, their professional context and immediate family constitute the only 'reference groups' as psychologists call them, that they have the time to invest in actively. Their work and family identity is the focus and, while they may look for other group involvements, these are often linked to professional interests. Sometimes these people depend on their life partners to develop other reference groups or to maintain important family and friendship relations.

While moving to another country might require immersion in a completely new culture, there are usually opportunities to live and work with other Global Cosmopolitans. For some, this can mean living partially or totally in an 'expat' community or in a subculture of people from the same country of origin, with little direct contact with the local community. Others try to find a flexible place that allows for different connections with people and groups that match their needs at a certain point in time.

There are a significant number of people who are ambivalent about strong group attachment and will choose their involvement with any 'club' carefully. They might see themselves as independent of spirit or so different that they do not identify with any group. Over time, however, even independent spirits may feel a shift in the types of people they want or need to bring into their inner circle. This can lead to changes in their immediate situation, a decision to go home, or the search for a differently populated professional context or social space. They may actively search for a way to reinvent themselves, creating a circle that will support their need to relate to different groups of people.

I just want to be comfortable when I go home at night. I want to live and work with other Global Cosmopolitans. I will only look for work in London, New York, Singapore, or Dubai, where people understand me. This is where I belong. Yet, will this work for me in the long term?

Needs can change, but Global Cosmopolitans are experts when it comes to the specific need for group involvement. Whether they are introverts or extroverts, skillful or less skillful in building relationships, with each new move they know they need to look for balance.

For people traveling in nuclear families, there is often a tendency to assume that the minimal time and energy left over from professional life will be devoted to their relational context. Relocation consultants will often advise people about where to live, appropriate schools, etc., based on a family's expressed needs for formal and informal identity groups.

There is no doubt that technology helps. People are becoming increasingly comfortable and inventive about how to maintain both loose and strong ties online. We live in a connected world, and the Internet provides support for a variety of reference groups. It also provides a great deal of support for all aspects of who we are—political, caring, funny, or ready to run a marathon a year.

Unexpected Crunch Factors: Travel and Time Zone Constraints

What I loved most about global living, I now like least – travel! What does that say about who I am?

It was only when I got to the region, that I realized how much of my time and energy would be spent traveling.

While professional identity may well become bound up with travel, after a while, other priorities can feel like a more fruitful use of time. And while there are some people who can exist on very little sleep, having work (or a personal life) that requires living in very different time zones can be taxing. Sometimes it takes an illness to reveal that the stress is just too much.

The truth is, if I stay up to learn about the markets in NYC from Hong Kong, I start to make poor decisions. Maybe it takes someone younger, but I don't know if I can do it.

The ability to cross time zones with ease can be an important part of Global Cosmopolitans' professional identity. But it will also impact on their lives in other ways. One of my interviewees recalled a conversation with his partner:

Talking to you when you are ready to go to sleep in France and I am just waking up in Seattle is a nightmare. For a minute, I love you, and then I see those sleepy eyes and I get angry. I can't help it. I'm used to sharing everything, and I often go to sleep feeling so alone with my little problems of the day.

Ultimately, this Global Cosmopolitan couple will have to find a creative solution or their relationship will fall apart under the pressures of 'jetlag.'

Challenges for Global Cosmopolitan Women

Change and reinvention, moving into new roles and opportunities, can seem easy or normal to you, but is it for the people you are working with? For example, moving to another country for a promotion or more interesting professional opportunity is simply not possible for women from certain cultural backgrounds. A decision to break with the cultural constraints such as their familial roles can feel so devastating that they return or stay home.

Awareness of such differences can lead to creative solutions for helping women to develop according to global norms, while staying loyal to their local community. There might be a different way to include them in teams and training. For example, one Global Cosmopolitan CEO told me about his project to enable women from Saudi Arabia to attend training outside of their country by sponsoring family members to travel with them.

Many of the women I have interviewed describe moments in their lives when setting different priorities forced them to look at who they are. A common theme was how much their financial responsibility or professional ambition was central to their core being, relative to their relational world. The combination of children and career makes it hard to play all the key roles that contribute to an identity, even for women who never leave a single cultural context. Yet geographical distance, different norms, and professional imperatives—as well as being the person they want to be in relation to key people in their lives—only add to the complexity of the challenge for Global Cosmopolitans.

Women without male partners, especially those with children, can be stressed by local rejection of their life situation. Excessive travel and long nights at work when they are the only parent available for the children can make certain roles feel impossible. While many of them can afford childcare, this does not substitute for the time spent with children or the rule that many couples are able to follow that, 'one of us will always be here.'

The number of men following women's global careers is still limited. While there are couples that 'take turns' or men who encourage their female partners to take the lead, the reasons for the lack of male 'trailing spouses' are multifaceted and certainly linked to the fact that women are still likely to earn less than their male partners or, worse, that organizations make assumptions about women being available to travel. There are organizations that make efforts to help both partners find work, and there are couples that use technology and creativity to find solutions, but female Global Cosmopolitans continue to face challenges that men do not, even in the twenty-first century.

Sometimes, opportunities arise that are not necessarily global but give women an opportunity to use the skills they developed on their global journey in a different way—and potentially contribute to a larger sense of meaning and purpose. For instance, a number of women talked about applying their skills to the issue of gender diversity in their organizations.

Kate has been working in an investment bank for more than a decade. Over the last couple of years, she has been contemplating 'what next?' So when an offer came to move to another European country as head of a gender initiative, she was thrilled. She knew that it was a risky step, but she was tired of seeing so few senior women at work. While she had not been a particularly active voice for women's rights to date, she believed that a cornerstone of her expertise stemmed from being different and managing difference.

While Kate never imagined working on gender initiatives when she started her career, she recognizes that what she has learned about being different on multiple levels has contributed to her skillset. She has also seen that there are numerous reasons why women have had difficulty maintaining significant global careers and wants to facilitate gender equity across the world. While she has been successful, she is sensitive to the political dynamics, cultural differences, and the process of inclusion as crucial aspects of maximizing the extent to which women feel they belong, will be respected for their difference, and listened to. She wants them to see opportunities that will make it worthwhile to put so much time and energy into a career.

However, I also heard many stories from women about difficult encounters with HR, when they sought the opportunity to use their global skills. In addition, many female Global Cosmopolitans described instances of lack of sensitivity to family constraints from their organizations.

Ambitious and hardworking, Lily, originally from Hong Kong, loved her work as a consultant in France and after many years of global living, built a family and a home there. Her mother, who she had been very close to, had just died and she was looking at what it meant to be a mother herself – for the third time. Her mother had come from China after the birth of her two sons and now she felt lost without her. After the birth of her daughter, her French mother-in-law, to her great relief, volunteered to help.

Six months after the baby was born, she was asked to work on a project in South Africa. While very willing to go back to work, she was not willing to leave the country at this time. She had two other children who were already in middle school and she wanted to be at home at night for them. She knew that once they went to bed, she could work long hours, but at least she could have dinner with them and be a presence in their lives. When she tried to discuss this with a senior partner, she discovered that he was unsympathetic. While she had given a lot to the company over the years, she felt like she had hit a ceiling that was crashing down on her and she knew that she would have to leave.

The Glass Ceilings of Global Cosmopolitanism

One of the professional challenges that both men and women describe is the limitation of being 'other.' A clear-cut example of this is when high-flying Global Cosmopolitans work for organizations that limit who gets the most senior opportunities and management board memberships. This can be a matter of company policy, but it can equally result from government regulation. And some people may not be able to transfer to the head office of their organization because they cannot get a work permit. Organizational and political glass ceilings can restrict people's futures and make them re-evaluate their plans.

Some Global Cosmopolitans' ambitions are restricted by their own desire to return home eventually. They may find this a major barrier to their long-term commitment to a company. Recognizing the issue early is important, if a creative solution is to be found.

If this organization is not able to facilitate my eventually going home, I need to start thinking about other possibilities. Although I like my current employer, I have to look for other opportunities that will open doors when I decide to go home.

People look to the top—and if it is viewed through a glass ceiling—they will be less committed to the organization. A move to a company or country where access to power is possible will be better for their professional development.

Identifying Global Cosmopolitans

How do we identify potential leaders with the skills and experience to create dialogue between different factions? How do we select the people who can—and are willing to—lead the changes that have to be made? Organizations may benefit from looking to their own Global Cosmopolitans for advice on change or leadership, rather than seeking them externally.

For many Global Cosmopolitans, especially those who are single, their colleagues have become their dominant identity group and their work environment has become their home. Even when they move countries, many aspects of their work or their organization will feel familiar. With the amount of time and energy they put into work and travel, the time left for investing in other relational spheres and opportunities for development in other aspects of life will at best be minimal. This can mean that their professional identity dominates other aspects of their sense of self.

If organizations can understand that their staff are starting to see the company they work for as home, they will be able to generate greater loyalty and commitment to their mission. In a turbulent world, full of travel and change, sometimes the most secure environment and stable culture is found in one's existing organizations. Home is where the heart is, but it is also where the work is.

6

The Relational Me

Identity stories are best understood in relation to the people in our lives. Many of our relationships help us feel connected to the important aspects of who we are and who we want to be. While 'the professional me' receives a lot time and attention, the members of our inner circle often have a major impact on whether we feel we are developing a consistent and authentic identity story over time.

Leaving a place called home can mean a loss of the social identity groups that gave structure and meaning to our existence. At the same time, the significant relationships left behind can contribute to a sense of home and meaning or purpose in life—even for Global Cosmopolitans who are creating new friendships and nuclear families on their travels.

For Global Cosmopolitans, understanding these connections and their need for intimate relationships is a precious part of building a life. Yet staying in contact with the intimate circle of important characters in their life story is particularly challenging when the development of that story also involves multiple global moves.

Global Cosmopolitans, like everyone else, typically need to resolve the 'who am I?' in their various relationships. The concentric circles of people in their lives—the most intimate relationships at the center and the most peripheral on the outside—are made more complex (or more interesting depending on one's perspective) by global mobility.

© The Author(s) 2018
L. Brimm, *The Global Cosmopolitan Mindset*,
https://doi.org/10.1057/978-1-349-95345-5_6

Back to Basics: The Development of the Relational Self

How do people start to learn about relationships? Along with genetic propensities, a relational world starts with its very earliest attachments, the people in one's inner circle, often parents, grandparents, and siblings. Throughout their formative years, children learn about how to be in relationship with others, a process that has both familial and cultural scripts.

What is learned very early in life, long before the development of conceptual frameworks or words in any language, leads to formative feelings about safety in relationships. While there are multiple opportunities to improve our comfort and skill at managing relational worlds over time, early experiences are a crucial basis for this development.

Global Cosmopolitans living far away from family and friends have to look for new ways to meet their relational needs. The people they encounter have different backgrounds—often based on significantly different cultural variables. It is easy to be unaware of our unwritten rules about how to be in a relationship, until confronted with someone who is different. Friends, lovers, or colleagues who have different values and constructs about relationships can help contribute to a broader view of the rules learned or constructed over the years, but certain differences can still be stumbling blocks to developing connections with people.

The Complex Circle of Family of Origin

If you never leave the city where you were born, you may or may not find that you create new ways of relating to your family and friends over time. Global Cosmopolitans, however, even those with strong family ties, spend most of their lives far away from their roots. This can lead them to feel distant and cut off the possibility of finding new ways to have a positive time together. At the same time, for many Global Cosmopolitans, maintaining relationships with their family of origin is central to their understanding of the meaning of family and to their lives as a whole.

The unintentional consequences of having little or no direct contact with one's family of origin can be a major concern for both parents and children. It is often up to the Global Cosmopolitan to look for ways of staying in touch. It is ironic that opponents of globalization often accuse people who choose to live globally of having no roots—even no loyalty to their country of origin. Yet the Global Cosmopolitans I have interviewed consider their roots and values central to their identity story and to their search for meaning. For them, understanding themselves means understanding where they come from.

Many Global Cosmopolitans begin their story with the experience of their parents or grandparents, or through the many stories that they have been told during their formative years. 'Where did my immigrant parents really come from?' and 'how important are their stories to me?' can become important questions as they develop their relational self. Ann, for example, has read a lot about the immigration of Vietnamese refugees to Canada and the USA, but she is only slowly learning about her family story,

They wanted me to succeed in their chosen country, Canada, with such a vengeance that they never helped me understand the importance of their history in Vietnam on who they were and why they acted the way they did. It took me years to have the courage to explore their link between their past and mine. Knowing their stories has helped explain so much about how they related to me, what they left behind, and how they related to their newfound country. I feel much closer to them now that I understand their behavior and their attitudes. Recently, they talked about moving back to Vietnam, which touched a deep fear of losing my parents as I know them and of losing my roots in Canada. I cannot imagine changing my deep connection to Canada. In spite of the many years I have been away. I have been spending vacations there with my family. If they leave, will I still consider Canada home?

Global Cosmopolitans' connections to their childhood home usually depend on families and friends. In spite of family problems, such as divorce or feuding, Global Cosmopolitans are often concerned about how to stay connected. Sometimes parents, other family members, and friends themselves move away, which raises the question: Will it feel like home if the people in my intimate circle are no longer there? Knowing that they always have a reason to go home to see family can abate the fear of disappearing roots.

When people talk about traveling to see family or organizing family reunions, they emphasize the need for elaborate planning. It is a subject that they often discuss with their friends, but ultimately they need to find their own solutions to resolve conflict and avoid misunderstandings. Couples, as we will see in a later chapter, often have to agree 'equitable' solutions, no matter what the history of the relationships has been.

My wife and I are French. My summer home in the South of France was home to me and now it is home to my children. They go there every year and spend time with their grandparents and extended family. Even though they go to a French-speaking school in Singapore, it is in the South of France that they learn about the importance of their roots and their cultural heritage. I could not live outside of France, if I didn't feel that my children were experiencing these connections. While our evening meals include conversations about global issues, there is a respect that is developing for their roots as well as their wings.

This couple shares a similar background, and they are in agreement about how to organize their time in France, which is not always that easy to arrange. But bicultural couples have the additional complexity of how to stay in touch with—and how be inclusive of—families of origin from two different cultures.

Some Global Cosmopolitans feel 'cut off.' Because of family history, they might have failed to develop a sense of their roots or a feeling of being at home in family relationships. This can put a lot of pressure on a couple and can be confusing for their children. Some people try to understand what the loss has been, what can be done to heal the wounds, and what other ways there are to stay connected.

Rohan's family was full of cut-offs. 'Walls' had been built to avoid conflict while everyone lived in the same city. Now, having made a life for himself in the US, he does not want this to happen to him. He returns to India whenever he can, at least once a year, playing his role of eldest son and trying to be engaged in his extended family – including a messy family business. With all that he has learned about diplomacy from his global life, he has been pushed to his limits when he finds himself trapped in roles and behaviors that he does not respect. Every year, there are some setbacks and some progress, but over time, he has realized that his desire for connection is much stronger than his drive to cut off. Being a diplomat has paid off.

Professional Relationships

In reality, Global Cosmopolitans tend to devote more of their time and energy to their work than to the rest of their lives. Not only can work provide a feeling of being at home (as we saw in Chapter 5). Work can be a source of friends and multiple affiliations that contribute to supportive networks and interesting people that can contribute to interesting projects or leadership opportunities. Career commitment takes time, and the challenge and excitement of meeting people that are different is a source of motivation for people on a global voyage. They describe feeling richer as individuals through engaging with and learning from other people.

Integration can be comfortable, and friendships are often made within these professional situations. However, not everyone wants to have friends at work, and hierarchy, language, or culture might prevent it. Many Global Cosmopolitans say that they hardly have time for their families, their family of origin, or the families they are creating, let alone create good friends.

Different Notions of What It Means to Build and Maintain a Relationship

As individuals differ, so do their attitudes toward initiating, building, and maintaining their personal and professional connections. Culture, personality, and experience all play a role in forming the attitudes and behaviors that affect both the ability and the desire to invest in new or old relationships. Rules defining the quality and quantity of our relationships are created. These relationships affect self-understanding. Some people tend to invest in a few key relationships, sometimes only one, and others like having many people in their lives, both close and distant.

Generally speaking, Global Cosmopolitans have developed the skills necessary to work across borders. Friendships that cross borders or cultures are a different matter. Yet many of the people I interviewed said that having the opportunity to get to know people very different from themselves added to the pleasure of their global adventure.

Managing relationships is rarely easy, but some extroverts say they thrive on it. They love the idea of having friends everywhere, or meeting someone they know from one place in an airport in another. Introverts can have very different perspectives. They are careful who they relate to and may use technology to manage the distance in relationships. Either way, the relational world has to be created and maintained if it is to provide support and become a source of growth.

Possible futures can also be a source of tension. Global Cosmopolitans may struggle to stay involved and caring with current contacts if another transition might be imminent. They must find a balance between developing relationships and supportive networks where they are, and letting go when the time comes to move.

One useful metaphor is characterizing maintaining different types of relationships to eating an artichoke. You have to find the right balance between the time you spend finding the edible parts of the outer leaves and the time it takes to savor the core. In the same way, one can spend too much time on peripheral relationships, neglecting core relationships and what they have to offer.

Keeping in Touch

There are multiple relational spheres of influence and support, and all of them demand a certain degree of investment and nurturing. Global Cosmopolitans do not always recognize the skills they use to do this, but their stories indicate that they have learned some valuable techniques. Indeed, they often push themselves beyond their comfort zone in order to maintain their various relationships. For many, in spite of being able to connect via technology, there is still a need for the personal touch with the people who really count. They take the time to write a personal email or make a personal phone call when it matters.

Seasoned Global Cosmopolitans understand that certain relationships cannot be taken for granted. They know that they need to invest in people to feel their presence. However, their perceptions about the need for investment, how to do it, and the ways they do it at different stages of their lives vary greatly. Young people seek to work abroad for a variety of reasons, but there is often an underlying desire to develop a sense of autonomy, even an attempt to build their relational sphere independently. More mature Global Cosmopolitans know how to blend both their past and their present into their relational world.

Social Identity Groups

It can be challenging for Global Cosmopolitans to find the time to meet people through sports clubs, religious affiliations, expat organizations, or children's schools. Knowing the local language or sharing a common language can help them to become involved in some local activities. Clients and colleagues who speak English or other languages used at work can also ease integration. Global Cosmopolitans need to balance the time and effort they put into their friendships and networks between: people in their past; people in their present situation; and people who might be part of their next step.

As Global Cosmopolitans mature, they talk about making time to reconnect with people from different parts of their lives. Some say, 'Now that my children are grown, I have a bit more time.' Others say, 'I'm curious to find out about my childhood friends,' or 'Now that I am starting another chapter in my life, I wonder who I want to reconnect with.' At the same time, they also describe groups (see Chapter 5), which they have joined to help set the stage for new projects and new life chapters. Their relational world continues to evolve.

As is the case for identity (see Chapter 4), understanding the complex circle of relationships is a multifaceted subject. The need to maintain important connections with people over time, space, and language becomes a challenge in itself. Global Cosmopolitans must learn the skills to create relationships they can trust and deal with the tensions that can arise between remaining connected to the past while living in the present. Their relational world is further complicated by the impact of culture. The necessity of balancing changing needs when moving and traveling becomes a significant element of life, as we will see in the next two chapters (on couples and children, respectively).

New Ways of Defining and Describing a Family Context

Global Cosmopolitans often make efforts to replicate a sense of family in their new locations. They describe cultivating a 'family' among friends who are interested in the same things or by finding new areas of interest. In the case of parents with young children, they often surround themselves with people who are in the same situation and can fulfill the function of an extended family.

Fabia has decided to make the city and country she is living in home. So she is making long-term investments for herself and her daughter. The local context she now calls home complements but does not replace the familial, friendship, and professional relationships that also contribute to her feeling of being at home in the world.

Fabia's local 'family of friends' represents different times and places in her life. There are people in the same profession whom she has gotten to know and like on a personal level. There are parents of children in the neighborhood that she has met through various children's activities and school. Many of them have lived in different parts of the world and speak multiple languages. Then there are old friends who have turned up in the same city. And the circle is an open one that allows further inclusion as her needs and interests develop. All of these relationships have required nurturing. And it takes time and energy!

Certain individuals can be very fearful of foreigners or might not be interested in expanding a well-developed network. That said, many Global Cosmopolitans want to get to know local people and there are some who make that goal the first item on their agenda when they move to a new place.

In very transient and diverse communities, this can paradoxically be both easy and difficult. There are often many other people looking to recreate a relational sphere. Equally, some people may be suspicious of short-term relationships and wary of investing in people who may not be around for long.

Friends and Family Can Be the Keys to Feeling at Home in the World

Knowing that there are family and friends to go home to often makes it easier for Global Cosmopolitans to continue on their global journey. Work can provide a feeling of being at home in the world, but friends, family, and colleagues are central to helping people remain connected whenever they change the place where they live and work. However, that does not necessarily make re-entry as easy as might be expected.

I have loved our years living abroad. While I never knew if the friendships that I made along the way would be part of my life after I left, I always kept one or two people close to my heart – as I did with my friends that I grew up and I knew would always be there. I have kept in regular contact with those key people in my life, often vacationing together in Greece or Sicily. Last year, we finally moved back home to England, but we decided to live outside of London so that we could raise our children away from the big city. I no longer have easy access to the people that were close colleagues and friends when I lived here. Commuting to work gives me very little time to grow the close, intense relationships that I love. I assumed that coming home, I would no longer have to worry about making time for my old friends. I still remember the heart-wrenching feeling that I had when I left. My desire to return was based on my appreciation of my friends and family and how important it is to nurture those relationships. Many of my friends are in a similar situation of feeling overwhelmed by what we have to do just to get through a day, so I am hoping that we'll eventually make more time for each other.

Relational Needs Can Change with Age and Experience

Seasoned Global Cosmopolitans understand that relationships need to be nurtured and cannot be taken for granted. They know that they need to invest in relationships to feel their presence. However, their perceptions about the need for investment, how to do it, and the ways they do it at different stages of their lives vary greatly.

Births, deaths, and illness are particularly powerful events that can bring people together as well as highlight changing needs. Seeing signs of aging parents or even missing important events in the lives of siblings and friends can shift priorities about spending time together. The years can go by quickly, and a decision to go on a short global adventure can turn into two or three decades away from home. Another global move can highlight shifting needs at any stage, and Rene could feel the difference,

> I didn't expect to live in Brazil for very long. But I had this great idea, and I wanted to see it through. Being an entrepreneur is incredibly time-consuming. I like it, but it means that I have no time for building relationships. I am at the age where it would be great to fall in love and develop a long-term relationship.
>
> When I first lived in Brazil, I was younger and working as a consultant. I had an amazing social life. But what was right in my twenties and thirties is not what I need now. I miss sharing my life with another person and having children of my own. I never thought that I would say that, but it is true. Unfortunately, I am spending most of my time developing my company. I know that I should set aside time for other aspects of life, but it's hard.
>
> Also, I am very ambivalent about staying in Brazil. I might, but I might want to leave, and I realize that if I fall in love with someone, I need to find someone who would be willing to either stay or go.

Putting Important Relational Events in the Calendar

Global Cosmopolitans describe flying home for a weekend to go to a family reunion, wedding, or alumni gathering. Others plan events, such as big birthday celebrations, that bring together their friends from all over the world. Even people on limited budgets will prioritize expenses to see their families or make sure that their salary packages include trips home.

These events are important in the relational sphere and can be well worth the time, effort, and money. A Peruvian banker, Valerie, told me about her upcoming trip to South Africa for an alumni get-together, which she insisted was 'a must.'

> *For family reasons, I had to come home to Peru, and even though I cannot earn the same amount of money as my classmates, I just need to be with my MBA friends every year. I am currently single and work most of the time, so this is also a way to clear my calendar for the type of relationships that help me feel at home in the world. Maybe in a year or two, I will feel more at home here, but right now, I am missing people that have had the kind of global experience that I have had.*

Loneliness Is an Occupational Hazard

Loneliness is one of the not-so-secret enemies of Global Cosmopolitans. Many people travel or try living in another country because they want to test their ability to make it on their own. Global Cosmopolitans frequently relate how much they love working on their own or the quiet moments of solitude on an airplane or in a hotel. But a dream come true can turn into a nightmare when you feel lonely. Surrounded by good friends, now, Leah is very hesitant to move yet again,

> *When I first arrived in the US, I missed my friends so much. My husband is very loving, but he was going through his own issues and to be honest, he does not really understand how much I need friends as well as him to care about me and to listen to me. I love it when a friend calls up and just wants to talk about her life concerns. For me, friendship is about openness and caring and being there when someone needs you. It took a long time to find and establish the type of friends that I had back home.*

People who travel extensively and have not developed significant primary relationships describe moments or periods of extreme loneliness. While work can continue to be exciting, loneliness can dampen our motivation in all other aspects of life.

> *How did I end up In Hawaii? It sounded great, but what a disaster! I have never been so lonely. It's beautiful here and I have a great job, but finding your way into the culture here is not easy. I thought I could keep hopping from one country to another, but I have changed.*

However, Rick listened to his heart and paid attention to his changing needs. Feeling that his life was unstable and lonely, he could see that he was more open to falling in love and making a commitment. Now he was ready. Within two years, he fell in love and got married, had a baby and moved to San Francisco.

But now, he sees other challenges to living in San Francisco, such as being far away from his aging parents in Australia and his global network. He will have to come up with new solutions.

The need to find a balance of belonging follows people across their lifespan. But over time, people learn what they need from relationships and attempt to develop the skills that will make their relational world work. This leads some to look at issues of commitment to a significant other or to friends and family.

Global Cosmopolitans can feel lonely even when outwardly they have a busy and exciting life and career.

Ellen pays a lot of attention to her relational world. It is her job. She helps others settle into new environments and develop the skills they need to be successful. She has lived in many cities around the world and has made an effort to participate in local groups that enable her to feel connected to where she is and to find new friends.

Although happy with her work, Ellen can feel quite lonely in Hong Kong. She raises many of the issues that Global Cosmopolitans talk about: being different and not really accepted by locals; not having an easy point of contact with them other than work; and social status changing because of the needs of the couple or the family.

Ellen had always found a way to belong in both local and global communities. While this was still true, she realized that her openness might be shifting.

'Some cultures are more inclusive than others. It has been hard for me to establish friendships here. I like to expand my social circle beyond work. The other big complicating factor is that this time my husband is often not here, since he has taken early retirement and is busy establishing our retirement house and community Washington. So, I am single – without being single.'

Given her personal awareness and skillset, Ellen has made sure she has connections that are important to her, finding some in the expat community in Hong Kong, so thinking ahead about what she will do to involve herself in her new community in Washington. Still in her fifties, she is beginning to design the next stage of her life.

Moving into a new context or category with a different set of needs—for example, a desire to be in a committed relationship—can be challenging. Some people say that they did not plan their existence this way, but time has flown by and they realize that they have neglected their personal lives. While the deeper reasons for this situation vary tremendously, the question often arises at a point when they no longer do the work that has become central to their life and identity. They experience a sense of loss at not having people who care about them—and whom they care about—close by. They have failed to expand their relational world through participation in different social identity groups.

Losing Someone Close

When people embark on their global adventure, they rarely think about the possibility of losing someone in their family or their close circle of friends. But over time, this becomes an issue. Sometimes enjoying being with family members while everyone is still healthy involves complicated planning; other times, a crisis raises the stakes for living so far away; and once in a while, there is just loss, a loss that feels so far removed from the global life that it is hard to assimilate. This can leave a Global Cosmopolitan feeling more alone than ever.

Marion went home to the Netherlands when her elder sister died. The loss was devastating for her. At the funeral she could express her emotions in Dutch, learn about her sister through the stories that others told, and feel that she had started the mourning process. Then Marion returned to London. There was no one to talk to, nobody who spoke Dutch or knew her sister. She went to work. It took a while to realize that she needed to talk to somebody. In this case, she found a therapist who spoke Dutch, since she knew, in this situation that understanding language and culture was important to her.

Designing Workable Solutions

As their relational needs become clearer, Global Cosmopolitans know that they need to look for workable solutions, even if they are not the most conventional or simple to organize.

One solution, although obviously not an option for everyone, is working from home. This gives a great deal of flexibility in when and how people can be available for their families. With many Global Cosmopolitans working outside the office when they are traveling anyway, working from home is increasingly accepted. Chris feels lucky,

The nature of my work does not require a lot of office or face-to-face time, which is fine for me. I need and enjoy the time I have alone to focus on my work. I have been highly successful working this way, and I am happy to use my free time to be with family and a few close friends.

I can be a husband and a father in a way that I never thought was possible. Both my wife and I have very busy and engaged lives, but working from home has contributed to improving my family relationships. Being able to pick up my children from school or take them surfing with me has been great.

Since I can work anywhere, we are considering taking a year or two off and living in Asia, which is far away from our home in California. We have travelled before and this would give us another experience of living in a different culture. I have actually established a project that would benefit from my being in Asia, so it looks like this trip is going to happen.

Generational shifts can also prompt Global Cosmopolitans to rethink their relational world and come up with new solutions. Mark knows how to appreciate the present, but he understands that his relational world will shift soon,

While my children are still in school here in Dubai, and my parents are both in good physical health and have relatively flexible schedules, they visit us here for a couple of months every year. It's a win-win solution. In a couple of years, our children will be going to boarding school in the UK, and we are sending them to schools near my parents, which is great but then raises the question of: where will we be? At that point, we'll consider re-entry, based on our immediate family's needs. Being realistic, I want all of us to have time with my parents like we have with my wife's family in Greece.

The Global Cosmopolitan Mindset, as we saw in Part I, involves learning how to live with difference and benefit from it. The skillset acquired as a result is as relevant to forging a relational identity as it is to building a professional self. If you are comfortable crossing cultural boundaries, then generational, familial, and emotional boundaries will no longer seem like a bridge too far, especially when you learn how to apply those skills to your own life.

7

Making It Work as a Global Cosmopolitan Couple

Establishing a resilient relationship is a challenge for most couples. Sustaining that relationship over the years is even harder, requiring commitment to its continuous development and evolution. From the outside, international couples might be perceived to be living a charmed existence. But the added complexity of their lifestyle means they have to make decisions that have an impact on their lives at all levels, and effect people in different ways. Frequent changes in cultural context can affect their entire family system in significant ways.

The differences in background and personality that individuals bring to a couple can be experienced at different points in time. This can lead to frustration, but it can also lead to opportunities for creative solutions along the way. Sharing the process of discovery, creating and recreating different patterns of living, and taking the journey in a new direction can reinforce the bonds between a couple. Global Cosmopolitan partners often describe sharing the high points in their travels. They talk about seeing life in a way they had never anticipated—together. They frequently recount who they are individually and as a couple after all the ups and downs in very positive terms. Above all, they talk about the fun they have had on their life adventure. It might not always have been easy, but they have had the opportunity of a lifetime. And, thanks to their Global Cosmopolitan Mindset and Skillset, they have made the most of that opportunity.

Openness to Change

Couples have to navigate significant turning points over time, and there are no clear solutions when you feel on the precipice of change. Although you

© The Author(s) 2018
L. Brimm, *The Global Cosmopolitan Mindset*,
https://doi.org/10.1057/978-1-349-95345-5_7

can work on long- and short-term plans together and may well have talked about 'What if?' for a number of scenarios, you often need to deal with the reality of a situation and your own reactions to it with no warning. If both partners are open to change and aware that another turn in the kaleidoscope will throw up new patterns that they have the skills to accommodate, you will be able to cope.

Challenges often come from family of origin and children. A crisis can occur at any moment—a phone call from home about illness or death, or a child who needs different education or health care. But equally, sudden change can result from a phone call offering a great new work opportunity.

Crises and opportunities can bring out the similarities or the differences between what each partner wants and needs in the short and long term. Global Cosmopolitan couples may need to develop a high level of flexibility so that changes to their lives can be made.

Some of these changes feel negative and limiting. A parent getting sick or dying can lead to questions and major differences about responsibility in relationships. Such situations raise questions like, 'Do we have to go home, or can my mother move across the world to live with us?' While couples do discuss the inevitability of family loss and change, reality brings the discussion to another level. And some people have to admit that what they thought they could live with, they cannot. A child in trouble for whatever reason can create a cascade of questions about what to do, while a change in the political or economic context that threatens your physical or financial safety can also be a game changer.

Other changes or opportunities can feel exciting and positive. A professional change can feel like a once-in-a-lifetime opportunity, but the couple has to decide if it will work for them and their family. A project that might be tangential to career progress, but is aligned with values around social impact, can become a real opportunity to make a difference.

When is the right time to change course? An opportunity for a child sometimes feels like the chance to change gear. When a son or daughter goes to college, a parent might glimpse an opportunity to switch roles, go back to school, or live closer to home.

All of these challenges, both positive and negative, require a couple to cope with change. Some changes will require adaptation, both major and minor. Some people can tolerate the turning of the global kaleidoscope without feeling dizzy. They are comfortable with the notion that the next move will have more x or y in it—and may cause some z. So what if they have to wait to work on other aspects of their life projects?

Sharing the Journey

Living internationally puts a lot of pressure on couples. Both members can feel cut off from their family of origin, old friends, and people who can be relied on to understand them. It becomes up to the couple to create a loving and vibrant context that will survive long-term transition and change.

Stan and Sara were excited about their move to Bangkok and both actively contributed to making it work for themselves and their children.

Both Sara and Stan put a tremendous value on their relationship. It is the key to both of them being able to lead the lives they want. They talk easily and have complementary skills. Stan likes to plan and structure things. Sara says that he is great at setting goals and making them happen. Sara is very organized and can realistically set limits about what is doable in the short and longer term.

Each of them can find it exhausting to have both of them working. But Sara believes that the fact they do so is important for their relationship. She has seen too many unhappy women living as rich expat wives, with too much time on their hands and no sense of purpose, while their husbands continue to grow and enjoy their international existence.

Both of their children were born in Bangkok. Luckily, they have a great nanny, who is very much a part of the home they have created there and is loved by both the children. Stan and Sara travel for work but have a 'one-parent' rule, which means only one of them is ever away at a time.

With their scheduling done, they have time to socialize in Bangkok and travel as a family. Meanwhile, one of Sara's key skills is the ability to say 'No, I can't,' at work and at home. They both want to pass the ability to have fun and excitement every day on to their children. They regularly text each other about their 'wow!' experiences.

Learning how to talk about thoughts, feelings, and differences takes time—and it is necessary to work on developing this skill before a decision turns into a crisis. When insecurities arise on a global journey and there are no support systems at hand, what starts as a pressure point can soon become a source of fear and anxiety and escalate into assumptions and inferences that magnify the original problem. Beneath the surface strength and self-confidence sometimes lie feelings that can erode an individual's well-being and the couple's resilience.

John loved the idea of following Beth's career to Argentina. Their two children were in boarding school, and they both felt flexible about the 'what next?' He is a writer and thought that he could work as easily there as at home in New York. This was his second career after more than 20 years as an investment banker.

He realized that this was a big step for Beth, who had been a 'third-culture kid' but at mid-career was getting her first opportunity to move as an adult.

Within no time, she was using her fluent Spanish and travelling extensively for her work. All of the skills that she had developed earlier in her life gave her a powerful sense of who she was and who she could be. And offers came her way for advancement.

John, on the other hand, had never lived anywhere but NYC and after his initial excitement started to feel lonely. His Spanish was terrible, and his progress was minimal. He was so happy for Beth, but started having doubts about himself. But instead of talking about his self-doubts, he started criticizing Beth and blaming her for things not working out.

Luckily, a friend came for a visit and got him talking about how disappointed he was in himself, helping him figure out a way to talk about it with Beth. She had already told him that he had to stop criticizing her, so he knew that he had to get past that and respond to her questions about what was going on. First of all he apologized and admitted that he was having difficulties and it was not her fault. They talked about small changes he could make that might make a difference.

On her side, she was also tiring of the travel and missing having time together. She was committed to putting certain limits on when and how long she would travel for work. He admitted that he missed having a place to go to work and people that counted on him. He started to think that, although he did not want to return to his previous career, he might need a structure that he respected. This discussion gave him just enough momentum to find a part-time teaching position at the local university and a group of writers that wrote in English.

One of the keys to happiness and success as a couple is learning how to make joint decisions that include career but do not exclude other important factors. Understanding not only the 'I' but also the 'we' involves a complex formula. Even defining what the 'we' means can be complicated by a decision-making process that is often dominated by career needs.

Creating a relationship that fosters growth and personal development over time for both partners, across changing personalities and circumstances, can be challenging. Some classic pressure points are as follows: the question of whose career is the more important; a widening difference in experience; shifting attitudes to moving; having the time and energy to devote to family life; extensive travel with extended separations; and financial security.

Applying the skills that you learn from living a global life—like listening and appreciating difference—can fall by the wayside when the single most important relationship in your life is threatened by change.

As we have seen in previous chapters, many Global Cosmopolitans spend the majority of their time and energy at work. As their confidence and competence matures in the workplace, they can feel that there is a widening gap between their professional needs and their needs as part of a couple. While Global Cosmopolitans might be considered experts in managing very difficult conversations and negotiations in their job, they might well leave their skills at work and forget to apply them at home.

Not Aarav and Sana. Sharing goals for their lives that were consistent with their values, respect, and caring for others was as evident in their relationship as in their professional lives. The energy that they create together is palatable. They love what they do and how they do it, Both of them have a lot to say about shared goals, values and the importance of being about to talk to each other.

Aarav: The first big move was from India to the US. My wife and I both went to graduate school in the US. My degree was in business; hers was in law. It was not easy, but we made it work and had a great time doing it. She worked as a lawyer and I worked for over ten years getting the corporate experience I needed. I always knew that I wanted to go out on my own and create an organization that could have major social impact. While we loved living in the US and might eventually go back there, we decided to move to Singapore. We were starting a family, and this way we were closer to our extended families. We would also be closer to where I felt I could have the most impact.

What a leap of faith! But after a few years, my company is growing fast and already making a difference. I have 50 people working for me, people from diverse backgrounds all over the world. They are also interested in the company goal of making a difference in the world, while all of us want to make some money. It's happening. I do not think that I could have done this if I had did not have the combination of wanting to make the world a better place and at the same time having the technical and relational skills to make it happen.

Sana: We have always been planning our lives around each other. We are on the same team and we always thrive on the energy of exploring doing something new. We give each other permission and we make sure that we allow the other to enjoy what they are working on. Both of us are very mindful of how engaged we are in what we are doing, how we are doing it, and how it impacts our family. The focus on who we are as people makes it easier to focus on who I am rather than where I am.

My Career, Your Career, Our Careers

The topic of careers becomes particularly thorny—if not taxing—when a option to go global or stay global is involved. Global Cosmopolitan couples have similar characteristics to those that stay at home, but many more complex challenges to face. It is hard enough to adapt family life as professional changes bring about personal changes and affect the time and energy you have available for home. But the consequences of moving globally add extra layers of complexity.

In some couples, one partner is willing to adapt—and possibly put his or her own career on hold—when circumstances demand. Some people, more often women even use the move to change careers, take a break, or spending more time with the children. Others make a point of ensuring that both members can pursue their careers wherever they go. And a few adopt a strategy of taking it in turns—prioritizing career development for one and then the other with each move.

While there are efforts to support dual-career couples, this continues to be a difficult issue for Global Cosmopolitans, who sometimes are faced with having to decide whether or not to continue on their global journey, which include practical considerations, such as getting work permits for spouses who do not have a job when they move.

Couples with a long history of global living know that moves can seriously impact the career of one or both members. Traditionally, it has been women who have reinvented themselves in order to facilitate their husbands' careers. This was the case for Rohan and Gita.

> My career would never have been as successful if my wife had continued the career that she wanted when we first started our global voyage.
>
> Starting out in the 1990s, working in what was then the USSR, was an adventure in itself. Gita and I enjoyed an amazing life, but there were trade-offs that had to be made. My career, which was enabling us to live with a certain security, lifestyle, and excitement that we both wanted, was highly mobile. We often moved every two years and to places where her career was severely limited. Her background was in education, and whenever possible, she worked as a teacher, but she had to give up the progression she would have had if we had stayed put. We are now in Abu Dhabi at a time in our lives when we can think about what next. There are no regrets about those career decisions.

More experienced couples are now taking turns or finding a place where both can work. But this does not always work out. Simon describes how he tried—and failed—to accommodate Agnes's career as a consultant.

> We tried moving back to London, but it didn't work out for me. I couldn't find work that was engaging enough, and then I was headhunted for a dream position in Abu Dhabi. I was already bored and restless and wanting to move globally again, and this was the opportunity of a lifetime. It was my turn to decide and so we moved the family to the UAE.

Agnes had to give up her career again in order for us to live here, and struggled with the loss of her work in London. It has not been easy for her; she's been incredibly creative in building a life for herself and the family, but lurking in the background is her need for career accomplishment and success.

The kids are fine, benefitting from a great school and the opportunity to know children from everywhere, but our next turning point will be coming up when we send our children to boarding school in England.

I envision a deep period of reflection. I love my job. Every day it is exciting, and I continue to be on a steep learning curve. I could settle here until we have to leave. I do miss my parents and friends, but up until now, I have managed to fly home for reunions and fly family here on a regular basis. But our parents are ageing in two different countries in Europe, and their health is starting to deteriorate. I have a strong sense of family responsibility. Also, once our children move away, I assume that my wife will want to return to a more active professional life, which she does not see happening here. It will certainly make it easier if she finds something exciting in the region.

Many couples at this key turning point decide to live more separate lives, but this is not what either of us wants. We have seen too many couples draw apart by living separately, and eventually divorce. We also know that if one of us feels deprived of having a choice, resentment can build up and make living together quite challenging.

Acknowledging that there has to be some career reciprocity can be the key to making a relationship work.

Sylvie, a French entrepreneur had moved to Dubai to start her own company. It had been difficult and she had invested a lot, but it was worth the effort and her business became very successful. She fell in love with another French entrepreneur and was hoping that he would take the risk of moving to Dubai with her and run his business from there. She was trying not to push him too much, since he had never worked outside of France, but she knew that the market and the possibilities could convince him to give it a try. She also made it clear that this was her moment, but she was very open to letting him be in charge when the time came for the next move.

Global Cosmopolitan couples also have to recognize that an agreement to take turns might have to be put aside when a particularly exciting professional opportunity is on the table. Prioritizing one career over the other at this point may be the answer. The interview with Emma was timely…

After getting their MBAs, both she and her husband, Hugo, moved back to Belgium. Both continued working after their two children were born. He continued working for a small start-up and she took the risk of slowing her career down and taking charge of a gender initiative. Her work became highly visible and she was offered a significant promotion – to the head office in the Midwest of the United States. Hugo was extremely supportive and said, 'Let's make this happen. It's your turn.' He knew that his work was easy to do from anywhere but he had to get his company's approval. His response to their initial refusal was, 'I guess I'll have to quit.' The company's no turned into a yes when he clearly showed them how it could work.

In the last interview, they were packing their things and ready to move. However, Emma and her husband's success does not mean that there is a formula for harmony. Global Cosmopolitans need to look for creative solution in each situation as it arises. Their skills of coping with change come to the fore, but so do their skills of communication and empathy. Each test of a couple's resilience strengthens—or weakens—their ability to cope with change as a couple. It has not been easy for Janice,

I am married, yet I feel like a single Mom. My partner and I met in the US. We decided to move back to Europe, so that I could be closer to my family in the UK and he could be in his home country. We both have excellent professional opportunities in Germany. However, he is in Munich and I am based in Berlin. I have made some concessions that I now see have made my professional life much less interesting for me. While this seemed like a good solution at the time, now that we have a young daughter, it feels like a nightmare. I have not had time to make friends in Berlin, and I am exhausted from trying to raise my daughter and maintain my professional responsibilities.

Being an introvert, reaching out to others has not been easy. My parents and friends feel far away, and I feel so alone. His family is not in Berlin, and in any case, while they are very nice people, they do not feel close or helpful. This is raising huge tensions with my partner, and I do not know what we shall do. Right now, I do not see how I can continue my professional career in Munich and he does not see how he can move to Berlin. While he tries to come home twice a month for the weekend, I am so exhausted and there is so much tension that we end up fighting rather than enjoying being together. Whether we make it as a couple or not, I cannot take the chance of letting go of my professional opportunities. It means too much to me.

There may also be other external factors that come into play. Dual-career Global Cosmopolitan couples frequently find that, in addition to working on their issues as a couple, they have to manage those who inadvertently judge them, including colleagues, family, friends, and different values about how things should be done.

Some of the women I interviewed in Middle Eastern countries described the challenges of being successful in the region, particularly the importance of having appropriate support to continue working.

This support needed to come not only from mentors, sponsors, and bosses but also from spouses, adding another dimension to the resilience of the couple.

Pamela lived in England, Ireland, and France for over 20 years. As an engineer, she was able to have a very interesting and high-powered career. She had met and married her husband, who was also Lebanese, in London. They decided to move to Dubai with their two children, to be closer to family.

She says: 'I wanted to be closer to home. I still have to travel for work, but the distances are much shorter. My position as a managing partner in a top consulting firm makes a huge difference. It provided the initial respect I need to succeed as a woman and makes a difference for other female colleagues. I have a great support system in Dubai, including my mother, who can fly here to step in when needed, and most importantly, my husband who backs my professional ambitions wholeheartedly. I know that I need all the support I can get, particularly from him, if I want to achieve my goals.'

Long-Distance Relationships

Some Global Cosmopolitan couples opt for a long-distance relationship when they cannot find a way to pursue both careers in the same location. But any couples where one or both members travel extensively for work experience problems. Throw in living apart, and the complexity increases exponentially. How long can we do this and call ourselves a couple? Does it work for both of us? If we want to have children, what has to change? Don described his experiences to me:

When we lived in Europe, I was working and travelling all of the time. We thought that it would get better once I was home. We tried but the tension about my ability to be there was red hot. We both felt that the constant negotiating was eroding our relationship and our children were not happy. Now, I work in NYC and my family life is in North Carolina, where my wife has family and friends. It works. Although I doubt it would have worked in Europe, where my wife did not feel fluent in French. There is no negotiating when I will be there. I fly home on Thursday night and return on Monday morning. When I am at home, I am totally there.

Time together as a family is crucial to making long-distance relationships work. But the quality of that time might be diminished by a difference in time zones—which brings jetlag and exhaustion into the equation. Both members of the couple have to understand and accept that allowances will have to be made. Lily is trying to make her situation work, but she has already set a time limit.

> *We are based in the Philippines. I work here and my children go to school here. My husband's work is mostly in Malaysia, and he travels extensively in the region. It is not the ideal situation, but he loves what he is doing. He is quite happy focusing on work and being alone – and then spending a lot of time working from home, before he goes out again. I find it hard, since I am much more of an extrovert and love sharing little decisions and tasks. I also need him to be here for the children when he is busy working elsewhere. I am making friends slowly and I am getting better at using technology to share important moments with him, but it is not ideal.*

Some couples travel so much that they might as well have a 'commuting relationship' like Lily's. The effect on constant journeys for work on the life of a couple or family can be significant. Dominika expressed her concern:

> *We thought that a move to Amsterdam would be a move to really living together. The truth is that we are often just managing our calendars to verify who will be in town for the children. We have great help at home and the children are in wonderful schools, but it has not been easy figuring out calendars and finding quality time together.*

Global Cosmopolitan couples whose children have left home or are in boarding schools often treat the 'empty nest' as an opportunity to rebalance their lives together (as we will see in the last section of the book). Rose is a poet and has been able to accompany her husband on his global assignments.

> *Now that the children are grown, I have been able to spend more time in English-speaking countries, where I am at home as a poet. Instead of returning to Australia, which used to be considered our home, we bought an apartment in London, and now my husband meets me there after his work related travel, instead of returning to our home in Madrid.*

Same-Sex Relationships

Same-sex couples often describe the difficulties that they experience just trying to exist in certain cultures. If they need to live in secrecy, there is an additional stress on the couple. If they decide that they want to have children, some cultures are much more open than others. While Global Cosmopolitans deal with difference on a daily basis at work, it is often the biggest hurdle to happiness outside the office. But for some people, the reality of being outside their own country helps when they experience rejection or just misunderstanding.

> *Matteo came out when he started dating men in New York. His sexuality had been a secret until he left Italy. Although out in New York, he still did not talk to his family and friends about being gay for a very long time. He knew that home for him was Italy, but he had to feel free of his secrets in order to live there.*
>
> *As he eventually began to tell people at home, he realized that many of them knew and it was not an issue for them. It was his own secretiveness that had been the problem. Little by little he opened up with family and friends. He eventually felt freer to find a stable relationship, and take the risk of bringing someone home with him.*

It is difficult to predict what the future will hold for same-sex marriages. Men and women, now in their 50s and 60s, who left their home countries to avoid family and peer judgment, have often settled into their lives away from home.

> *Over the years, one couple found it easier to be open about their sexual orientation. Now in their late 50s, they feel accepted as a couple. They found a solution that worked for them by creating more than one home. Their professional lives had them based in different cities in Asia. While not ideal, both were totally involved in their separate and very time-consuming careers. But their real home was in Thailand, where they felt they could be themselves and create a sense of being together within a larger and more like-minded community.*
>
> *Preferring a context where he could settle down and have children, John decided to move back to the US after years of being a Global Cosmopolitan, so that he and his husband could raise children in a context of relative acceptance. John had grown up in a loving, open-minded family and wanted to recreate that for his child. Now a father, he could still benefit from his own father's presence. In addition, his mother had died, but in America he could also create a loving community of friends who supported his decision to adopt.*

The Two-Edged Sword of Adaptability

Unfortunately, some of the positive characteristics that define the Global Cosmopolitan Mindset and Skillset also lead to difficulties in relationships.

Many of the skills that people develop through living globally, like being able to adapt to new professional situations and demands, help personal transitions to work smoothly as well. However, the impact of individual adaptability on the couple can be double-edged. Seeing yourself as adaptable can strengthen your confidence about taking risks. But adaptability can have its disadvantages, for instance when someone feels they are losing a part of their identity. They sense that their selves are slowly disappearing in the adaptation process, and this can be devastating.

Nadia and her family immigrated to Massachusetts from India when she was a young girl. Her mother, although trained as an economist, stayed home to raise their three children. Her father, a surgeon, worked long hours. Although her mother spoke some English, she did not really adapt well to living so far away from her family and friends. Nadia became the responsible adult at home, adapted very well to life in the US and was an outstanding student. Armed with her MBA, she quickly moved up the corporate ladder. She was clearly a high flier.

She fell in love, got married, and was happy to move to Bangalore. She knew she needed to get away from home, where she was always helping family members. She was not thrilled with her job there, but she adapted once again. Then she and her husband moved to Singapore and Nadia took a corporate post that allowed her to travel less, now that they had children. She adapted. While she did not mind being more available to her children, this tipped the scales.

She could see that she was losing her enthusiasm for work and for other life projects. It took a colleague to point out how rarely she shared her ideas. Without thinking, she would help other people articulate their ideas, but not share her own. If someone asked her to do something, she did it, even if she had more important things to do.

She had the good fortune to have had really good mentoring at work, which helped her start to articulate what she thought and felt. The next step felt harder, but doable: setting reasonable boundaries on the needs of others and speaking up for herself. This served her well, since her husband came home the following month with an offer of a job in London. She really needed to understand what she wanted and be able to share her preferences and ideas for them to make a joint decision about whether to accept it.

Different Perspectives Within a Couple

It is important to remember that each individual experience things differently, and each half of any couple may experience what is outwardly the same life event in radically different ways. For instance, the individual impact of an international move is affected not only by individual differences between partners but also by factors such as whether both are working (or just one); where the work is (based in the new country or travelling widely); and what expectations exist about roles in the family. These are familiar themes to couples everywhere, but Global Cosmopolitans are often cut off from traditional sources of support and understanding. This lack of support in a new situation can be experienced as a hardship, even when the move opens up opportunities to have experiences they never dared dreamed of.

Just like at work, developing the ability to understand and articulate what you *want*, what you *need*, and what *you are able* to do becomes increasingly important over time.

Encouraging a partner to speak up constructively can help both the couple and the individuals in the long term. It can be hard to recognize when there is a potential conflict of interest. An unwanted move can lead to a sense of loss of self or even depression, and this is often a signal that something has to evolve. When one person starts to change in a way that feels negative, both members of a couple can panic, and they will need all their skills and resilience to make the new situation work.

As we have seen, women who are unable to pursue their careers are particularly vocal about the need to create and recreate a life. After everyone else is taken care of, what do I do? In typical 'expat' communities, there are international schools with very active parent, teacher, and family groups. These provide opportunities to network, find out what is going on, meet people with shared interests, and organize activities together. Many women—and increasingly men—feel saved by the support and stimulation they receive from such communities. Some even discover new interests that change the course of their lives.

There are many situations that make a move problematic. Trailing spouses who are not parents or teachers may find it hard to identify groups of people in a similar situation to themselves. In some cities, they may be severely limited in what they can do. Boredom and frustration can seep into the life of someone who had been anticipating a stimulating adventure. This can lead to loneliness, depression, and excessive drinking for the half of the couple who is not caught up in the excitement of a new job and travelling for work.

Divorce

Divorce is painful and complicated. Global Cosmopolitan couples share a unique life, and when they decide that they cannot continue the journey together, breaking up that primary relationship is difficult, even traumatic. Grace admits that she had a wonderful relationship with her husband until they became parents.

I met my German husband when we were graduate students getting our MBAs in the States. I am from a traditional family in Korea, but I went to a US boarding school and did my undergraduate and graduate studies in the US. We are both investment bankers and have been working in NYC for over 15 years. We have two beautiful children and we are divorced.

We did not disagree about many things, whether it was where to live or whether both of us should actively pursue our careers. What we disagreed about was how to raise our children. He really believed that I did not love our children enough, because I did not look them in their eyes or touch them very much. That was how I was raised, but my husband was raised by parents that hugged him, played with him, and made eye contact. We needed help to figure out how to be good enough parents and how to accept difference. Unfortunately, we started blaming and judging each other, fighting… and finally separating.

It is actually calmer now. Living separately, we have more respect for each other's parenting styles and are less threatened by our differences. The children are fine, but it is not easy for us. Initially, my career took a hit and I decided to change career direction. The children are based with me, and even though I am lucky to have the finances to get good help, I decided that I wanted to be more available than before. Now that they are absolutely on track, I am scaling up my career.

My parents and friends from Korea still have a hard time with the notion of divorce. While I was a superstar in their eyes for so many years, divorce has tainted that picture, and this is extremely painful to me. I carry their values, so I have needed a lot of support to handle the feelings of failure that I have experienced.

Divorce for Global Cosmopolitans is often subject to constraints that derive from cultural backgrounds and contexts. People from different cultures may have different notions of how to use support, and unfortunately, many couples are unable to get the kind of help that could enable them to preserve their relationship and create a family that works or find a reasonable way to separate. The impact of shame, and the fear of rumors, can also keep people from getting the type of help they need.

Significant legal and financial realities can inhibit or prolong divorce proceedings. One or other of the couple might end up losing the status required to work—or even remain—in the country they are currently living in. Different cultural traditions and laws can also compromise parents' rights.

When one partner has the knowledge and wherewithal to file for divorce, it can leave the other, all too often the woman, living in fear of the consequences of separating.

On a more positive note, I have also listened to stories of Global Cosmopolitans learning from previous mistakes, when they seek a new partner to share the journey. Others describe using their distinctive Global Cosmopolitan Skillset to maintain strong contacts with their children from a previous relationship. This is the challenge that Felipe faces, having drifted apart from his first wife because of their very different ideas of how to build a life together.

> *For Felipe an important part of being a Global Cosmopolitan was having the opportunity to spend time in other countries and satisfy his need for the excitement of new places, new food, and new ideas. He traveled with his first wife for many years, but when their children went to school they decided to base themselves in Florida, close enough to Latin America where he was often working at the time.*
>
> *Born in Colombia, Felipe felt at home in Latin America and enjoyed the chance to see his family of origin regularly. He traveled extensively, loved it, and felt a growing distance from his wife, who was at home – working, raising their family, and feeling his absence. It was not good for the marriage or his role as a parent and eventually they separated and divorced. While he had been comfortable leading parallel lives, his wife had wanted a different existence.*
>
> *Felipe's work now brought him to Asia, where he fell in love again, this time with a Singaporean woman who had been traveling for work for most of her professional life. Although she had always loved traveling, she had been offered a government post that she could not refuse. He managed to find work based in Singapore to be with her. While they both prioritized travel, they now agreed it was something they would choose and do together. With a new commitment very far away from his children and parents, Felipe's is determined to make sure that he plays an active part in their lives.*

Becoming an Ex[1]

Among the people I talked to, there were many who were newly single, whether through death, break-up, or divorce. Being an 'ex' or a widow(er) means the loss of status, as well as the loss of a significant other and the relationship itself. This can be very painful, even if separation was a choice.

> *It's hard to be a Global Cosmopolitan when you have just broken up with the love of your life. Feeling alone is bad enough, but it's even harder being away from family and friends who know and love you. Yet, I like myself and my lifestyle more than the idea of moving back to Sydney, the place I call home. My ex and the children live there. I fly home to see the children as much as much as I am able to. However, while I still receive the affection and reassurance that I need from some of my friends and family, Sydney is the place where I feel the most like an ex.*

Some exes start to re-evaluate the importance of context, a larger purpose in life, or another commitment in order to feel a sense of connection. These can be drivers of change for people dealing with the loss of a partner while on a global journey. The changes can be big or small, as long as they help fill the void.

Relationships with family members, friends, or colleagues can change significantly without triggering a move, which some might find daunting. Being somewhere where they feel rooted or where they will be with like-minded people can be more important. Others will respond differently and consider whether it is time to learn how to be on their own. Seeking another direction or adventure will often facilitate this learning process.

When they lose a spouse, some people suddenly find themselves rethinking past assumptions: 'I thought I always wanted to go back home. That was my voice, but is it my voice now?' Others will realize that, without a partner, they need to invest in a new place or different relationships.

Some people find themselves alone in their ex's home country, asking, 'Do I want to be here on my own and do I even have a choice?' Various factors such as life stage, financial situation, and family can influence their answers. While some of my research subjects in this situation were comfortable enough financially to go elsewhere, others had developed their professional identity and knew that it was not the right time to leave. Children were a major factor in trying to figure out what to do, especially if there was a contentious divorce. Women with grown-up families were trying to figure out where they wanted to be in relation to their children or grandchildren.

Even if the separation was a mutual and amicable decision, the pieces of the global kaleidoscope will have shifted and redistributed. Life looks very different. Along with the emotional aspect of being alone, logistical issues to do with shared assets, citizenship, and rights take on a new significance. Individuals, often women, who gave up their own earning power and subsequently found themselves on their own with inadequate knowledge of their finances or the resources they needed to create another life chapter.

Longer Lives Mean More Decisions

Many couples that have reached their 50s, 60s, or 70s together find they need to grapple with what has changed and what has remained the same, as they think about the next turn in the road. 'What next?' looks different than what they expected as the kaleidoscope turns once more. Fault lines can appear around what to do next. Learning how to dream together and enjoy time together without the structure of work can be confusing for people who have depended on their careers to structure their lives, supply outlets for their needs, satisfy their ambitions, and structures for their relationships. Writing new life chapters with a co-author often requires a whole new set of skills (as we will see in Part III of this book).

On the other hand, barring health or financial constraints, this is opportunity for some couples to continue expanding their Global Cosmopolitan Mindset by experiencing further new adventures. Why don't we spend a year living in Greece or buy a holiday house there? Could we spend a year sailing around the world? Just remember that such questions may lead to conflict with a partner who says, 'At last I have time to be with my friends, my children or to get more actively involved in philanthropic projects.'

However, in some cases, after years of living or working in a certain country, the political and economic environment can undermine plans to stay put and settle down into peaceful retirement with grandchildren running around the garden. This is just one of the harsh realities that Global Cosmopolitan couples must put into their personal kaleidoscope before making the final turn.

8

Raising the Next Generation

Becoming a parent can change everything. In addition to worrying about one's own career, one has to decide how to bring up children, what values to impart, how to ensure the best education, and how to help children through the crucial developmental stages as they go from infancy to high school and beyond. Being a Global Cosmopolitan parent makes all these issues even more complex, and people respond in very different ways.

Global Cosmopolitan parents describe various strategies that they actively use to prepare their children to enjoy a global life and gain a global perspective. While some describe their wish to repeat—or not to repeat—their own experiences, many look for new ways to give their children an appreciation for difference and the type of resilience they deem necessary for growing up in a globalized world. Their own experiences, whether one-off or recurring, hold lessons for the next generation and impact the decisions they make for their children.

Tatania was born in Siberia. Growing up was not easy, but she found the motivation and determination to forge ahead with her life far away from home. Her voyage had included many twists and turns across the globe. That too was not easy, but she felt she had developed her own resilience by learning how to confront the many challenges of living in very different cultures. While she had always been a brilliant student, with a highly inquisitive mind, she would never have had the confidence to fulfill her potential if she had not learned how to overcome her shyness and assert her ideas in multiple languages and cultural contexts.

© The Author(s) 2018
L. Brimm, *The Global Cosmopolitan Mindset,*
https://doi.org/10.1057/978-1-349-95345-5_8

Before I met her, she had already made one successful move to Brussels with her husband and son. While they had built a comfortable life there, now Tatania and her family were moving to London. Even though there were new possibilities for personal and professional growth in Belgium, Tatania wanted her son to understand the challenges and the benefits of change. He was already comfortable speaking Russian at home and Flemish in school, and the move to London would give him another cultural immersion.

Tatania felt that her global voyage had taught her so much that she wanted her son to experience the same challenges and changes. She knows that he will never experience the same leaps that she had to make, but she hopes that he will understand what it takes to forge a path for himself and find his own success in a different culture. For her, the Global Cosmopolitan Mindset is all about developing an openness to the world and the survival skills to do well in it.

The Importance of Roots and Wings

In discussions about parenting, it is generally accepted that children need both roots and wings: roots to know where home is and where their core values start, and wings to give them the ability and interest to leave the nest and create their own lives. Global Cosmopolitan parents face distinctive challenges, as they work hard to help their children grow both the roots and wings that they will need for whatever path they choose.

When Global Cosmopolitan parents talk about how they raise their families, they describe varying degrees of concern that their children will lose a sense of purpose and meaning if they are not connected to their parental cultures. Their discussions of cultural expectations or desires to give their children roots are often blended with discussions of the relationships with families of origin, the meaning of home, and the possibilities for re-entry.

Daan was very clear about his plan,

My parents moved extensively when I was a child because of my father's work. Now that I am a parent, I am actually repeating the pattern of moving internationally every three to five years. I have let my organization know that when my son turns ten, I want to go home to the Netherlands. While I know we shall keep the global perspective alive in our home, I want my children to have friends and family and a sense of belonging that I never really had growing up. I have to admit that I am also looking forward to developing that home.

Parents often want their children to have special relationships with grandparents and other relatives. The choice to live far from home might have been voluntary but it does not mean a rejection of family ties or values. Including their children in their 'larger background picture,' as David, puts it, becomes essential for some.

My wife is Israeli and I am American. When our children were small, we always wanted them to have a strong sense of family. My parents lived in the city where the children were born, but my wife's parents were very important to us as well. When they were younger, my wife's parents travelled to visit us two or three times a year. We would spend our summers in Israel and managed to buy an apartment when real estate there was more reasonable. Then we moved to Brazil for a few years and had to work out arrangements for both sets of parents to spend time with the children. We are so thankful that we made that time for family. They know that they have aunts, uncles, cousins, and our childhood friends that will always welcome them with open arms. Our children are grown and living in different parts of the world; we are back in the States. Our parents have died, but at least we have so many wonderful memories that we created together.

Learning from Children: A Growth Experience

It is important for parents to perceive the risks but also the rewards for children of living a global lifestyle. Some Global Cosmopolitans decide to cut their journeys short when they become parents. Others share their ideas of how to make it work and how to see—and react—when it is not working. While it is crucial to pay attention to the needs of children, some of whom do not reap the benefits of frequent change or immersion in new languages, it is also important to discover what children do gain from their global experience—and to learn with them.

Listening to even very young children can give an understanding of how global development begins. Building a learning relationship with children can open a door to another fascinating world. One personal example involves my four-year-old granddaughter, who recently came from London to spend the weekend with me in Paris. I asked her if she wanted to speak English or French with me. She said that she would like to speak both languages but that her English was stronger. She then continued, 'You know that you speak American and so does my mum, but I speak English.' She stopped to reflect. 'It's okay,' she said, 'since we really understand each other.'

Stages of Parenthood

Birth and Babies

Having a baby always stirs up a range of emotions. Having a baby in another culture—or with someone from another culture—broadens that range, particularly around questions of identity, culture, and relationships. Becoming a parent is often the most significant event that shifts one's thinking of the meaning and reality of having a global life. And, as with many other life-stage issues, one cannot always predict how one will feel when it actually happens.

Well before a baby is born, the Global Cosmopolitan faces a set of questions that might not have arisen in a local life. Every culture has traditions embedded in the mindsets of parents, traditions that only become relevant—often in unexpected ways—when a baby is due. Rather than settling into the current location, with all its known commodities and comforts, the decision to have a baby can become a catalyst for changing places, as it did for Pierre and his wife Stéphanie.

It's been over ten years since we left Singapore. Living in Asia had been fantastic. We are both French, but we actually met while working in Asia. I was traveling to China often and my wife was traveling at least four days a week. In spite of the travel, both my wife and I had developed solid professional and personal relationships in Asia, as well as a great circle of friends. We thought we would live there forever, until we found out that we were going to have a baby and we re-evaluated everything. While we both loved our work, as older parents (we were already in our 40s), we wanted to be very present for our children and wanted our parents to get to know them.

Expecting a baby made us both realize that we wanted to be closer to home. Our best professional options were in London. We started talking to our respective offices in London, and they were both interested. Of course, our families were thrilled. Our parents lived near Paris and our siblings were living both in France and London.

Now we are living in London. Our parents are retired and they can actively participate in the lives of our children. Yes, we had another little girl two years later. It was absolutely the right decision at the time. Our global minds are contributing to how we parent and how we work out of our London offices. We kept a house that we bought in Bali and mange to go there every year. Who knows what we'll do when the children go off to university?

Even if the impending arrival does not result in changing countries or moving home, there are plenty of other issues to tackle. Thinking about what languages the child will be exposed to and learn to speak is one. Choosing a name is another. Many Global Cosmopolitan parents enjoy the process of thinking about names for their coming child, but they might be obliged to consider names that will work in various languages, names that recognize the child's—and the parents'—cultural backgrounds, or names that will blend in anywhere.

Some people love the adventure of having their baby in another country, as it gives them a new opportunity to learn about the local culture. It can be exciting to have a baby in a context where your ability to communicate is limited. But for others, it is just another aspect of global living.

For others, it can be a source of unexpected challenges, such as trusting the local healthcare system. While friends and support groups with local knowledge can give advice about the best hospitals, couples can feel quite alone with their fears. If a previous experience during another posting included certain examinations and birthing options, expectant parents can feel vulnerable when those are not available in a new location. Along with the healthcare benefits, there may also be questions around parental leave. A previous position might have included extensive paternal leave, but what if it is not on offer this time around? Worse still, what happens if the father misses the birth or has to leave for a business trip as soon as the baby is born? Who is around to pick up the slack or just be there for the mother?

The issue of passports might have to be considered long before the baby arrives. Some Global Cosmopolitans have multiple passports. Others have passports that their parents considered safe, because their parents ensured that they were born in those countries. Some might find that their child only qualifies for citizenship in their home country if they return there for the birth, which almost inevitably means a lengthy separation for the parents, as the mother will not be permitted to fly as her due date approaches. Yet others might choose a third country for the birth.

Nationality or place of birth of the baby is just one of many issues that the new parents must negotiate. For Global Cosmopolitan couples, it is a time when their natural adaptability can make it both easy and difficult to discuss differences. Once again, the Global Cosmopolitan Mindset and Skillset turn out to be double-edged.

Aisha, whose parents are Lebanese, grew up mainly in London, where she completed her university studies. Her parents traveled when she was young, following her father's consulting career. She lived in Germany and France before she started secondary school in London. Every summer she went 'home' with her mother to the family's house in the mountains and soaked up the Lebanese traditions that are so central to her identity.

Her husband, Lars, an investment banker, is Danish, while Aisha herself works in industry. For years, disagreements were rare, since neither one of them liked conflict.

Aisha describes herself as a third-culture kid, knowing how to adapt to most new situations. This background also contributes to her being agreeable with others even if there is an underlying tension. For her, open conflict should be avoided.

Her parents live close by in London, which she appreciates, but she also knows that she has to put up some clear boundaries. She waited a long time to have a baby, so at age 43 she at last has to assert herself with Lars as their cultural differences emerge. Now, she has to be able to say what she wants and she cannot please both her husband and her parents at the same time, particularly given their very different cultural backgrounds.

Traditions associated with giving birth are carried in the minds of parents, no matter how much time they have spent away from their cultures or origin. For instance, in spite of being extremely worldly and completely integrated into other cultures, many Chinese new mothers feel they should spend a month at home after their baby is born. According to Chinese tradition, this brings luck to the child. Similarly, in certain Middle Eastern cultures, mothers are expected to return home with their babies for 40 days. The roots and traditions that give a sense of identity and belonging can be an integral part of the parenting journey. James believes that being able to stay open and try different cultural perspectives has been one of the key factors in building a solid relationship with his wife.

We met and married in London when we were both in our 20s, each having a successful career. Our cultural differences – she is Chinese and I am Canadian – seemed amusing and inconsequential at best until our first child arrived. Her mom arrived from China, wanting her to 'sit for a month', which we both reacted to, but my wife was too sensitive to the traditional idea of creating a lucky life for her daughter, so decided to do it. We even tried the Chinese method of toilet training.

That was a phase in our relationship where I think we handled our differences very well. I think it was easier because I also was not sure what my role would be as a parent, so I was still in a state of wonder and watching. Over the years, our cultural differences do come up from time to time, but the ability to take enough distance at that time helped me understand that some of our differences were really not that important.

How Do You Manage Family Life?

Once the baby is born and returns home, who should be there? What form should the initial childcare take? Does one parent need to stay at home with the children? This last question can arise either because of a lack of childcare options or because of strong feelings about children needing to have a parent at home. Some say this is the case only when they are small, while others think a stay-at-home parent is most important for teenagers.

> *Luckily, my wife, Elsa, had a mobile career in education, so whenever possible, she worked. Given that we traveled in many outlying places during the 90s, and I had to travel a great deal of the time, someone had to maintain a life for our children. Also, change happened frequently and often, so creating stability at home was extremely important.*

Living in a cosmopolitan center, far away from home, couples can usually find a variety of people and resources to help them with general, personal, and cultural parenting questions—although the opportunities will depend on income levels.

In Singapore, many Global Cosmopolitans and locals have live-in maids to help. In France, there are government-sponsored crèches and approved child minders who take preschoolers into their own homes. But for outsiders, particularly those who do not speak French, navigating the state systems can be a challenge, and such people often look for private solutions. In the UK, a typical option is to hire a nanny or an au pair, a young person who lives with the family and helps with the children in order to learn English. Wherever you live, the difficulty—and cost—of finding someone trustworthy to look after children should not be underestimated.

Protecting Your Children as They Grow up

The desire to protect your children is universal. But a crisis can happen anytime anywhere. When it involves children, it can make a complete change necessary.

> *Farid realized that, as long as he worked in a small town, there was a great risk of his children being bullied. He never wanted his own children to experience what he had lived through growing up in the Netherlands. While he knew that children*

can be bullied anywhere, he hoped that moving to a large city would allow them to go to international schools, which might make it easier. That might mean a pay cut, but it would be worth it.

Alice's son was on the autistic spectrum, but it took her a long time to get a proper diagnosis. Once she understood what the situation was, there was no question of staying put. Alice and Rick both wanted to move to a place where they could get the best care for their son – and they needed to make that happen. For Rick it was a great relief to see how understanding and helpful his employers were. It would take some organizing, but he had two excellent options. For Alice it meant leaving the business that had just started to grow. She had put her heart and soul in her work, but she knew that she had a good team working for her. She was ready to leave first and find another job later.

A Global Education

Questions about schools start early, sometimes before birth, since deciding where to live might depend on what type of education is available. The early questions tend to focus on: language of education; whether the child should learn alongside other Global Cosmopolitans or in the local system; and whether to choose a school that will reinforce certain values, religion, or cultural identification.

Children of Global Cosmopolitans start to learn about the world as part of their daily lives. They see maps and globes marked with where they have lived and where their wider family lives. Many learn more than one language from infancy and notice very early on when another language is being spoken. They appreciate that there are other languages in the world that are quite different from those spoken at home. Even at two years of age, they can often name the languages that are spoken in their nursery schools. Becoming bilingual or trilingual is normal for many of them.

Parents with multiple cultural connections often want their children to attend schools and have friends that reflect the diversity they have come to value so highly. For this reason, bilingual or international schools can seem attractive. Alternatively, local schools, if they are available to non-citizens, can offer integration in the local culture and wider diversity of social class. They can be the first choice for parents who want their children and possibly themselves to be able to be integrated into the local community.

In the urban centers where Global Cosmopolitans abound, such as Dubai, Singapore, London, and New York, there are plenty of bilingual and international schools to choose from. Given that many children with a Global Cosmopolitan background go to these schools, they are a popular option, but they can be very expensive. For people earning significant salaries or employed by organizations that pay school fees as part of a package, this is no barrier. The less fortunate may have to settle for a limited choice of schools or seek scholarships.

Even if the financial situation is secure, getting a child accepted by a preferred school can be a significant burden. Understanding the admission system and coping with the potential challenges of switching from one education system to another can take an emotional toll.

It is not unusual for parents to turn down potential moves if one or more children are at a crucial stage in their education. But even if they stay for several years, the children will probably experience the emotional upheaval of having friends move away on a regular basis. The populations centered on international schools are notoriously transient.

Some couples know that they will move at least three times or more before their children graduate from secondary school, so they might consider a system that is generally available throughout the world. On top of school, some families feel that their children should attend weekend language and culture programs or summer camps in order to inculcate important values and strengthen links with the culture of origin.

Simon and his wife have loved giving their children to go to school with children from all over the world. Choosing schools has been central to Simon's discussions with his wife,

First we tried putting our children in the French school, given that my wife is French. Our first child was fine. But when the second one had trouble, we moved both of them to the British school – which, given our hope that our children will go to British universities, was a very wise decision. They are still required to keep up their French by going to French school on Saturday. Every summer they go to visit my wife's family in France and we just bought a home in the South of France, so I know they will always be quite fluent in French.

Whatever you have thoughtfully chosen, it may or may not work out. Not all children can thrive in the schooling that is available, and this can become a turning point. Parents in this situation may dedicate as much energy as possible to changing the educational system where they are. Others decide that they need to look elsewhere, which might necessitate a family move or a change in the couple's living arrangements.

It is important to underline that while parents may love changing cities and countries, frequent moves are not always good for children. This can prove to be a contentious issue. Many Global Cosmopolitan parents seek outside help to understand the problem and the possible solutions. If it is a couple or parenting issue, the child might not be the deciding factor. But for many families, the discussion leads to staying in the same place to create stability or going 'home' to build a base where their children can thrive.

Boarding schools may also be the answer for parents who feel their children should be educated 'at home.' Alternatively, some parents spend time apart so that one can be close to where a child is being educated, while the other keeps them all financially soluble from the other side of the world.

The choice of school can also come into play when considering potential university education and even where a child might live after graduation. Korean parents often want their children to succeed in the US or UK educational systems and send their children to the appropriate schools. They may even dispatch them to boarding schools in the USA or UK, so that they are in the best position to continue to higher education there.

University and Beyond

Many parents are surprised by the desires and possibilities that their children consider when it comes to higher education. Remember, children who have moved extensively while growing up are exposed to many alternatives for university-level education across cultures and languages.

Certain parents do not believe that their children should have a choice, which inevitably leads to family tension. Others, give the children more voice. One child may opt to be educated in one country, while a second child decides to go elsewhere. Parents sometimes struggle to understand the underlying issues for these choices. One Italian father, Luigi, put it this way:

> We returned to Italy for our children. We wanted them to develop their roots in Italy and know the language and the cultural references. All three of them have chosen to go to the UK for university. While they appreciated the sacrifices we made to go home, they had been educated in very international schools, and they believed that they would not find the same atmosphere in Italy. Now all three of them are in England, and happily planning international careers.

Conversely, one American divorcee, Lynne, lamented her inability to offer her children the choice of studying at US universities:

After the divorce Lynne continued living in Spain. The divorce proceedings had been difficult. The father of her children did not see it as his responsibility to pay for an education and felt very strongly that his children should go to school in Spain. From his point of view, the children had to get scholarships if they wanted to study in the US.

The Single Global Cosmopolitan Parent

Single parents who are not in their 'home' country can feel the weight of responsibility, as they make the multiple decisions involved in parenting. At times, that all-important career pales into insignificance next to the sole responsibility of raising a child. In addition to time-consuming logistical challenges, they have no ready-made local support networks. Staying late at the office or traveling for work may prove impossible.

Some decide to stop moving so that they can create a sense of belonging to a place and build a close circle of friends or family. It may feel easier to be a single parent in a large cosmopolitan city where there are many others in a similar situation, rather than in countries where being a single parent is frowned upon.

Ana, a Columbian, decided to move to New York from Paris to raise her son when she became a single mother. She had a portable career and felt that she would have a more supportive environment, given the number of friends that she had cultivated when she lived there. She also liked the person that she was in NYC and felt that the place and its pace brought the best out of her.

Building Resilience so that They Can Fly

At some point, the children will leave home, whether for boarding school, college or to take a gap year and learn more about themselves in the world. Either way, they will start to gain a perspective on who they are and who they can be as adults. This is where the resilience—the roots and wings—developed through the education and experience provided by Global Cosmopolitan parents can make a difference.

Gabriela lived in 21 cities across 4 continents growing up. Her parents were Mexican, but she had only lived in Mexico when she was very young. Their early deaths, just as she was starting her own family, left her feeling very uprooted and homeless, given the number of times she had moved as a child.

Married to another Mexican, also a Global Cosmopolitan, for the past 17 years Gabriela has been living in Atlanta. Like many parents, she pays close attention to the life experiences that she wants for her children. Central to her parenting is the desire to give her children a sense of home – and in particular a sense of home in the US and Mexico. Her husband also wants their children to have roots in Mexico.

Atlanta is a wonderful place to raise children and her husband's career is best managed from there, so her future might be to remain in the US. But she is working on redefining what it might mean to be a local cosmopolitan for her and her family. She and her husband have two homes, one in Atlanta and one in Mexico, and speak two languages, Spanish and English, with their children. They also travel widely, exposing the children to different cultures and the notion of traveling.

Based on her own experience of moving globally, Gabriela sees how her children could benefit from developing resilience wherever they are.

In many ways, there is no predicting what children will do with their lives. It is hard to predict how the family global journey will impact their lives. Letting go when they take their own path toward being global has its own set of challenges for parents. Their lives keep evolving, and creating an appropriate dialogue and family time together becomes more and more difficult. And so it has been for Thierry,

We lived in Asia for many years. It was a great experience. But when our children were approaching adolescence, we decided that we needed to move back to France. We were in Singapore, which is a great place to raise children. They were in the French system, yet we felt that it was important that our children experienced living in France for their secondary studies. We wanted them to develop a cohort of friends and be closer to family. Our yearly visits during the summer holidays were not enough.

This was an extremely difficult transition for me. I loved working in Asia, and I had developed a lot of confidence, expertise, and an excellent network. It was a shock to me to have people in France, even friends, wondering how loyal I could be. They also had trouble seeing what I could offer and how my skills would apply to their organization. I decided to start my own business, which I had already done more than once in Asia. It has not been easy, but I am happy to say that I am quite successful now.

My children adapted quite well to their schooling in France, but they both missed the cosmopolitan atmosphere they had experienced in Asia. Now, my son has decided to go to university in England. He has made it clear that he misses the diversity that he grew up with and wants to go to school where there will be students that have a similar international experience.

Nurturing Family Ties with Adult Children

Along with ensuring that their children can fly when they need to, the Global Cosmopolitan parent also has to work to keep the roots strong. For some people, it means regular trips to be together or buying a house to create a place that will be home for the family.

Parents have often spent a lot of time trying to provide their children with both the advantages of a global life and the stability that grounds them. But whatever the parents do with their own lives, controlling the impact on children is another story. Parents are often shocked, confused, and yet fascinated to see the different choices that their children make as adults.

Global families can become very tight knit as a result of moving together, and the expectation might be that this will endure. While some adult children choose to continue a life of exploration and adventure, others find a different—more local—road to follow. Either can be experienced as a break from the family. This adds an extra level of complexity for both parents and their adult children as they strive to maintain the core family. Clement lamented his new reality:

> I had in my head that I would go home to Belgium when I retired and enjoy the community work that I could do, but mainly I looked forward to spending more time with my wife, my children, and my grandchildren. It was one thing to realize how busy and integrated my wife became when she returned, but it was a shock to realize that my children, who I adore, are now living in England and might move to Asia next year. I have not been known for my flexibility, but this is the quality that I will need to keep our loving family strongly connected. I know, I raised my children to be open to the world and they loved the life we had. Now I have to accept that the values I gave them through our lifestyle and our many discussions have contributed to who they are. I love them, and now I will have to see how I will create family time with them, wherever they might be.

Many children of Global Cosmopolitans identify their nuclear family as their home. Once they have started on their own global journey, they are often surprised when their parents make decisions that appear to disrupt their sense of home. For those who have become attached to a particular house, they may feel hurt or angry when rooms are reassigned or redesigned, particularly if it is 'their' bedroom. They might understand the change logically, but resist it emotionally at the same time.

Even more unsettling from their point of view is when parents choose to reinvent themselves or move to another city or country. Their concept of home must now take on a new shape and adjust to the new reality. It may feel as if the possibility of moving back home has been changed forever.

Living in a Changing World

How do you raise children who will be resilient in the world as it develops? Global Cosmopolitan parents are often particularly sensitive to changes in political, geopolitical, and economic contexts and how these might impact the lives of their family.

Attempts to develop awareness of many issues, from climate change to anti-immigrant policies, can start quite young. The impact of globalization can be the topic of discussions at school and at home. Some parents mention using travel, vacations, and sustainability projects that they are involved in to help their children understand issues such as the effects of deforestation or the plight of people less fortunate than themselves. These experiences lead to broader questions about how to make a difference responsibly and how to be a good global citizen. And how better to raise a good global citizen than by passing on the Global Cosmopolitan Mindset?

9

Creating or Re-creating Home

Discussions of home with Global Cosmopolitans are lively, filled with emotion and at the same time, particularly meaningful. People have a lot to say, and the stories they tell, illustrate how important this issue can be. The question of home permeates the considerations of how to make the most of a global journey. Their stories reflect their deep concerns about how emotions associated with home impact decision-making when creating new chapters in their lives.

Associations with the concept of home vary significantly. Some people may no longer use the language of their childhood, but their bodies still hold memories of place. Talking about home often includes associations that are visceral, captured by different senses, from the scent of trees in bloom or the taste of favorite childhood candy to music attached to memories.

It can easily start with a discussion of food. Imagine the flavor of home cooking… Rodrigo, a Peruvian who lived in Korea for three years, put it this way: 'I knew from my first meal in Korea, that life was going to be different.' Anticipating cultural differenvces, he had forgotten about the basics of human existence—like eating. One taste of Korean spices and, he said, 'I felt like I had a different digestive system. That was only the beginning.'

And the smell of home cooking! That was enough to make one Mexican, Antonio, gather up his courage and knock on his neighbor's door. He had detected the unmistakeable aroma of meals from home wafting from within.

Some people go so far as to turn their desire for home cooking into business plans that involve importing spices or opening restaurant chains in other countries. Others develop Global Cosmopolitan taste buds to go with their new mindsets. Learning how to eat or prepare different food often feels like it goes to

© The Author(s) 2018
L. Brimm, *The Global Cosmopolitan Mindset*,
https://doi.org/10.1057/978-1-349-95345-5_9

the heart of appreciating another culture. Many people enjoy and accept food of other cultures, particularly if adapted to their own basic tastes and styles.

For many Global Cosmopolitans, creating a home in a new place starts with creating traditions around food. They describe attempts to bring family and friends around the table in order to develop a sense of belonging, often with food from their country of origin. It is also a usual part of parenting to look to establish family traditions. Decisions, for example, to wean small children onto hot spices, start early—whether in an attempt to connect them with their parents' culture or to integrate them fully into the country where they now live.

The irony of course, for many Global Cosmopolitans, is that they often live in cosmopolitan cities, where cuisines from different parts of the world are readily available. Sometimes all they need to do is go out to feel as if they are coming home, particularly if loyal to their familiar flavors rather than adapted to the new location.

One family, in anticipation of an eventual move home, always kept pictures in the kitchen of places and people in their country of origin. Since the kitchen was also a 'family room,' it seemed the perfect place to introduce images of the country they called home. If only it were that easy…

Easy to Talk About, Hard to Resolve

One of the easiest topics of conversation with Global Cosmopolitans—and often the hardest to resolve—is home. No matter how long they have been on the move, they have plenty to say about the concept of home, how it evolves, and where they have tried to create new ways to understand and experience it. What does home mean, is it connected to place and/or to people, and what does 'creating a home wherever I am', entail? As they talk, however, it often becomes clear that not having a home or not being at home anywhere some experience as a form of existential angst.

Those who never embark on a global journey often look at where is home from a perspective of staying in one country, but those who live around the world are very different. While they may have one concept of home tied to their origins, they will most likely have another that reflects the origins of their spouse and children, and yet another based on where they are living at the time. Indeed, some even take their definition of home as the workplace as it can feel like the one constant in their lives.

There are multiple starting positions for Global Cosmopolitans' discussions of home. Some start from longing and nostalgia and an assumption that certain events will bring them back home. Some begin by describing their ambivalence. Others talk about what they are doing along the way to meet their need for belonging or to supply the things they really miss, while others will wax lyrical about the joys of otherness.

However much they long for their roots, most people are also trying to create a sense of home where they are currently living. This can become a key aspect of their happiness and the way they define (and redefine) the benefits of moving globally. It touches on a fundamental need to belong and an evolving need to define what belonging means, as well as understand the evolving impact of long-held values and attitudes.

Given the variety of different experiences that people have over a lifetime, the concept of home can evolve over time. Even though 'where are you really from?' is often the first question we ask when meeting a stranger, the Global Cosmopolitan may not really have a simple answer.

Home often becomes a relative concept for the Global Cosmopolitan, who must develop creative ways of describing its meaning. Although the idea of living without 'home' is unthinkable to many, for some it can feel liberating to reinvent themselves and have greater freedom of self-expression. Others may make tireless efforts to set down roots, whether in their country of origin or elsewhere. For others still, home is an idea, perhaps simply an image of somewhere from their past frozen in time—and which may not exist any more.

While people starting out on a global journey seem less concerned with leaving a place called home, those well into the voyage tend to describe many moments in their lives when they have addressed—directly or indirectly—the question of where they belong. As the discussion deepens, multiple layers of meaning and implications unfold: home is where I work, where my parents are (even if that's not where I grew up), where my partner is, where the family I travel with are, where my piano is, or even where my books can be found.

Over time, people shift from cultural and parental definitions of home to understanding they need personal definitions. On a daily basis, 'home' moves from country of origin to the place they return to every night after work, wherever that may be in the world. Messages about home are deeply engrained, and some people revisit them at different points in their lives, particularly when they have children. Redefining home and resolving when and whether to *go* home continue to need attention as people move through different life stages.

'Home is emotion; it is where I grew up.' Maxime was insistent about this. He said that his parents' house in France represented a physical connection to the child he once was and his permanent emotional headquarters. He insists on taking his own kids there every summer, even though it is half way across the world from the home that they are living in now – and he throws everything into making sure they have a good time. 'They call it the happy house,' he said proudly.

Some couples feel it is important to create roots in neutral territory—where they are both outsiders. Others are happy to have multiple homes.

> *Giles had settled in London with his boyfriend, the place they'd first met. But he was happy to move when his partner got a better job in Amsterdam. 'This is our opportunity to create a life together, away from our roots and our old friends. Now we have two homes,' he said. 'And there may be more to come.'*

The presence of family may also be central to feeling at home in another country.

> *Setting up a home in Toronto, after living in New York and London had not been easy for Emily a management consultant born in Hong Kong. 'But it only started to feel like home when my sister and her family moved into the neighborhood after living in Australia,' she admitted.*

Defining home and creating a feeling of being at home is an ongoing process relative to changes in yourself and the life you are composing.

It Might Not Just Be About Place

Many Global Cosmopolitans do not associate home with a certain place, or at least the houses or locations where they grew up. Different global living experiences spark different memories and often bring out a sense of choice about where home should or could be. Positive or negative associations with place can be based on how much they liked who they were in a particular setting. This leads to comments like 'I really felt my best in X' or 'given my linguistic fluency, I was able to be myself, understand and be understood in Y, but I loved the landscape in Z.' Thus, home is intimately bound up with a sense of identity and the growth mindset that is integral to the Global Cosmopolitan Mindset.

As Global Cosmopolitans become increasingly mobile, it appears that they look for new ways to feel a sense of roots—whether people, values, or meaning. When they describe their own pathways to defining home, they often raise issues of family history, their experiences on their global journey, the importance of people, along with a notion of how they want to see their life developing over time. Such was the situation of Richard.

> *Is home where my brother is, where I grew up in Argentina and where my parents are or where we have been raising our children for the last 15 years? My brother and his family are in the US and we live in London. As a Jew, am I a cosmopolitan like my*

grandparents and great grandparents? For their generation it was a dangerous label that caused rejection and ultimately death. They had moved to Paris from Russia and loved Paris so much and felt so rooted there that they did not see that they would ultimately be seen as outsiders and escape death by moving to Argentina with my parents. For the first time in my life, I now understand how important place, belonging, and feeling accepted can be, especially when I think of my children and the legacy that I want them to have. I know that they will make their own decisions eventually, but I, or actually my wife and I, would like to be living in a place that we call home.

Many families begin to define their nuclear family and often their friends as home. According to Margaret:

Home is a feeling of being held in a space, I feel at home when I am with the family I have created. I even feel at home when I think about them. Now that our children have children of their own, we try to create times to be together in our summer home and create family events that allow that feeling of home to be communicating to our children and our grandchildren. We try to include friends or members of our family of origin to enrich that feeling. It is not easy to do, but the feeling of providing a sense of home together makes it worthwhile.

For one Canadian, Ludovic, the word 'home' subtly shifts its meaning from one sentence to the next.

I always thought that after all my travels I would want to return to Montreal, where I grew up. On one level I knew that I had moved on, but it did not stop me dreaming about returning home. Once my home was sold when my mother died a few years ago, I knew that I would never go home to live in Canada. We have created a wonderful life in England, and it is my home now. Retirement gives me the time to solidify friendships and be actively involved in the type of charity work that gives my life meaning now. Wherever I go, my professional skills are valued and I am able to contribute.

The Impact of Regional Affinities

Regional affinities, such as to Latin America or Europe, have taken on an interesting role in the trajectory of some Global Cosmopolitans. Despite cultural and linguistic differences within the region, similarities or shared history can stimulate a strong sense of belonging. Many people only discover these affinities when they return after a long period away.

One entrepreneur, Véronique, characterized her feeling of being European only after significant experience of living globally. She grew up in France, with parents from different non-European cultures. She feels French and European, and will use both words under different circumstances to describe herself. Her linguistic ability contributes to this feeling along with her relational network.

Latin American, Asian, and Middle Eastern Global Cosmopolitans frequently describe the tension between wanting to maintain a feeling of belonging to childhood friends or family and knowing that their nomadic lives have changed them in significant ways. Those changes might draw them to accept work and lifestyles that are more global and less local, but within their region of origin.

One couple moved back to Brazil after years in Europe. Camila and Paolo thought that São Paulo would be their final stop – and then she had a professional opportunity that she could not refuse in Chile. Camila and Paolo both spoke Spanish and he easily found another position in his organization. Two years later, they were happy to stay in Chile for a while. It was easy to make friends there and they felt close enough to family and friends at home. Their children were fluent in Spanish and they felt at home in Latin America.

One English woman with Nigerian roots made a decision early in her career that changed her life. After graduation Victoria worked in finance for a few years before she following her dream of working in development. She took the best opportunity she could find, which sent her to Ghana and then South Africa and finally to Nigeria, where she met her husband. Having spent time in multiple countries in Africa, she realized that she felt comfortable on the continent, but her time in Nigeria gave her insights into her history and identity that changed her perspective on her own story. Getting married and having children in Nigeria helped solidify pieces of her identity story that gave more meaning to her work and her life goals. Established financially, she started advising people on their new business ventures. Then her husband was offered a wonderful professional opportunity in London, just as the children were preparing to enter secondary school. The time was right to move back to the UK. She started to fly regularly to Africa to continue her work there. At this point in her life, having two homes, one in the UK and one in Nigeria, worked very well.

Finding Ways to Feel at Home

Finding a way to connect to the local culture helps some people to feel at home, although sensitivity to how the locals respond to them varies. Being asked, 'no, where are you really from?' or told, 'you have a lovely accent!' can challenge their sense of belonging. Questions such as 'when are you going home?' or 'did you go home for the summer?' only confirm that allegiance to this new place will not be possible.

However, learning the language, working in a local environment, having children attend local schools, and making good friends are among the many ways people put down roots in a country. Others are just waiting for the next move, which might mean upheaval to yet another country with yet another linguistic base, or it might mean going back to their *real* home.

Feeling Safe

For most people, home represents a feeling of safety. This can be particularly challenging for people with histories of feeling unsafe. When we are confronted with 'clear and present danger,' we usually need to reconsider where we want to be.

On a personal note, this crucial aspect of home was highlighted for me last year. I was in a restaurant very close to a terrorist attack in Paris. While our cell phones alerted us—my daughter called from London—we had no idea what was happening and where it was safe to go. All we knew was that the violence was to our left. We did not stay in the restaurant, which in hindsight would have been safer. We just wanted to get home. It was instinctive and home felt safe. It certainly got me thinking about what happens to people who really have no place to go home to or move to? What happens to their ability to be—and feel—safe? How does the thread of safety or creating safety for our families impact on the story we create about home?

Many people associate home with the experience of certain safety despite childhood experiences to the contrary.

One senior executive talked about growing up in a home where violence reigned, even though the family lived in a context of relative calm in the world. While he could move away from all the scenes he encountered as a child, they still haunted him. He will never forget what it felt like to be so scared, and how much he searched for ways to feel safe. His motivation to escape and his determination to get out helped him build a life that his parents could never dream about.

Now, whether at home or at work, his mission is to create an environment of safety that allows his children and the people on his team to take risks. For him, the two go hand in hand, and he is well known in his organization for excellence in bringing out the very best in people.

The stories he recounted to me about his children included descriptions of sport as an opportunity to teach children how to develop enough self-confidence to take reasonable risks. Other anecdotes revealed how pleased he was that he had helped his children experience their difference in positive ways, as they travelled the globe and learned how to reach across difference to connect to others.

The visceral experience of being safe at home is something that many people try to create or re-create when they live in different places, however temporarily. It can become an important family value.

> A family of white Kenyans had constructed elaborate systems to ensure maximum safety for their family, as they were living in an area of considerable tribal warfare. Occasionally, as the only 'white farm' within miles, they were attacked and had to create safe hiding places.
>
> They also lived on the edge of a nature reserve, where the animals felt at home and occasionally broke through walls, causing major damage to houses and people in the way.
>
> Yet, this was their country, and they felt safe. The guards, the methods for keeping snakes out, the early warning systems helped create a sense of tranquility and belonging, in spite of the dangers. They were at home in Africa and, while they had spent extensive time elsewhere – and would continue spending time elsewhere, being at home, affirming a connection to the place where they were born, helped them feel peaceful.

Two Homes (or More)

Growing up in one culture and living in another can leave someone feeling that they have split loyalties and a sense of always longing for the 'other place.' The original culture can mean family and friends that give connection and meaning to life. Even moving to another culture for love can lead to confusion and ambivalence. Living and investing in the present becomes a key question. For those who can afford it, the answer can be to have two homes.

A growing number of Global Cosmopolitans are exploring this option. A second home not only helps them to deal with different allegiances, it can also be an opportunity to create a place—and ties—where you would eventually like to settle. It represents an acceptance of the bimodal experience of wanting to be at home in at least two places—and helps balance two important aspects of identity.

> Even though Stan and Sara have done all of the paperwork for staying in Bangkok, Stan has also made sure that he has a family home in Switzerland. Sara has made Bangkok her home, yet she still feels connected to her family and friends in Canada. For her, Canada is part of her definition of home.

Sometimes what feels right for the next step comes as a surprise.

An entrepreneur in Hong Kong had just sold her business. Meera admitted that, almost out of nowhere, she really wanted a home in India, even though she had not lived there in 35 years. There were many factors that could have affected her decision: financial security, a changing landscape in India, children going off (possibly to India themselves), or the insecurity of only having a home in China. Now, she will have two homes.

Another Global Cosmopolitan who was born in India, but had gone to school and been very successful in private equity in London, talked about having sold his latest investments and was now helping his son develop a business in India. While keeping a home in London, the family was spending enough time in Bombay to establish his son's entrepreneurial efforts. Home was a fluid concept in terms of place, but the relational threads of building both homes were extremely powerful and meaningful.

The Importance of Language and Culture

Culture and its representation through language can have an important impact on how we define home and how we feel about the need to go home. Traditionally, people have referred to a mother tongue as a reference to a personal and cultural history. It often is, and individuals often talk about wanting to go home, which is linked to language. However, Global Cosmopolitans frequently describe being parents from different cultures.

At the same time Global Cosmopolitan parents are very conscious of the possibilities that more than one language can offer. Increasingly, children are maturing with two or three languages at home and the expression 'mother tongue' is confusing. These children can feel at home not only in more than one language but also in more than one culture or place.

Stan is teaching his children Hungarian as well as English. They are learning Thai at school. One could say that he is setting the scene for his children and their comfort with finding new definitions of what is home.

Even my four-year-old granddaughter can explain to me that she speaks English with her friends at home, but she wants to be more fluent in French with her friends in Paris. That way, she says, she could be at home in both places.

For many Global Cosmopolitans, feeling at home in the language of a culture is a significant factor when considering where to put down roots. If they cannot understand, they cannot feel at home, which translates to, 'I am just visiting.' While the language at work is frequently English, the language of the support staff and local community may be different. The expat community can provide friendships, but that may not be enough to feel at home in the long term.

Even discussing the meaning of home brings out different linguistic and cultural references and attitudes about the importance of belonging.

People have very different associations with the concept of home, depending on the language they are using.

Family Background

Notions of home start developing in early childhood and often define how to relate to extended family. Over time, it is possible to learn how to live with different definitions of family and family structures.

Multigenerational homes are the norm in some cultures. People from these backgrounds may change cultures and feel at home elsewhere but often dream of building a house for their extended family. While wanting to recreate the essence of his childhood, Dev, looked for a way to bring everyone together in a different cultural setting.

Dev, an entrepreneur in the UK described living around the corner from his mother and father. His parents had been born in India, but raised in the UK in houses that were home to very extended families. In spite of their financial success, they still chose to live with their extended family, so that he grew up with feeling that both his mother and his aunt were his mothers, while his uncle and his father were equally important in his life. While he described the many battles in the house – from how to run a business to who is cooking the meal and how the girls should be educated – he felt enriched by the diversity of thought.

Before Dev returned to live in the UK, the entrepreneur's own life experience included different places around the world, but now in his early fifties, he was convinced that he wanted to benefit from living as close as possible to his family, before the previous generation started dying. He wanted his children to have the same rich family life that had nourished him.

Dev was also very sensitive to having gone to university with people who saw family and home very differently. He had seen how it created a certain distance between himself and his friends. And now that he was choosing to replicate his own experience of home, he wondered about its long-term impact on his children.

Do I Really Know Where I Come From?

Individuals who moved frequently as children, often remark that they cannot easily describe home as a place 'where I am from.' For many Global Cosmopolitans, the solution is to create a secure sense of home in the nuclear family. For Gabriela, the tragic loss of her parents highlighted this issue.

Gabriela's parents were Mexican, but she has no memories of living in Mexico. Unfortunately, before they could go back and create a home there, her parents died. She had moved all around the world in a family unit, and for Gabriela her immediate family and friends were home. It probably was not by chance that she fell in love with a Mexican. As a dual career couple, they enjoyed moving around the world, but as soon as the children came, they set up home in the US.

But Gabriela was determined that this would not be their only home. She tried to build a base with distant relatives in Mexico, but it did not work out: they were too distant and different. That did not stop her. Her husband had family there, but that was not enough. They wanted their own base and so they bought a house in Cuernavaca.

They go to their home in Mexico with their children on a regular basis. Creating two homes has helped. Although Gabriela and her husband remain Global Cosmopolitans, they will not move their homes. They travel for work, they travel for fun, their friends are very cosmopolitan. But in many ways Gabriela is a local cosmopolitan in each home. Although her parents have gone, she now feels she has roots once again.

Most stories are less extreme than Gabriela's, but many Global Cosmopolitans did move around significantly as children, often going to international schools rather than local schools. The impact of early lifestyles varies—and even the impact within families varies. For every person I interviewed who just wanted to plant roots after his own children were born, there was another who felt happy that her children would experience the same lifestyle, with a sense that home can move.

Children of immigrants have different ideas about how to create a home that feels rooted for them and eventually their children. If their parents had particularly difficult journeys, learning about lost connections to place can be challenging, especially for someone, like Ly, who is trying to understand the importance of belonging in a place or a country.

My parents were Vietnamese refugees who met and married in the US. We lived on the East Coast for much of my schooling, before moving to London and then Australia as a family.

My parents stayed in Australia, but my brother and I are living in different parts of the world and I do not know where I want to put down roots. After university in Canada, I started a successful career in Vancouver, but I felt uprooted there. There is no one from my family living here.

I was just offered a job in Vietnam, which I am tempted to take. I do have family there, and I am curious about the roots of my family story. So far, my parents have told me very little about my background. I know that having a better sense of my family history, however grim it might have been, will help me feel more rooted and more accepting of their ways. My parents were so happy to be alive that they have never wanted us to have to look at what they have been through.

Leaving Home

Without ever leaving home, it is hard to imagine how deeply the impact of uprooting will be felt. It can start with a relatively mundane moment, as mentioned at the beginning of this chapter, maybe smelling a new type of food or recognizing that the way you dress makes you stand out as different rather than being invisible in sameness. The first day of work can also be an eye-opener for people landing in a new cultural and linguistic context like Elias. The sudden loss of competence at work felt like homesickness for him.

For my first global move as a manager, I started work in Russia. I went to a crash course in Russian, but it never prepared me for the feeling of incompetence that was so pervasive during my first weeks in the office. Without language, I felt like a child trying to communicate with adults – and I was the boss! I made a lot of mistakes, but I also learned to listen and learn from my team, even if it was often in translation. This was my biggest lesson. It was not my best career move and I was lucky to have the opportunity to move elsewhere where I had stronger language skills. As much as I love the adventure of traveling the word, if I do not feel at home enough in a language, I cannot feel at home enough to function well.

The process of leaving the place called home can also have a major impact on the way we define it. Generally speaking, the people I talked to were not motivated by a *need* to migrate. While their parents might have been migrants or refugees, who communicated messages about nostalgia and the possibilities of integration, the people who are now questioning the meaning of home and its role in composing a life are doing so from a perspective of *choosing* a global lifestyle.

Nevertheless, remembering the loss of leaving can bring up a plethora of issues that influence the process of going home. Albert still talks about the identity loss of leaving his village in France. While leaving was his choice and he has no regrets, at this stage of his life he feels the loss of roots and connection. His identity is still linked to being the one who left.

> *I was raised to stay in my village, marry someone from there, work there, and give back to that community. I believe that I have lost that piece of who I was and was supposed to be. Now that I have started a family, I want to bring them back to my village, at least on regular visits, to find a new way of relating to the place where I am from and where I developed my fundamental values.*

Creating a Home: Can We Agree?

Defining and creating a home is an ongoing challenge for Global Cosmopolitans. It is not always easy to agree about where home should be with life partners children or even grandchildren. As the reader will see in Part III, home is a key aspect of the dialogue and decision-making process when considering the creation of new life chapters. While home may be where the heart is, this has not held many of the Global Cosmopolitans that I know back from finding creative solutions.

10

Embracing Complex Change

One defining feature of Global Cosmopolitans is that change is normal for them. While change is happening at an accelerating rate, affecting the lives of everyone. Global Cosmopolitans describe the levels of complexity of change in their lives that contributes to having an interesting life adventure, while at the same time, providing challenges that often force them to confront the limits of their resilience and their ability to alter their fundamental values. Their success in life and in work has involved embracing complex change. Many of those I interviewed were managing major change in their organizations and/or in their personal lives at the time, or were anticipating a change on the not-too-distant future. In the stories of Global Cosmopolitans, change is a positive force that opens up new possibilities.

The Global Cosmopolitan Mindset contributes to the ability to be motivated by new challenges, to learn from those experiences, and to gain the skills that facilitate the transformation of challenges into opportunities for personal and professional development. The experience of having done it successfully before contributes to the desire to try something different, yet again. Their dynamic resilience they have built over the years, helps them succeed.

Many of my interviewees have been experiencing a world of fast-paced change for a long time. They have personally witnessed a shift in the world order—with significant impact on their careers and life experiences. A post-MBA opportunity in the early 1990s after the fall of the Soviet Union, the opening of the Chinese market, and the growth of Dubai were three of the many examples that people mentioned and had benefited from. Well aware of some of the challenges facing them, their attitude toward taking risks, finding adventure, and trying to find or create organizations where

© The Author(s) 2018
L. Brimm, *The Global Cosmopolitan Mindset*,
https://doi.org/10.1057/978-1-349-95345-5_10

they would be successful outweighs the fear of future change. Living in a technologically advanced world has also helped them to see new possibilities where once there were barriers.

Life Stages

In spite of a huge range of differences in style, personality, professional ambition, and financial status, Global Cosmopolitans take complex change very seriously in every aspect of their lives. Their reserve of positive attitude, resilient dynamism, and cross-cultural know-how all contribute to their decision-making and the confidence that they can make the next life chapter work. However, woven through their global journeys are significant variations in the perspective on what they want and need at different stages in life.

Certain marker events often signal a change in perspective. Along with multiple changes in professional opportunities and responsibilities that come with maturity, changing perspectives on the global journey and its impact, are affected by changes in relationships such as making commitments, breaking up or losing a loved one. From having a baby to various stages of child rearing, parents often have to re-evaluate their lives. Each time there is a decision to be made, the pieces of the puzzle, along with the personal mosaic, have evolved.

Alex and Lina met in university in Germany and decided to follow their hearts and live a life of adventure for a few years. They always thought they would go home when they decided to have children, but that did not happen. Both of them were working in finance in Hong Kong, when their two children were born.

We assumed that we would go back home when the children were born, but we loved living in Asia and put off the decision for a few years. When the possibility to live in Beijing came along, we still felt that we could wait. Having children ready to go into high school changed everything for us. The decision to move home to Germany was complex, since both of us wanted to continue developing our careers. Given our expertise, both of us would have to travel extensively. Both sets of parents said that they were happy to help us out, and they were still young enough to do it. We knew it would not be easy, but we knew at this stage in our lives, we wanted the children to develop roots in Germany.

Before we knew it, our children left for university. In the meantime, China was changing so rapidly, and we thought about going back. But, we had settled into a comfortable life and began thinking about projects that would take us out of our life on a part-time basis. This is when we got actively involved in working with the challenges of migration.

Perspectives on aging differ for personal, familial, and cultural reasons. For many people, growing older means taking on traditional age-related responsibilities, while others glimpse the possibility of living to a hundred and are focused on remaining healthy and active.

In certain cultures, it seems easier to reinvent yourself as you age, which can affect your later choices about where to live. Going home can be a way to perpetuate change or return to your roots. Remaining on the move can be a way to stay young at heart. Whether solo, coupled, or in a family, your perspective on change and its implications will inevitably vary with time and you will have to remain proactive about the evolution of your developmental and identity stories. To complicate the matters further, new models of family life are emerging, women are giving birth later, and human beings are living longer. The kaleidoscope keeps on turning over the life spectrum.

Crisis Management

Some decisions have to be taken so quickly that it is difficult to analyze the different implications. Sometimes, the skill is the ability to seize the moment and know when an immediate response is necessary. This is never more obvious than when a personal or family crisis arises.

Ilke is German and her husband is English. They had been living in London, where he was a consultant and she had her own, thriving business. Ilke had already developed a can-do attitude through her various professional experiences in the world.

She says: 'I thought that I had ticked all of the boxes and everything was moving forward as planned. The children were in good schools. We loved our lives and our work. Then our daughter got dramatically ill at age 11. Within a month, she was in hospital and could not move. She apparently had an autoimmune disease and her body started destroying itself. She survived with medication, but nobody knew what she had. The doctors disagreed vehemently, but generally said there was no cure, only ongoing treatment. It was a difficult time for the whole family, but there was an expert in Canada and we decided to move there. It was the best decision of our lives. Our daughter was cured, and we built a wonderful life there.'

Ilke's story emphasizes that some changes are made in reaction to a crisis. People with a global perspective will look throughout the world for the best health care, even if it requires a new move or a family separation.

Although it is easy to make a quick decision about a positive opportunity, a move halfway around the world to cure a serious illness, though urgent, may be a more challenging choice, as it will also impact the lives of the healthy. Couples with a strong track record of making decisions together have often done the groundwork in their relationship, so they can respond more quickly. In the case of Ilke and her husband, they had already made some hard calls together. They had built a relationship with shared values and goals and knew how to be attentive to their differences in decision-making style.

A crisis can also focus the mind and shorten the reaction time. It is not unusual for people to wait for crises or surprises to push them into a decision, even a very important one!

Being Opportunistic

Even in the midst of preparing for quite a major change, it is possible to take advantage of a sudden opportunity that leads in an entirely new direction. Taking risks in order to generate additional opportunities seems to be another success factor of the Global Cosmopolitan Mindset.

The Global Cosmopolitans I meet are very professionally oriented, but rarely use the word 'career' or describe a standard professional pathway. Taking responsibility for composing an international life can mean going off-script and not depending on organizations for professional advancement, or personal growth. Instead, opportunities are seized whenever and wherever they arise.

Victoria had taken some time out to get her children settled in Kuala Lumpur. She soon realized that she wanted to stay active professionally, but she wanted to make a career shift into a socially responsible sector. She knew that she had certain constraints around travel and flexibility for the time being. Just as she started to feel ready, a colleague contacted her to apply for a great opportunity, working out of KL but involving significant trips abroad. While it was not the perfect job, she decided to apply. She was invited to interview immediately, so she knew that the company was very motivated to hire her – which meant that she could ask for a certain flexibility in her work. She could have waited for another, maybe better, opportunity, but in the end she decided not to. She would make this one work for her.

Fabienne happily followed her husband's career to Bangalore. She knew that there would be work opportunities for her there, which made the choice relatively easy. She had been working very hard for years, and was happy to take a break and enjoy spending time with her daughter. She also appreciated the opportunity to get involved in some entrepreneurial projects, which allowed her to follow her heart and still have time for her daughter.

Once she felt her daughter was firmly established in school, she decided to return to a more traditional career. She is traveling more than she wants to, but she has an agreement with her husband that one of them is always in town. She is ambitious and hard working and actually prefers the structure of a large organization.

Internalizing the New Reality

Change involves transition. This may sound like a tautology, but change and transition are two very subtly different concepts. William Bridges[1] identified that the change is something that happens to people, whether they like it or not. Transition, on the other hand, involves internalizing the new reality— coming to terms with the change, which may well mean letting go of old ways as well as adapting to the new.

> *My first experience of leaving home in the UK changed me forever. I went to New Guinea to do some research and to work on a world health project. I made the decision to go there quite easily, but once I got there, I had to decide whether I would stay or go back home and call it quits. It was the most humbling of experiences. I was lonely. I was uncomfortable and anxious about my health. I wanted to go home.*
>
> *The first phase of learning was about myself. All through my life, I had liked to be the expert and I had to admit, while I did have some knowledge, I had much more to learn to make it useful. It took a while for me to come to terms with the situation and try to make the most of my two-year assignment. Reaching out to others helped, one of the many skills that I needed to learn. What I thought was my intrepid independence was gone forever. Learning how to work with a team became second nature. When it was time to leave, I almost signed on for another couple of years, but I decided to go home long enough to finish my education.*
>
> *That was over twenty years ago, and I have lived in three countries since then. I am staying put for a while, as I raise my two beautiful daughters in New Zealand, but the kick-start to my Global Cosmopolitan Mindset happened during that amazing experience.*

Regardless of life stage, when contemplating a global journey and seeing doors opening that you never imagined, the question of feeling capable of dealing with the complexity of the choice, as well as the capacity to cope with leaving the security of what you know. Looking at previous patterns of dealing with different kinds of change and transition can give you a clearer perspective on your attitudes and strengths.

This was the case for Juan, who was born in Nicaragua. From very poor origins, he was very smart and managed to get an education that gave him the stepping-stone to change his life. While academic work was easy, being so different from his more affluent peers was painful. Yet he knew that he had to take advantage of his situation to help his family and his country. He learned to work hard and to be recognized for what he could do. This enabled him to get scholarships abroad to further his education. The more educated he became, the lonelier he started to feel. But he did fall in love and started developing his family and professional life away from home in the US. There he still felt close enough to home to sustain his desire to make a difference.

Then he was offered an opportunity to develop even further by taking an assignment in Spain. For him, this step meant diving into a global life that was appealing, but he wondered if it was one step too far away from home. He concluded that establishing himself as a Global Cosmopolitan was the best career option. It would give him substantial financial security, which in turn would allow him to contribute to solving some of the problems in his country of origin. He just did not know if he had it in him. He was unsure if he had the kind of confidence it would take to be on his own.

Realizing that his sticking point was confidence, he started working on it by looking at his life story and seeing what he had already learned about dealing with difficult situations. While his country did not provide economic security, it did provide security in terms of knowing how things are done and reminded him of his life mission.

Could he now act on a bigger stage? Sharing his stories with others was a big confidence boost, along with the knowledge that others, too, had issues with confidence. Seeing the power of good advice helped him focus on what would make the difference for him in a new setting – coaching.

Taking Time Out

Taking time out to experience life from a different angle or gain a perspective on your life can be a great way to create a window onto a potential new future. For many people, a sabbatical is a catalyst for change.

Aharon was financially independent and thought that he was retired at 42. He tried various opportunities for personal growth. He taught math for two years in a junior high school, he studied, he climbed mountains, he tried golf, and he took acting classes. He had no time constraints.

Initially he did not want to want to go back to investing, but in a weak moment, he decided to have fun with friends and start a small investment group. Later he turned to working on his own.

He loves making his own decisions and making things happen. He is now working at his own rhythm as a consultant to founders and CEOs. He says that he has been lucky, which is true, but he has also taken the time to create his own professional pathway.

Ashwin was doing very well and working very hard as an investor, but decided to take a year off for reflection. It was a great opportunity to slow down, invest in his personal life, and to recognize what made him tick and what he really wanted to do. He watched TV for a week, and then started looking at who inspired him.

He recalls: 'A friend's father had retired and now spends time volunteering as a teacher. This helped me think about what I want to give and enjoy. Another friend was making necklaces. She loved it so much and it brought her such happiness that she did not want to get paid. I realized that if I was free, I would also give. I take great pleasure in giving my skills away. Now my year is ending and I am thinking of starting my own business, where I can share what I know and do best. I want a collage of personal careers, which will certainly include teaching.'

In order to make complex transitions in their lives, Aharon and Ashwin benefited from learning how they needed to make the best decision, both in terms of their own needs and those of others. Even if the sabbatical is enforced, it is possible to turn time out into an advantage.

It was not Alan's choice to take time out, but the position that had brought him to – and kept him in – Europe, came to an end. They had lived in London and in Amsterdam, but this became an opportunity for him and his family to go home, albeit without an offer.

Thanks to his salary, they had become used to a relatively comfortable life in Europe. Now that they were home, his wife could go back to work and the children could go to local schools, so some of the financial pressure was off.

Alan took advantage of the situation and started opening his eyes to a larger array of possibilities. While the decision is not made yet, he has found a great position, which is not nearly as remunerative as his previous job but offers exciting challenges. In particular, there is an opportunity to use his skills for projects that will directly contribute to the greater social good—something that he now knows is important to him.

Taking time out is also a way to slow down, reduce stress, and stay healthy, all of which are typically at the top of people's change agendas. This could mean getting more exercise, using mindfulness, meditation, neuroplasticity, and retreats, or just learning how to get enough sleep. Taking time out for some individuals is a new source of stress and helps them gain perspective on the role that work can play in structuring their lives.

Cycling Through the Seven Cs of Change and Development

While, Global Cosmopolitans have traveled the Seven Seas, they often lack a comprehensive framework for the personal and emotional journey that accompanies their global journey. The model I developed working with Global Cosmopolitans has been useful for individuals and couples and for coaches and mentors. The model keeps a focus on the task required at each step, what helps and what hinders.

The Seven Cs of Change and Development is designed to be useful as both a descriptive and a diagnostic tool for greater clarity in decision-making. Each of the Seven Cs represents a stage of the change cycle where issues have to be resolved before advancing to the next step. At each stage, it is important to understand what facilitates the task and what might derail it. Thoughtful reflection about previous experiences can provide insights into what contributes to successful completion of a cycle of change. Recognition of what is different about *this* change is an important part of the reflection process.

The Seven Cs of Change and Development

After identifying the trigger for change, at each stage, ask what helps and what hinders you moving forward.

- Complexity: identifying and understanding the variety of implications created by a change.
- Clarity: bringing coherent understanding to the complex issues raised by the change.
- Confidence: developing the belief that one can be successful in the changed situation.
- Creativity: finding new options or solutions.
- Commitment: taking the first steps to implement the change.
- Consolidation: adopting the new identity and ex-identity that this change represents.
- Change: living the change.

Successfully used for changing behaviors and even attitudes, the power of the model lies in giving people a framework that can stimulate a deeper dive into what the change is all about. It can be used to facilitate discussion about change and theories of change with groups of people from diverse cultural or professional backgrounds.

Embracing complex change can be invigorating but daunting. Aligning this process in a relationship can be exciting but complex. The Seven Cs framework has helped many executives and their families break the process down into workable parts. While sharing the process of global decision-making is not easy, understanding the impact of individual needs on the process can facilitate acceptance of a decision, clarify sources of resilience, and help take the cycle of change forward. Following this framework can become the cornerstone of an even more successful future life.

Using the 7Cs for a Complicated Move

Amy and Jeff both love working in Singapore. Growing up in England, they had never imagined their global lifestyle. They had been living together for 15 years and had already lived in Malaysia and Indonesia before they moved to Singapore five years ago. Their two children are in an international pre-school and they have a live-in maid who enables their busy lifestyle. Decision-making had been pretty simple for them... until the events of last month.

Amy had already been contemplating a career move in Singapore, when she received a fabulous offer in Dubai. Jeff was happy with his career options in Southeast Asia, so he was not excited about moving away. Then he received a phone call from his mother, which changed everything. His father had just had a second heart attack. While Jeff had been highly career driven, he found himself starting to question what was important in his life. For Jeff, it was now about discovering what was best for his wife and parents, as well as for himself.

1. Complexity
The first stage consists of identifying and understanding the complex variety of implications created by a change.

Amy and Jeff started making lists, but neither knew how to set priorities. Jeff, who hates indecision, said that he wanted to quit and go back home to London. Amy, who has always been open to multiple possibilities for major decisions, knew that time was not on her side. She realized she needed help and started asking for it from friends, co-workers, and her current boss. Jeff felt he had to make a decision, and that he had no need to talk it through with anyone. Amy feared regrets on his part and wanted him to be able to live with the consequences of this decision. Speaking with friends and coaches ultimately helped them decide that Dubai would work for both of them. It was closer to London and could provide interesting opportunities for Amy and hopefully Jeff too.

The issue of aging parents becomes bigger over time but in a mixed family, country of origin can add to the complexity both culturally and professionally. In some cultures, children are expected to care for their parents and move home to do so. Identifying all of these variables helps a couple or family frame the challenge.

2. Clarity

The objective of this stage is to achieve a coherent understanding of the complex issues raised in the first stage and start to form a plan.

Jeff realized that getting closer to London would make a difference for him. He envisioned five years in Dubai, if he could find work that he enjoyed, to build a pathway to working in London. He also had a long talk with his parents, which helped him calm his anxiety and focus on his family's move. Amy sought information from her prospective employer on the type of travel commitments involved with the new role, with an eye to being present with the family and supporting Jeff's ambitions.

It is important at this stage that couples identify options for their children, such as schools, social activities, and networks of friends. This particularly helps with the next stage.

3. Confidence

Jeff was willing to explore options in Dubai, but he knew that he needed more time to address his concerns about having the right contacts in a new region. Amy negotiated a later start date. Just knowing he could have more time gave him the confidence that he'd be able to find something ideal.

It is not just partners who worry about a move. Children might be concerned that their parents' new jobs will mean more travel and time away from home. Hearing the concerns of others can be useful. In reassuring them, you will also reinforce your own confidence.

4. Creativity

By this stage, it should be apparent that new solutions might be needed to tackle the problems at hand.

Jeff realized that a number of options would emerge if he had some more management experience and training. Until now, he had only managed people who were experts in the oil and gas industry. He recognized that he might have to move out of his area of expertise and considered working in alternative energy, or another area completely. But he knew that he could not move to Dubai without a job offer. If he wanted to change industry, he needed to go somewhere where they were willing to invest in his development as a manager. He found that looking outside of his comfort zone felt right and opened creative ways to develop his career.

Creativity can sometimes mean letting go of the idea that you must continue to follow your current path. In Jeff's case, this meant looking at alternative career options, but it could also mean a staggered move, with one partner moving first and the other taking time to find the right fit before committing to the change.

5. Commitment

At this point, it is necessary to understand that there is no single right or perfect answer. Successful change is based on commitment to a good, realistic solution that is well implemented. However, taking the first steps can often close options and generate anxiety, making this a difficult stage.

While Jeff and Amy remained committed to moving back to England within five years, they recognized that the move to Dubai was a better way to begin the process of re-entry for both of them. They knew that the transition would not be easy. Amy had to start her job while Jeff was working out the details of leaving his old firm and joining a new organization. Saying goodbye to friends, finding schools and live-in help for their *children*, and managing all of the appropriate paperwork for the move were complicated and time consuming, but they started to see the move as a fresh start.

6. Consolidation
Jeff and Amy realized that in order to make this move, they needed all the help they could get, since both of them would have to travel significantly to get started. Just telling their parents of their long- and short-term plans helped them let go and invest in their new *possibilities*. Their parents even offered to help with the transition by coming to Dubai and thus became part of the solution.

Consolidation involves adopting the change and leaving the old situation behind. Difficulties can arise when one has trouble letting go of the old life, but new possibilities, for example involving other family members, may emerge.

7. Change: Living the Change
In the final step of the process, you start living the change, but it does not end here.

*This is just a new beginning for Amy and Jeff. Unintended consequences can arise. For example, the choice of school might be linked to a longer-*term question about whether they want to maximize the children's British *identity* or whether they want to maintain as international an environment for them as possible.

Mistakes and discomforts should be seen in light of learning opportunities rather than feelings of regret, which can lead to a sense of loss and aversion to future moves. Helping others accept the change can be half the battle, so it is important to work through the change in as structured and considered a way as possible.

Working with Global Cosmopolitans on change reveals that people can fly through some of the Cs, while getting stuck at others. This insight provides a way to look at coaching another person through a process of change or transition and reinforces an understanding that what helps one person is not necessarily what helps another.

The Seven Small c's of Change

This Seven Cs model is useful for complex transitions and major moves, but it is just as useful for changing the smaller behavior patterns and the decisions that contribute to success on a global journey. While some behaviors and attitudes seem to change without visible effort, others can become stumbling blocks.

In fact, the model can be a way to look at any process of change. Working with it in a classroom setting, as well as with individual clients, I have used it to kick-start change projects, such as getting back to healthy exercise, listening to others before making assumptions, or sharpening the skills necessary for career advancement.

Working on relatively simple but difficult personal change can contribute to someone's understanding of the process of more complex change, their attitude toward change, and what it takes for them to change a behavior or even an attitude. It is also an opportunity to look at what helps or what hinders behavioral change more broadly.

Overcoming Resistance to Change

Even people who pride themselves on seeing change as normal have bad habits or weak points that they may want to work on but are not sure how to do it. Some people also talk about the positive energy that they have gained from overcoming resistance to change and what they have learned from the process.

> Sebastian wanted to prepare for a major transition involving a return to the US. He initially looked at how he managed two previous major transitions, including a move from Chile to China, which also meant quitting his consulting position to take responsibility for a social innovation project in China. While he had been very successful, he had faced unnecessary challenges both times. He did not want to make another major transition without understanding how he could improve the process. He knew that he had to look at his way of approaching change every carefully.
>
> Very competent and confident, he realized that his confidence could turn into a two-edged sword when approaching change. His can-do attitude could cause him to turn a blind eye to details that needed addressing. He found that he needed to examine his over-confidence. He spent time attempting to slow his involvement down and become more observant, and he did this with a coach.
>
> That led him to approach his forthcoming decision very carefully. Using this framework and working with this wife, he realized that his need for clarity pushed him to minimize the complexity of a decision. Not getting bogged down in complications was one of his strengths. However, it led to him avoid certain aspects of complexity that needed attention. Understanding how his strengths could also be his weaknesses helped him to start paying appropriate attention to details, without the fear of losing his desire for clarity.

As we can see in Sebastian's example, the concept of two-edged swords can be used very effectively along with the 7 Cs of Change.

Seeing a positive change on the horizon can be very exciting, yet the complicating truth is that it invariably involves real loss as well as potential gain. While people have various degrees of desire to change and differing levels of confidence in their ability to cope with significant change, experience is an excellent teacher—although not the only one. Identifying the patterns that contribute to a positive transition and seeing ways to improve the process of change through the use of the 7 C's framework can be particularly helpful.

Preparing the Next Step in the Journey

Mariana wanted to reinvent herself as an orator. In moving countries, she had seen how she was able to evolve her identity. As a Spanish speaker going to university and graduate school in the US, she says that her personality expanded because she wanted to adapt to the American environment. Earlier, when growing up, she was very tall and awkward, and needed to work on being accepted by her peers. As a woman, working in very male and English-speaking environments in the US and Australia, she deepened her ability to balance belonging and feeling different.

Now, more senior and experienced, she was offered her dream position in London, which would involve new levels of leadership. She realized that she had to learn to speak in public, not only to tell her story but to motivate people to support her organization, which was in the business of making a significant impact on the lives of others.

Looking back at other changes she had made, she knew that motivation was key. She knew that she was motivated by learning and by making a difference. She knew that her seamless adaptation to the needs of others, which she had learned when she was young and moving between countries with her parents, made it difficult for her to speak out. In other words, she had to battle one of her greatest strengths to articulate her own beliefs.

She started working on a one-to-one basis with people she knew well, but speaking in front of large groups sent her into a total panic. Her coach helped her find acting tutors and situations where she could work on talking to an audience. A course on public speaking was very helpful. Today, she speaks in public with ease. Change mission accomplished!

Typically, Global Cosmopolitans have to constantly probe the attributes that will make them successful. In Mariana's case, she knew that integrating a change into her identity story could happen, as she had made this type of adjustment before. She also used the Seven Cs framework, which was helpful for understanding her attitudes toward change and how they impacted the process. While understanding does not necessarily guarantee new attitudes or behavior, it can generate insights that help to facilitate the process. I will leave the final words in this chapter to two Global Cosmopolitans in the hope that they will resonate with—and inspire—my readers.

I have decided that I often go into a shell during periods of change. In other words, I am often a slow starter in times of great transition and this is a behavior that I would like to examine and try to adjust.

As a Global Cosmopolitan, I have experiences that should make me more open to change, and I need to tap into those internal resources.

For the majority of trigger events, I feel that I am quite capable and comfortable in identifying the implications and starting to understand and prepare the change. This is partially due to the logical approach I often take to changes in my life. I now see that my logical approach has been my strength, but it can be my weakness if I do not learn how to pay attention to my feelings.

Part III

Creating New Chapters in an Already Interesting Life

Introduction

Global Cosmopolitans lead busy, engaged, and often passionate lives that involve many turns in the road. Along the way, they have to make numerous decisions about where to go, who to go with, and what to do. Having made decisions that will fundamentally change their lives, many will be quite articulate about the choices that have made all of the difference in how their lives have unfolded, just as Robert Frost described in *The Road Not Taken*:

> Two roads diverged in a wood, and I–
> I took the one less traveled by,
> And that had made all the difference.[1]

As they rise to the challenges and seize the opportunities in their path, they come to understand the extent to which they are authoring a life story comprised of multiple threads that give meaning and definition to their existence. Despite the many obstacles they have encountered, they emphasize that complex change has been a positive force in their lives.

While they might describe themselves as lucky, most Global Cosmopolitans also know that they have worked hard to gain their success and build their confidence. Their stories reflect the opportunities they have created and the life lessons they have learned as a result of dealing with the challenges they have faced. Change becomes increasingly normal for them. They give us a glimpse of what it is like to build a life and a career across the world and multiple cultures. The stories they shared reflected moments in time when their authors were able to give a certain perspective to their journeys.

Although no two of these stories are the same, they all have something in common. They are writing new chapters in their developing lives, which define them as individuals, as well as providing examples of answers to some universal questions, such as how to satisfy the need to belong, what gives a sense of meaning to life, or how to have an impact.

As more people face the possibility of leading longer lives, learning to create new life chapters out of the opportunities that arise or that they create will be an increasingly relevant life skill. Their sensitivity to what gives their lives meaning and motivation offers lessons to us all.

As the framework of this section evolved, the notion of creating new chapters in a potentially long life story increasingly took hold. I was reminded of my son's interest in the children's game book series *Choose Your Own Adventure* (bestsellers in the 1980s), in which the reader faces choices that can lead to a variety of outcomes to the plot. The questions are different in real life, but the principle is the same. What turn do you want to take? And what are future choices that will cascade from your decision today?

As this book has emphasized, Global Cosmopolitans have had to recreate their lives and even their identities in new cultures and new languages. Given the complexity of their existences, they are aware of the trade-offs they have to make to succeed in a new country or new market. They adapt to the changes that are necessary, but are open to draw on their strengths to meet new possibilities head on. They are able to turn their personal kaleidoscope to focus on filling in the gaps or developing new perspectives that offer new solutions and patterns of life.

They have applied their confidence and creativity to reshape their lives in very interesting ways. Even brief versions of their stories can provide inspiration to others at crucial times of reorientation or relocation. The stories in this section describe varying responses to creating a sense of home, resolving certain relational complexities, or focusing on a sense of purpose and meaning in life. They are particularly concerned with experienced Global Cosmopolitans who are balancing their identity issues with other dilemmas.

Timing and location are key factors in these stories. A proposal to expand or sell a business can spark new possibilities or other unforeseen changes. At the same time, the reality of significant investments—literal and metaphorical—in both work and life can create major constraints.

Proposals from colleagues or even strangers can be seen as turning points in the path of life. Sometimes a suggestion from a friend or a loved one can lead toward a new change, new interests, or new skills—or simply affirm the importance of old interests. A significant number of people talk about the excellent help they have received from family, friends, colleagues, networks, coaches, or therapists in writing their new chapters. Knowing when and how to reach out appropriately is a skill that successful people usually know how to apply.

'If you are used to questioning your life and your possibilities, reflection and personal growth will continue'. At least this is what Global Cosmopolitans have taught me. After all their rich experience, they still take great interest in what others are doing and what they can learn from them. When they have opportunities to get together with people who share their concerns and interests, they seize them with both hands.

Each Global Cosmopolitan story in this section illustrates a design for a new way of living. The protagonists are just leading their lives, but at the same time—having gained a level of confidence and the capacity to reinvent themselves by taking risks—they model the futures of generations to come. There will be new rules and new dilemmas. But composing a life that allows the continuation of personal growth and commitment, professional success, and the contribution to larger social goals will become even more relevant. In the end, each generation has to find its own 'road less traveled,' but there is no better guide than the maps drawn by the previous generation.

11

The Global Cosmopolitan Odyssey

Global Cosmopolitans often mention Homer's epic poem the *Odyssey* when talking about their voyage. The *Odyssey* is typically referred to as a ten-year struggle to go home, with its eponymous hero, Odysseus, facing numerous trials and tribulations as he attempts to return to Ithaca from Troy. Some see the story as a metaphor for life itself: man's journey from birth to death.

Many generations later in 1911, C.P. Cavafy[1] wrote about the same journey home in his poem, *Ithaca*. Cavafy could be described as a Global Cosmopolitan by birth (his family roots extend from Constantinople to London via Alexandria, Trebizond, Clos, Trieste, Venice, and Vienna) and through his own experience of international living. 'Hope the road is a long one, filled with adventures, filled with understanding,' he wrote, capturing the benefits of a global journey in terms of treasures and learning. 'May you stop at Phoenician trading posts/and there acquire fine goods…To many Egyptian cities you may go/so you may learn, and go on learning, from their sages.' He comments through metaphor on what many Global Cosmopolitans try to resolve for themselves, not least to remember that the journey is every bit as important as its destination.

Are all Global Cosmopolitans trying to go home? And what might they find when they get there? As we saw in Chapter 9, Global Cosmopolitans have many ways of defining 'home.' Not all of them, by any means, choose to return to where they came from. Indeed, many do not even have a home—as traditionally defined—to go to. There are a variety of reasons, for this from having a Global Cosmopolitan background themselves to the risk of physical danger or economic hardship. For some people, home is a

© The Author(s) 2018
L. Brimm, *The Global Cosmopolitan Mindset*,
https://doi.org/10.1057/978-1-349-95345-5_11

complex construct that keeps evolving. Some individuals say that they see home as a place that they will create or chose and that their global journey gives them the possibility of searching for the place they want to call home. Other say, They may choose to take home with them wherever they go, to create a concept that is a hybrid (defined perhaps by a combination of their family, professional life, and travels), or to move to places where their differences are appreciated and understood.

Nevertheless, as we have also seen earlier in this book, going back to their country or culture of origin is a dream that many Global Cosmopolitans are driven to realize. It might be a move they make when they start a family, the arrival of children raising the importance of roots, culture, and education. It might be a return mid-journey, when they are still active professionally but beginning to think about how they can make a difference in the place they came from. Alternatively, it might be a belated homecoming, for the sake of aging parents or simply retirement.

Taking the decision to re-enter the country called 'home' can be difficult. And while each decision to return home might be made for different reasons, some of the issues surrounding that decision will be the same.

Unlike refugees or economic migrants, many of the Global Cosmopolitans have the luxury of freedom of movement. They have passports, sometimes multiple passports, and most can choose to go back to their roots—and visit whenever they want to. The issue of home without freedom is a subject worthy of many books in its own right. But most of us, fortunately, are free to move. Whether we define ourselves as Global Cosmopolitans or not, we have much in common with this group and much to learn from what it means to them to 'go home.'

The Decision to Return Home Is Multifaceted

The decision to return home is just as complex as any of the other choices that Global Cosmopolitans have to make as they navigate the world. The factors involved are too numerous to list, but several are worth highlighting.

Life stage is a factor that reappears in several different guises along the way. Going to college, formalizing a relationship, having children, choosing schools, midlife career change, and approaching retirement can all serve as focal points for thinking about a return. The issue of roots and wings, as discussed earlier, becomes a crucial topic of discussion and decision-making for parents.

Feelings of security and confidence can impact decision-making on whether the journey continues or takes a homeward direction. Family and friends might be concerned and believe that the solution is to 'come home.'

But they tend to offer—or demand—that solution without examining what the Global Cosmopolitan actually wants for himself or herself. This can be confusing, since it raises the question such as: Whose needs am I meeting? What is my responsibility to my family of origin as opposed to what I want or need to give me a sense of connectedness and belonging in my life? What if home feels like a more complex notion than the place I grew up in? Do I still identify with home as a key cultural context of my personal development? Learning how to manage these voices can often feel more cumbersome than the decision-making process itself.

Equally confusing and upsetting is the message: 'Do not come home.' This could be qualified by: 'It is not safe here'; 'The economy is a mess'; or even 'You are better off away from the political events in the country right now.' Worse still are the more personal comments, such as: 'There is no place for you in the family business'; 'We need you out in the world'; or 'There are messy family issues that have arisen in your absence or have not disappeared.'

Memories of home are also key. Certain memories draw people back home, while others contribute to wanting to stay away. But maturation and personal development may have opened different perspectives on past experiences. Global Cosmopolitans may have to reconcile the differences between the home they left and the home they return to, as well as what their international experience has taught them about their current needs.

There may also be a tension between the 'new' family and the 'old,' especially if extra cultures have been added to the mix. As Global Cosmopolitans identify increasingly with the family life and friendships they have created on their journeys, they wonder if they will find a place for themselves with their families and cultures of origin.

You Cannot Turn the Kaleidoscope Back

When they think about going home or 're-entry,' most Global Cosmopolitans know that it will never be the same as it was. The kaleidoscope will not replicate the same pattern it showed all those years ago. Hence, negotiating a changed sense of self becomes central when people talk about the possibility of going home.

Learning how to manage a global life involves a process of maturing and developing competence and confidence. Yet, at different points, no matter how successful people have been, questions can be raised about settling down, especially in the place that used to be home. Will there be pressure on me to be the person I was? Will I be able to see myself as the person I feel I have become? Will I be able to function in my different roles, the way I do now? Will I find the right people and responsibilities, professional or otherwise, to be seen as the person that I have become—and to have the impact that I am used to making?

Fears of reverting to the person that began the voyage can bring up similar concerns. How much have I really changed? And how can I communicate that effectively to the people who knew me before I left? Knowing that you have matured does not always give you confidence that you will hold onto the person you have become on the global journey, when you return to the circles of family and close friends who did not travel with you.

Some Global Cosmopolitans describe having learned another 'language of existence' that feels consistent with their new way of being. They are concerned that speaking this different language back home will lead to misunderstandings, particularly with people who are not open to learning through the dialogue of difference. They worry they will have to return to speaking the 'old language' and thus lose the capacity to express the new identity that they have nurtured and developed. Facing this loss of self and the ability to communicate can touch a deep concern about who one is, who one can be upon return, and who they will be able to relate to in the community back home.

Another worry that is frequently raised is the potential loss of excitement and interest. Will I stop feeling that life is an adventure that continually opens doors to learning and growth? For people who have had particularly exotic global lifestyles, the idea of going home raises fears of boredom or of no longer being able to learn from the kind of difference that they find stimulating.

Above all, people fear that their Global Cosmopolitan Skill set will not be appreciated or used. They feel their Global Cosmopolitan Mindset may not be respected, or that they will find it difficult to adopt the local mindset required to cope with their new professional and personal lives.

Yet, despite all these fears, for many Global Cosmopolitans, going home after their long and successful odyssey represents an opportunity to invest in the country that they call home and to make a difference there. It is strongly linked to their sense of identity, purpose, and responsibility.

Are There Differences for Women?

Sue's story of going home is influenced by the fact that she is a single woman grappling with where she thinks she wants to belong.

Should Sue return to Hong Kong? She was not even Sue before she left, but Su Ling, a symbol of the differences she anticipates dealing with if she goes home. After completing secondary school and university in Canada and the US, she worked as an investment banker in London and obtained her MBA in Switzerland, where she continued working in private equity.

While it had been extremely difficult to leave her family, she had adjusted and flourished on her global journey. She loved her independence and the fact that every day felt like the beginning of a new adventure. Nevertheless, she started to experience a growing desire to return home. She had broken off a long-standing relationship with a European and had recently started dating an old colleague who was based in Singapore.

Returning to Hong Kong could work for her if it meant finding an exciting career path and feeling confident that she could enjoy her relationships with parents, family and friends. How could she integrate those relationships and her career potential into the life of the new Sue – the woman that she has become?

Sue is not alone. Globalization has facilitated the possibility of education and work abroad for many women, which can be an exciting opportunity offering multiple new lenses through which to see the world. However, many women choose to head home hoping to integrate what they have learned from their global experience. Re-entry can be one of the most challenging aspects of their global voyage.

Asian Global Cosmopolitan women who have the potential to become leaders in Asia know it is an exciting time to work in the region, but they are concerned about ending their odyssey. They are also unsure whether the opportunities to flourish in the Asian markets are greater than or equal to those they already have elsewhere.

A useful first step in the decision-making process is taking the time to understand and articulate their personal narratives. By voicing their own stories, they clarify the meaning of the journey so far and how to negotiate the next career steps. The gains from a global journey can be invisible even to the individual who has reaped the rewards.

While women need to know their stories, a second step in the process is identifying the skills that they have gained from their experience—and which will contribute to their future success at work. If they are unable to engage in a constructive dialogue, many women find that they fall into the trap of adaptation. Adaptation is one of the numerous two-edged swords of mobility—it can facilitate re-entry, but it can also result in alienation and loss of the creative voice developed through a different experience. The desire to please others and adapt to new situations can work against the need to hold on to the changes that have taken place in a globally developed identity.

Global Cosmopolitans are looking for employers that are open to change and difference, which often translates to being open to women. Many women envision nightmare scenarios if they return to very bureaucratic organizations. They often see multinational corporations, experienced in managing re-entry, as better able to offer them positions of interest and power.

In order to change cultures and succeed, the women have learned how to find creative solutions. They are used to seeing the spaces in between cultures, possibilities that are available in one culture and not another. Some want to work with start-ups or to launch their own businesses. Networking and funding can be challenging—they might need some serious help on this front—but facing challenges and taking risks are not unusual for Global Cosmopolitans.

Concerns about the personal sphere are often kept private by women, yet a crucial piece of the re-entry puzzle is the recognition that family and friends can make all of the difference. While their entourage can be proud of them and happy to have them home, Global Cosmopolitans want them to understand and facilitate any changes of identity, ways of relating, or decisions about lifestyle.

They express concerns about losing part of their newfound identity if they return home. While it can be easy to change certain behaviors, they know that the new attitudes that they have developed will be very hard to change or hide. While they are often prepared to engage in a dialogue around these issues, they fear they will never be accepted. One way that they choose to overcome this apparently insurmountable problem is by seeking the support of an international community or other Global Cosmopolitans. Men and women who understand the challenges of re-entry can contribute to their ability to manage a crucial cycle of change in their lives—from finding new solutions to bringing their newfound selves into their old relationships.

Is Making the Decision Twice as Hard for Couples?

Navigating the rough seas of re-entry is difficult enough for an individual. But managing couple and family relationships adds another degree of complexity, particularly if a Global Cosmopolitan is returning to a home country that has changed radically since he or she set sail.

On the one hand, having a partner can make it easier to share the complexities of transition—you are not alone in facing the challenge. On the other hand, Global Cosmopolitan couples often find that returning to the place they call home quickly turns from a dream into a nightmare. When they have formed a relationship abroad—away from cultural messages about how to behave in relationships—local pressures can alter both the individuals and the nature of their dialogue.

Dangerous remarks can creep into the conversation. 'I thought that I was number one in your eyes until we moved here.' 'I thought that I knew who I was.' 'I am turning into someone that I do not like.' People may even find themselves saying: 'Who is your confidante, me, or your mother?' Trying to manage a relationship according to old cultural norms about family, while remaining true to the new rules developed overseas can seem impossible.

If a couple is starting a family together *and* making significant career moves, *as well as* returning home, it is particularly difficult to remain on the same page. Close as the two individuals might be, it is still important to remember some challenges that are particular to couples (see Chapter 7). Talking to a trusted advisor and developing a new dialogue is more important than at almost any other point in the odyssey. Alex needed to talk about the possibility of moving back to Europe from the US.

Sitting on the beach, relaxing after surfing, Alex had received a call that he knew was about to change his life. He was being headhunted for a dream position in Germany – and had about two weeks to make up his mind. He turned to Sophia and said, 'In two weeks, we could move to Germany. Should we stay or should we go?'

He was French and his wife of five years, Sophia, was from Portugal. The recent birth of their son had 'changed everything' for them. They had already started discussing their thoughts about the future when Alex received this offer.

'I did not see it coming. I never thought that the invisible threads that tie me to my European roots would take me away from my California dream,' he said. 'Both my office and my apartment look out over the Pacific Ocean. Everything about my life here reflects my desire for a healthy lifestyle. But I fell in love with another European, and I feel a commitment and sense of responsibility to my family. So, when I was just headhunted for a position in Germany this week, we were ecstatic. Home is Europe.'

Alex and Sophia had both gained their MBAs from top-tier schools and had excellent CVs. If they moved to Germany, their parents and friends would be just an hour or two away. They both agreed that stability and family attachments had become priorities now that they were parents. Another small detail that meant a lot to Alex was that Sophia's parents had a house near the beach!

Sofia's decision was made. She wanted to create her home in Europe, near family and friends. She did not have the same kind of friendships in California. She wanted her son to be educated in Europe, learning the languages and cultural norms that reflect her background. Sofia had already started her own business, which she could operate from anywhere, but she preferred to run it from Europe.

Alex called for professional advice, knowing that he needed to be clear about his own decision to leave California. He was surprised to see how open he was to letting go of a dream that had been motivating him for several years. But letting go without regrets was a key element of his dilemma. He loved his lifestyle. While he was getting a bit bored with his current position, he had discussed possibilities of moving to new and challenging projects in his current company.

When he had left Europe, 15 years earlier, he knew that he was leaving familiar opportunities and networks for the unknown of being a lone foreigner. But it was relatively easy to close the door on that chapter of his life. This seemed harder. He wanted to open the new chapter with the same kind of motivation that had helped him overcome obstacles when he left Europe, so that this move did not just feel like 'going back.'

As he spoke, Alex started to understand more about the sources of his ambivalence. Talking to someone he trusted helped him see that he had the confidence and the motivation to move forward. It also helped him discuss the importance of the changes in his life and how motivating his dreams had been in the past. What would motivate him now? That was the big question.

For Alex and Sophia, it was the beginning of the new adventure. Barbara was at an earlier stage in the process. Her dilemma was how to say to her partner, 'I want to go home.'

Barbara, an American, and her French husband, Eric, went to business school together in Boston. On graduation, they both found their dream jobs in Paris.

As a consultant, she traveled and loved it. Her work gave her regular opportunities to go home to New York. Then Barbara gave birth to twins. Although she had excellent childcare, continuing as a consultant meant too much time away, and besides, she had been thinking about starting her own business.

Barbara also felt limited in France. While she spoke French, she felt that she lacked an understanding of how people related to each other and she knew that she could not survive in a very French organization. As a consultant, she was able to work in English by frequently traveling outside of France. Barbara was an excellent networker and people who knew her thought that she was extremely talented.

Her dream was to start her own business. While she was able to get involved in startups in Paris, they were not her own and she wanted to get involved in a big project. She also missed her family and would be living love to in NYC, where she grew up, and could be nearer to them.

Then, a great offer came from startup in New York. She knew her husband could find work anywhere, but she hated to pull him away from work that he enjoyed and his friends and family. It was very hard for her to tell him that she really wanted to go home. She knew that she could be very powerful in the US, but the biggest place she had to assert herself was at home. This was particularly difficult, since they were expecting another child.

It was not just about Eric either. Barbara's father had been the breadwinner in her family and, in spite of the generational changes, she worried about what her parents would think of the whole family moving for her sake.

Eric and Barbara had a number of open and honest discussions; confronted some of the more difficult pieces of their decision-making process. In the end, they chose to move to New York.

Children Make It Even More Complex

When children are onboard for the odyssey, there is no doubt that the process of going home is even more complicated. Sumitra and Anita's story is typical. Now that they were both in their 40s and had children of their own, they did not want to feel like the children they had been when they left India. When I interviewed Sumitra, they were still at the stage of mourning their lost life and trying to figure out how to integrate into a new life in the new India—with all its emerging opportunities.

No matter where I was living, I always enjoyed my home visits to India. I loved being treated as the old Sumitra, and I reacted as if I had not changed in my years away. I soaked up all the affection from family and friends and then returned to my global journey and the 'me' that was developing abroad.

In actuality, I have changed significantly over the years of living globally. Since leaving, I have finished two masters programs and have started two successful businesses. I met Anita, my wife, while working in London, then we went to the US.

Ironically, while we were enjoying our very American lifestyle in North Carolina, we would look at our two children and face serious considerations over whether or not we should move to India. The question focused on, 'How American did we want our children to be?' But there were other tugs on our heartstrings too.

As we saw it, moving to Bangalore seemed like a perfect solution for us. Our families lived there, there were interesting career opportunities, and it was the perfect place to start the business that I had been dreaming about.

Now, we have been here almost six months. There are aspects of re-entry that are wonderful. I feel like I belong here, with my extended family and friends. Despite all of the complexity and contradictions, I find a strange comfort in the smells of India and the food that I adore. Here, I can actually see endless possibilities.

However, the move has not been easy. We had a huge home in North Carolina; now we are living in an apartment. My daughter carries a picture of our old home on her phone and shows it to me at least once a day. She reminds me that she misses her friends and the fun that she used to have in school. I know that this will pass, but it does hurt.

One of my biggest challenges has been being a good enough son for my parents. They do not understand my relationship with Anita, and they have strong expectations of our involvement with my extended family. While they are very loving, it puts pressure on me to be the son that they thought that they knew, not the person that I have become.

Anita is feeling the brunt of the move. She enjoys having family nearby and significantly more household help, but she wants to use her management skills beyond home. While her parents live in Bangalore now, she grew up in London. She has trouble accepting the pressure placed on her to alter her career dreams so that she is available to ensure our children's education in the Indian manner and attend to other extended family commitments. She does not want to be a stay-at-home Mom. She is afraid of feeling trapped.

While I am focused on the issues of career and family, I feel I lost my blinders to aspects of India on my global journey and I see the complexities in the place I call home with different lenses. I am no longer living in someone else's country. This is mine and what do I need to do? How will I create a meaningful life here, maintain an inner respect for myself? I find it hard to see myself turning a blind eye to the inequities and corruption in India that seem so much more visible to me now.

It takes work, both separately and together to make the most of this important transition, so that the relationship can survive the internal and external pressures. Some simple truths—often forgotten in the midst of change—can prove helpful.

- Talk to other people, especially couples, who have experienced re-entry. There are no formulas, but it can be comforting to know that you are not alone. The discussions can lead to new approaches and creative thinking when you feel blocked. Small breakthroughs can help a couple get unstuck and find new ways forward.
- Personal reflection is crucial. As we have seen in previous chapters, Global Cosmopolitans can benefit from reflecting on their experience of previous changes and transitions in their lives. How have you managed change in the past? And how can you lever this learning to manage change in this new situation, which just happens to be an old place?

While Sumitra and Anita's decision to move to India was behind them, they still had a lot of work to do to navigate the impact of that decision on their lives. As in any change process, it is the implementation and sustainability that count in the end.

Planning for Re-entry

Some people put a great deal of thought into re-entry. They know where home is for them—and want their children rooted in that same place. They encourage regular visits to families and friends. They have pictures of their home country all over the house, so that discussions about 'home' can flow easily, helping their children to imagine a life there. Matias, for one, wants to forge a meaningful identity for himself and his family, so the focus for his next life change is on going home. What started with questions about whether to stay on their global journey or go home brought up many other questions about values.

Living in Dubai has been great. I love my work and the life we have created here, but something is missing. We have a wonderful circle of friends, but our deep connections to both people and place are in our home country. Since we met, we have managed to create a life over the last 20 years that has allowed us to live in different cultures and travel for fun. We have worked hard to develop a relationship that allows us to discuss even the most challenging of issues. Luckily, my wife is a planner and has helped us share our values and our desires for the next stages in our lives. As soon as our eldest finishes elementary school, we are heading home. We know that we want time with our families of origin. There is no substitute for that feeling of being part of a family and a community. We want our children to also appreciate and experience the feeling of connection and the deepening of roots in a country.

We are well aware of the challenges that re-entry can entail, not the least of which is my opportunities for career advancement. I can see the writing on the wall that I might not find a position in my organization as exciting as the one I have now. Right now, boredom is not part of my vocabulary, but it could be if I return home. While we might consider a stop closer to home, in another South American country, it would have to be very special in order for me to take a detour.

Before I did my MBA and before I started a family, I actually launched two successful businesses. While I like the security and the challenges that my current company has provided, I think I am ready to start my own business again. It will not be easy. I have a limited network at home and the market is quite restricted. And I know how easy it is to focus on the business and lose the time that I want to devote to my family.

As for our friendship network, it will take work. Our old friends relate to us based on our childhood experiences. Now, our outlook is very global, and our interests are not very local. We want to return as locals and as cosmopolitans. Maintaining an interest and involvement in the world will be crucial for us and for our children.

Cultural mandates about the role of family are changing around the edges, but many Global Cosmopolitans come from cultures where family and friends are central. Matias appreciates this and is already making attempts to mitigate the challenges of re-entry, although he also recognizes that there will be additional levels of challenge once he and his family move home.

Many people are not planners like Matias and his wife. While some have already talked about what they will do if they go home, the discussion is left at that, and they continue to focus on maximizing the present. Some couples assume that certain key events will color when, how, and if they return home. They are aware that a crisis at home or a decision to send children home for secondary school or university will be an opportunity to look at re-entry.

Living with the Decision to Go Home and the Realities of Re-entry

At a seminar in the south of France, I met with a group of experienced French business executives who had made the decision to come home after years of working abroad. They talked about how challenging re-entry had been. Men and women who had led organizations and had exciting roles in Asia found that people at home did not really respect their experience in the way that they anticipated. Having moved back to France to deepen their attachment to the place where they grew up, they were shocked at times by the way people questioned their experience and loyalty. While they had developed excellent worldwide networks, their compatriots back home only seemed to ask who they knew in France.

Several had decided to start their own organizations or become interim managers, since the skills that they had honed working globally were highly applicable. They could go into a new company as they would go into a foreign country and quickly figure out how it worked, what needed to be changed, and make it happen. Then, ready for a new 'country,' they could leave to help another company in trouble.

In addition, while many had returned to ensure that their children developed roots in France and friends for life, it did not always work out that way. Some children integrated quickly, as if they had never left, while others missed their international friends and big-city living and left as quickly as they could for studies in the UK or America.

The French group proved that you are never re-entering the culture that you left. You have changed, the people you know have changed, and the context has changed, even if it has only changed because you are seeing it with different eyes.

Bringing home a relationship or entire family that has been nurtured and developed elsewhere can be a source of stress until there is clarity about whether the family can function in a situation that will place new expectations and responsibilities on them. Once they have settled in, understood that the kaleidoscope has turned, and accepted that some parts of their lives will look and feel quite different, they can start to build a place for themselves anew.

Initially, there are multiple aspects of re-entry that need attention—often all at the same time. Finding a place to live and work, settling in, and re-establishing old ties are all priorities. If there are children, easing their entry can take both time and energy. Your old information about accommodation and schools probably needs updating, and even with connections, getting children into the appropriate education and activities can feel like a nightmare.

For children of all ages, there can be confusion. They need to go through the loss of what they had before and find ways to adapt to their new situations. While they might have been told that they are going home, they will not necessarily experience it that way. Home is supposed to feel familiar and safe, but in this new place that everyone else seems to know so well, a child can feel more like an outsider than ever.

There are also multiple career adjustments to be made. Some people return with a great work opportunity, which eases the process. They might even find a good position in the same organization. But they still face the question of whether they can have an impact locally and at the same time be recognized as a global thinker. Will the work be as interesting? Will their new colleagues believe that they are loyal? Will their local networks be strong enough? And—the big one—will their organization care about what they have learned from working globally, rather than focusing on what they can do locally?

Re-entry might also be the time when a couple finds a different balance in careers. One half might need to take a sabbatical to find another professional role. It might even be his or her chance to work professionally for the first time in years. There are usually gains as well as losses.

The Backdrop of Choice Is Often Colored by Lived Experience

Some Global Cosmopolitans enjoy the sense of being an outsider. Not having to abide by the local rules or to identify with the culture can offer a feeling of freedom, as well as the distance required to learn about another way of being in the world. To a lesser or greater degree, they can feel at home in their difference. When discussing the possibility of re-entry, they balk at the loss of this comfortable—to them—position of outsider.

Others have their choice eroded by factors beyond their control. They may be unable to go home, because they place they grew up in is no longer welcoming. Or they may *have to* go home because their contracts are not renewed or their residency rights lapse when they retire. Alternatively, politics may play a part. For example, many Muslims who have lived significant parts of their lives in the USA—or even have an American passport—are confused by the rise of anti-Muslim attitudes and potential laws. Like other Global Cosmopolitans based in America, they feel they are living in a culture that is not what they bought into. EU nationals living in post-Brexit Britain are having similar reactions. But it is not just the USA and the UK. A Canadian consultant describes feeling torn apart by an incident on a recent visit 'home.'

Walking with his parents, someone leaned out of the window and shouted at them, 'Why don't you go back where you came from?' His parents had moved from China to make a home in Canada and he had been born there. He was furious but silent, since he knew that for his parents, this town would always be their home. Yet this type of incident had reproduced itself too often for him to feel that he belonged there any more. He knew that he would have to create his own home in a place where he would not feel this anger and rejection. From a position of relative privilege in terms of his professional and life options, he wanted to live and raise a family somewhere he would experience no fear of prejudice.

Thanks to the Global Cosmopolitan Mindset, ending the odyssey does not necessarily mean 'going back to where you came from.'

12

Choosing a Place to Call Home: Why Not Here?

Place is complicated. The people I talked to about creating a home had sufficient global experience to understand the importance of having roots in a place where they wanted to be. They often described the changes in perspectives on many issues as they aged or when they saw changes in their careers or in their personal relationships. Given that many key life decisions are linked to the decision of whether to stay, try a new country or go home, with each potential move, they described the need to update how they felt about the impact of aging and their changing relationship to work and the people in their lives.

'Should we settle here?' Why not let this be our home? We can have two or even three homes? Or, Maybe, will it ever be time to go home? These are the questions that maturing Global Cosmopolitans often find themselves asking. Their answers can evolve over time depending on various factors: having the requisite papers, where the children are living, a long-term career opportunity, creating a new business based in the region, or buying property as an investment. While not always set in stone, the commitment to their current location can be very strong.

It is not unusual for people to be seduced by the idea of settling in Paris, London, or another metropolitan center—or conversely somewhere calm that is a contrast to city life. Either way, the attraction is down to a feeling of being at home.

Yet, deciding on a place to call home is not necessarily straightforward. Choices become complicated by conditions that one cannot control, both personal or professional. Political concerns and attitudes toward

© The Author(s) 2018
L. Brimm, *The Global Cosmopolitan Mindset*,
https://doi.org/10.1057/978-1-349-95345-5_12

globalization can have a direct impact on how countries do business and people work on a global scale. New regulations or changes in policy or government can impact residential status or a company's workforce.

Denise and Joe had lived in Europe for 10 years before moving back to New York. They both had American and Italian passports.

After the children grew up, we started thinking about where in the world we wanted to create another home. The East Coast in the US had been the base from which we traveled for over 15 years. Given the mobility and the global nature of our work, we could really be based anywhere. We started taking longer and longer sabbaticals in different places around the world. We are both Italian Americans, so we already felt a certain affinity to Italy. We found a way to build a house, which is now our home there. I know that many people try this and are disappointed, but not us. We are living out a dream, which has even allowed both of us to take different directions with our professional lives.

After years of traveling and moving across the world, Brian and Jen, originally from South Africa, followed yet another direction. This time, they bought a home in Paris—and a second home in the south of France.

We have spent more time in France than any other country since we started traveling thirty years ago. We love South Africa and it still feels like home, even though we'll never live there. Our friends are in Europe and, in particular, in France. Our children finished secondary school here and this is where their friends and ours are now.

Meanwhile, Claire was excited about being back in Massachusetts.

I never thought that I would see the day that my French husband would want to live in the US. It's not because he loves the current president, but he loves the life he can have there. We have not lived in the US since we went to graduate school together. We decided to create the next chapter of our lives in Massachusetts, where I was just offered a great career opportunity. I also have some ideas of other projects that I will be able to work on in Boston. While my husband is officially retired, he is thrilled with this new opportunity and already sees projects that he can pursue, and people he wants to spend time with. Our daughter is living in NYC with her family, which means that we can easily spend time with them. At this stage in our lives, this has become very important.

As people age, and their children grow up, some professional opportunities re-emerge, even for people who assume that they have put down their roots once and for all.

For Lou, a senior executive, the opportunity arose for a move to Asia after several years in New York. He and his wife had enjoyed their previous experience of global travel and now, well into their 50s, the idea of moving to Asia sounded very exciting. The children were at university and she had a mobile career as an editor. They thought through the decision very carefully and decided to try it. The professional move opened new doors for Lou, but his wife found it difficult. Her friends were far away, the children found it hard to visit even during vacations, and although an editor can move, her professional support system was in the US. She also realized that she no longer enjoyed living the adventure of a global lifestyle. She decided she needed to spend time in New York, so for the first time in her married life, she moved away from Lou. The arrangement is working better for both of them. She was used to her husband's frequent absence through travel anyway. However, they know it is a temporary solution, and that they need to be creative to make sure that their time together as a couple and a family will really work out.

Choosing to settle into another country or another city can happen at various stages of life. It can be a very calculated choice based on professional opportunities for one or both partners in a long-term relationship, a choice to be near home, a choice for the education of the children, or just a choice about place.

Martin and Zeynep decided to create a home in London. He is Swedish and she is Turkish, although she grew up in Germany. They decided to move to the UK so that their children could finish their schooling and they could put down roots. They chose to live near an international school, but eventually the children, one after another, decided to go to English schools, something that Martin and his wife could not have predicted ahead of time. Or could they? He told me his own story.

As early as age 16, I wanted to get out of Norway, so I went to high school in the US as an exchange student. I grew up very quickly. I wrote home just once a week. I lived on the East Coast with a family that had just lost their son so I became the new elder brother. At dinner we talked about everything – so unlike my stiff-upper-lip background. I learned a lot about difference. I did not expect it and I liked it.

It was challenging to go home. I was different. In the US, I had learned so much that I was able to start university early. I went into the army, which was an extremely formative experience.

I married Zeynep before I went to business school. We both shared a desire to look outward and travel. My wife had had an international experience as a child. We moved around the world together.

We started out as a dual-career couple, but when we had children, Zeynep stayed home. For us, home has always been where Mom and Dad are. My wife was always ready to move – we wanted to learn languages and about different cultures. We pulled up the roots we put down six times, in Germany, France, the US, Russia, Italy, and the UK. I started six country operations in eleven years. I was Mr Fix-It.

As the children became teenagers, we decided to settle down. I still wanted to work in industry and London was my first choice. I liked the people, which is always my deciding factor. We decided to put our children in an international school. They did not spend too much time in that school, and one by one they made the decision to follow the English system. They wanted to have friends where they were planting their roots. By settling down, we changed the rules of the game and they adjusted accordingly.

Have they benefited from moving around? They are definitely global thinkers. It's hard to know what the long-term impact will be.

I believe that you need to have a place that is yours, will always be yours, and will not change too much. It gives a balance of stability to all of that change.

Elise, whom we met in Chapter 1, took the time to create a new home in the UK and settle her family before she felt ready to send her career in a new direction. Her existing Global Cosmopolitan Skillset was vital, but she also added new skills to make her vision of another new chapter in her life possible.

Ambitious, hardworking, and successful, Elise started her global journey in childhood and continued her voyage by working in multiple countries around the world. In her mid-40s, she moved with her new husband and her two children to the UK. First things first, she established a new home, helped the children integrate, and at the same time found a new way to use her skills as a consultant. In her limited free time, she also managed to go back to school herself.

Although the journey was interesting and enriching, it took Elise time to feel that some of the new threads she had been developing were starting to come together. Once she was confident that the home base she had helped to build was solid enough, and that the children were old enough to enable her to work on longer-term projects, she opened the door to opportunities that she would not have considered earlier. And they came.

Two of her consulting projects are going full steam ahead, with the first two taking her to Israel and Italy. Now she has to decide how many to take on as they come in. Her family is doing well, and with stability at home, she can travel, even though that might mean being away for a month. She has added teaching and coaching to her very full CV, finished a degree in tourism and risk, and can see possibilities for publishing parts of her Masters thesis.

Elise combined the understanding that her relational world was the first priority with the recognition that she could not let her own growth and development stop completely while she helped everyone around her to adjust to their new life. Her thirst for new skills provided her with a stepping stone to the next stage of her journey. And her devotion to her family meant that they would be ready and able to cope when the time came for her to take her career in another new direction.

Sometimes it is the Global Cosmopolitan Skillset that defines the new direction. Ilke described what it was like to move back to the UK, her husband's country of origin, after years of living in Canada. Initially, they had moved there because of the treatment that was available for their daughter's life-threatening disease.

The treatment worked and life went on in Canada, where Ilke started a new chapter developing a major tourist resort. The children returned to Europe for university and England started to feel like the family's center of gravity again. They had continued visiting the UK regularly to see family, friends, and colleagues, and now Ilke and her husband decided to return there, reconnect with their network, and look at new employment opportunities.

As a consultant, Ilke's husband made a smooth transition back to the UK. But Ilke had to create a new chapter that would work for her. She began looking for a house near London, recognizing that pulling together the threads of her professional life would take some time. She did not waste a minute getting the context of her life settled so that she could focus on what she wanted to do. At 50-something, with plenty of energy, and an excellent reputation, she was optimistic that a new entrepreneurial idea would present itself.

Six months later, the move to London had happened and house searching and family issues were time-consuming. However, they did not stop Ilke from studying. She signed up for a course in philanthropy, where she discovered social enterprise. She found an immensely creative world where businesses had goals that were about much more than making money, something she had not been aware of before she moved to England. Her willingness to begin a new chapter took Ilke in an unexpected direction, one that she now relishes.

The idea of developing a new career in your 50s might be daunting, but the Global Cosmopolitan Mindset includes the resilience and inner reserve to make such a proposition less frightening. Even so, it takes time to feel that you are really living the new chapter. Letting go of some of the old professional structures does not necessarily allow for an immediate dive into a new professional life. Enabling measures—such as working on boards, volunteering, going back to school, or trying out different possibilities—can be part of the process of change.

Akiko also decided to create her home in London.

Akiko had gone to university in Japan then moved to the US to work. She got her MBA in Boston and subsequently worked in New York and Brussels for five years. After joining her bank, she moved to London and worked in the Japanese equity department for 20 years, traveling at least three times a year to Japan.

Akiko's relationship with Japan is now relatively detached. Both her elderly parents are in residential care and she keeps in touch with her younger brother and sister and friends in Japan, whom she sees once, maybe twice, a year. Having been away from Japan so long, she feels foreign in her own country and finds many things about Japanese society strange. She and her husband have no children, so only had themselves to consider when deciding where to call home as they approached retirement. For Akiko, home is wherever they are as a couple.

They felt they could 'live anywhere', having friends who had made homes all round the world. They were drawn to Spain but did not speak the language, 'so London is the place', as she put it. They have friends there and cultural activities that both love. Akiko observed, 'Having a choice is not always easy, but it is nice.' Although Akiko does not miss full-time work, she is always open to different projects. Meanwhile, she is playing golf, learning the piano, traveling for fun and socializing a lot. 'Our friends are cosmopolitan, open minded,' she said.

Felipe and June chose Singapore.

June has moved so often that, although she was born in Singapore, she feels as much a foreigner there as Felipe, who was born in Colombia. They met while working together in Singapore but dated on six continents. Now Singapore, where June's parents live, is their home. June says Singapore allows her to be both American and Asian at the same time. Having created portfolio lives and skills they are both immersed in interesting and new professional opportunities.

For Felipe, the decision to make a home in Singapore was more complicated. He has children from a previous marriage, who were living in the US, and his mother was far away in Venezuela. But he had started getting tired of moving around the world, and when the opportunity came up to settle in Singapore he saw the potential to make it the hub for his life. His children were in university, he wanted a domestic role for himself, and he finally felt 'nowhere is as nice as here'.

Felipe does not talk about putting down roots at this stage in his life – he talks about putting out branches. Professionally, Singapore is an interesting place and he feels he can make an impact. 'Singapore is bite-sized, you can construct a life, you can move fast,' he says. In addition, 'It's easy, stuff works here.'

For June and Felipe, Singapore is the place that they can call home, not least because it allows them to feel comfortable being both insiders and outsiders.

We have seen that Global Cosmopolitans develop a range of essential and portable skills during the course of their voyage. But a new chapter, involving major change and different goals, may require new skills to supplement the old. Charles, now in his mid-50s, is settled in California, and at this point, his Global Cosmopolitan Mindset is just part of who he is.

> *In China I was completely immersed in a foreign culture and it was a life-changing experience. I had to accept to become Chinese, which helped me tremendously. I learned Mandarin and was 'reborn'. In my second year there, I was selling programs. And for four or five years afterwards, I traveled regularly to China, using my knowledge of Mandarin for negotiations.*
>
> *While I was in China one time, my father died, and my mother was not well. I decided to take an MBA in France, and although I had places at Harvard and Stanford.*
>
> *After completing the program, I was very career-oriented, and got involved in biotech. Through networking, I found a great job in one of the top three companies and was there for more than two years. But at that time, start-ups had a hard time getting funding, and there was little career movement, so I knew I needed to move to make progress.*
>
> *The next chapter was a move to London, where I stayed for five years, working for a major pharmaceutical company. In the UK, I had to adapt again. I had to play by the rules, behave, and respect distances between people. I learned that there was no simple model. I realized that I always needed to reinvent myself. Each time, I gain from it, although it is not an easy process.*
>
> *Once more, events outside my control prompted a change – my company was acquired and my mother died during this time. I decided to go to California. The early 2000s were my years for making a lot of money. I wanted to be in the forefront of technology, and I had to break the mold. I found California very different again, for instance, the unwritten rules, the need to be politically correct, the level of competition in the workplace… But I also found working there easier than in England – you did not need the correct pedigree to get a job and get ahead.*

Charles, a French entrepreneur living in California, married an American and it looked as if he would stay in the USA. His wife had not traveled as much as he had and did not speak any languages other than English. But, like many Global Cosmopolitans, Charles still feels connected to his country of origin, even after nearly 20 years in the USA. At this stage, he wants to explore how to develop possible connections that will open doors to an eventual move back home.

> *The environment in France for start-ups is very different now, and it is becoming much more exciting to develop new technologies there. I want a job that has meaning, and I can see how biotech can be good for the planet. Also, it is becoming very crowded in Silicon Valley, and the industries that I want to be involved in –*

which are for the good of the environment – are more respected in Canada and in Europe than they are here. I also share the French perspective that government should support working for a clean environment.

I'm certainly not ready to retire at 54. In the fall, I'll take a long trip to France with my wife to start bridging the culture gap. My roots are there, but it has changed since I left, and of course it will be a big change for my wife. We will have to process things, so that when the right opportunity arises, we are ready to possibly move there or at least become more actively involved there.

In his career and location choices, Charles has developed the skills he needs to adapt and grow each time he is ready to start another new chapter in his life. He also knows how to use those skills, along with the Global Cosmopolitan Mindset he has built over the years—in his personal development and relationships, as well as in the workplace. Right now, he is immersed in his company. He wants a workforce that is ready to challenge ways of thinking, recognizing that most people do not take the time to do this. He is developing techniques, debating, and brainstorming to work on giving people the time to think differently.

He has also developed an awareness of loss and how it has shaped his life. Personal loss can be a driver of change, but so too can travel. Charles believes that when you travel you lose pieces of your identity. He refers to his home village and France as his 'terroir,' an expression used most commonly in the wine industry to define the soil, rainfall, sunshine, hills, and valleys—multiple aspects that are crucial to the nature of the product. For him, there is a sense of loss if he is not contributing to his 'terroir.'

Like many Global Cosmopolitans, Charles knows there are multiple professional reasons for staying where he is right now. He also knows that he will find a creative way to start investing in his home village, starting with a summer home.

Is Home Where I Can Have the Greatest Impact?

Across a broad spectrum of individuals, young and old alike, the issue of having an impact and concerns about social responsibility arose. Recent MBA graduates raised questions about when and how to have an impact and described making choices at a relatively early stage in their lives and careers that reflected the importance of social responsibility.

Traditionally, people tended to wait until they had the power, personal resources or time—often when they retired before attempting to have   an impact in their home countries. Today, there is a new cohort—very global, very cosmopolitan, and often quite young—who want to make a difference right now, for example, by educating others, speaking out for the rights of others or through the social entrepreneurship projects that they are in a position to manage.

Pamela moved her family to Dubai after years of living and working in Europe. She is already known as an active advocate for the rights and opportunities of women in the region. She is a partner and managing director at her consulting firm.

Pamela has a bicultural background: her father is Lebanese, while her mother is English. After her undergraduate education in the UK, she went on to get a PhD in engineering. She worked in the UK and travelled extensively for her a large and prestigious multinational. After completing her MBA, she continued working in Europe, but this time in consulting.

Now she is back in Dubai, leading education and human capital development for her company in the Middle East. She takes advantage of knowing how to be different and her different levels of prestige which give her both power and opportunity in her work. As she indicated in Chapter 7, having a supportive husband and a mother who is able to come to Dubai when she needs extra help with the children are additional assets.

Pamela represents many women that recognize that they have had the privilege of a good, even outstanding, education and life experience and now feel a responsibility to other women or minorities in need of a voice. Their sense of purpose is woven through their very active professional lives. They believe that the time for them to make a difference is now. With a Global Cosmopolitan Mindset and the skills to make a difference, they often choose to return home as soon as possible.

When Mira's father went to study in the US, he took his family with him. Mira's has fond memories of her move to Houston from Kuwait as a child. She remembers that her parents helped her and her siblings adapt to the new culture, but at the same time encouraged them to demonstrate their difference. They were encouraged to show what they wore at home and why, and to be proud of their roots. For Mira, this has contributed to her ability to be proud of who she is, even if it is not always easy for others to accept, and at the same time to show how she can adapt.

After her MBA, even though it was a ticket to working anywhere in the world, Mira return to home. She is committed to leading the way for women to become leaders and bring their values to the table. She believes that her childhood experience of guided global mobility has prepared her for dealing with difference in many situations, including working as a senior woman executive in the male world of Kuwait, and as a 'local' collaborating with teams of 'foreigners'. While less global in her adult life experience than in childhood, Mira is well placed to bring what she has learned both inside and outside her country to bear on making a difference there.

Worldwide Opportunities for Impact

Stories of creating a life that fuse a sense of adventure with building a better world are emerging across the globe. These can inspire other people to see what they can do. They also demonstrate that it is possible to combine a professional career, a global lifestyle, and a sense of global responsibility.

Aarav and Sana exemplify this growing trend. They share common goals for their lifestyle, their focus, and their desire to contribute to humanitarian issues by advising on and disseminating new ways of handling serious challenges.

Currently, Aarav and Sana are living in Singapore with their son. Singapore has proven to be an excellent base for their humanitarian projects throughout the region. They see that they and their skills are portable and have particularly enjoyed the opportunity to have an impact on India, where they were born. Although they have chosen to create a home in Singapore for now, they are open to change later in their lives. They are very articulate about living in a place and creating a sense of belonging to that place. Sana's life experience has taught her that, after every decision they have made to date, they have thrived. So the decision to live here did not feel like a risk, even though they gave up a lot of security by leaving the US.

Aarav is currently working for a data intelligence company, which partners with organizations around the world to make data-driven decisions easier and more effective. With headquarters in New Delhi, their mission is to confront the world's most critical problems through data intelligence. Working with them combines a link to his Indian roots and his vision of making a difference on a global scale.

Sana, who worked as a lawyer in the US, has been able to use her legal skills and consulting ability to help create communities of dialogue with a start up in Singapore. This company is piloting some of the first circular economy projects in waste management in Asia. It is active in reducing the eight million tons of plastic that are going into our oceans yearly and building business/brand value in areas such as water, sustainable sourcing, healthcare, aging, and education.

Stan and Sara are currently based in Bangkok for similar reasons.

Both medical doctors, Stan and Sara have been able to create mobile careers, which have helped them lead lives of global adventure and impact. After leaving their home in Canada, they moved to Philadelphia and then Paris before deciding to move to Bangkok, where Sam did an Executive MBA. Sara found an opportunity to run a clinic there and has since become the Asian expert in her field. She has been treating people and contributing to groundbreaking research, as well as transforming her clinic by changing key systems.

Stan's earlier experience as a doctor gave him an opportunity to help people in the midst of trauma worldwide, flying out from his Canadian home. Today, while he has to travel more than he wants to, he is the regional medical director for corporate solutions across Asia.

Stan and Sara have created a home in Bangkok, raising their two children, and enjoying new and exciting professional opportunities. While, they do not know how long they will live there, it is their home – thanks largely to the impact they feel they are making. They are creating a sense of belonging, even if they might decide to use their talents elsewhere in the world one day.

Meanwhile, Victor, an Australian with Chinese heritage, is living with his wife in Hong Kong and living out a long-held dream.

After years of experience as a consultant, working on sustainability projects in China, getting his MBA, and then working for a strategic advisory firm in Mumbai, Victor chose to join forces with some previous colleagues to start a nonprofit dedicated to building engines of economic growth and social impact. Although the organization is headquartered in Washington, DC, Victor has chosen to live in China so that he can see the outcome of his work close-up.

Aisha has chosen to be globally minded but locally grounded. Having benefited from the best possible international education, Aisha has had an amazing global career. Her goal has increasingly been to combine her business acumen with important development projects. She is definitely not someone who looks back…

I have developed many strengths on my global journey. I was painfully shy as a child. Suddenly at university in the UK I was a woman on my own. I had to reinvent myself. When I went to the US, I had to learn how to subscribe to an American way of life and I tried to be part of the melting pot.

My MBA program was not a melting pot. Diversity was its strength and the idea of being myself was very liberating. As I gained confidence in becoming who I was, I knew that I could return to my culture.

When I came back for my work in Pakistan, I did not move back to Karachi right away. I needed a smaller city, easier to get around. Work also contributed to a professional identity and a certain freedom. We had our first daughter there and our next when we moved to Karachi, where I worked for the family business, was appointed to a number of corporate boards, and started getting more involved in the volunteer space. I was rewarded for work with European organizations. Building bridges with people from diverse backgrounds was easy. My reputation in Europe continues to grow, even though I was committed to living at home.

One of the things that I know about myself is that my best ideas come to me when I go to bed. I wonder if women are more creative, given both the constraints and opportunities that their roles in society give them. I have needed to be exceptional to be accepted. Even when I worked in NYC, female empowerment had a long way to go. Expressing some ambition can still feel threatening to many men. The good news is that women are being educated to higher and higher levels. I still believe in the importance of women having champions and I am contributing to making sure that it is happening here.

While Aisha is totally immersed in building a local life, raising her child, and developing her professional identity in Pakistan, she has used her Global Cosmopolitan Skillset to build successful relations with foreign investors—for which she has won many awards. Along with her investment in Pakistan, she is also putting time and energy into worldwide ventures that can make a difference.

Far-Reaching Impact from a Place Called Home

Many Global Cosmopolitans described their involvement in social impact projects while working in parts of the world far away from their home countries. Here are a couple of examples with global reach:

Lisa and Bob, an American couple working in Brazil, managed to start schools for children in lower-income communities, in spite of being very active parents to their three children and having very busy professional lives. They have since left Sao Paulo and their investment careers, but the projects have been very successful and have served as models for other schools around the world. While Lisa and Bob moved on, their schools have developed and they still stay in touch.

Aharon and Yael have a number of philanthropic projects, both in the USA and in Israel. They have not only given financial support but also shared their time and their expertise.

Yael described the importance of their philanthropic projects and the know-how that both of them were able to pass on to social entrepreneurs. She explained their hands-on approach as well. Every day, she is involved in projects in their two home bases, both in the U.S. and Israel, which helps both of them feel that they belong to two countries and to a global social impact community. From an outsider's point of view, they are doing well managing two 'homes'.

Yael has admitted that it is not always easy for her to live in both worlds. There are difficult moments when she leaves Israel, where she feels most at home. She hopes that one day they will be able to return permanently. For the time being, the projects in Israel help her feel more connected to the country and its challenges – and have helped her children see what they can contribute to the countries they call home.

With a Global Cosmopolitan Mindset and Skillset developed over a lifetime, many ideas emerge about what to do and where to do it. All kinds of different choices and projects can contribute to a sense of purpose or meaning in life. Often, it is these choices that define home.

13

Who Says This Is the Last Chapter?

The human life journey is changing. This is not just because so many more people are becoming Global Cosmopolitans, but also because life expectancy itself has increased so dramatically over the last half-century. Reaching the age of one hundred is becoming increasingly common. Our lives have more chapters than before—and it is up to us to write them.

In mid-life, many individuals understand they are young enough to develop different aspects of their identities and careers, wherever their global journeys take them. Whether 40, 50 or 60+, the stories in this chapter reflect the choices that they are making as they create new chapters in their lives. Many Global Cosmopolitans reconsider the meaning of home and the meaning of their lives. The decision to go home, or to create a new home, rather than settle wherever they happen to be working can be a very different type of choice than those made earlier in life. The realities can be exciting, but complicated.

One of the key assets of Global Cosmopolitans is the extent to which they have created new chapters in their lives over the years. Moves, career changes, and personal reinventions are familiar experiences—and the idea that there are always new possibilities around the corner feels normal and energizing to them. This population has been managing change across the decades and is adept at finding a balance between being global and cosmopolitan on the one hand and feeling rooted on the other.

However, when these people enter midlife, they find that the importance of having a sense of purpose is magnified, particularly if they have been busy raising children and making an intense commitment to their careers.

© The Author(s) 2018
L. Brimm, *The Global Cosmopolitan Mindset*,
https://doi.org/10.1057/978-1-349-95345-5_13

The Mid-life Transition: Three Personal Stories

Letting go of certainty and security in midlife is not easy. People do not always have the confidence, competence, support, or ability to risk making a change at this age, even though they may wonder whether they want to do something different. Many Global Cosmopolitans are able to take that leap of faith and try something different, when—to the outside world—continuing on their current path appeared to be the easier option. As they describe their decision-making, it becomes clear that, for them, this was just another step in creating a life.

For some, the preparation starts early. With enough financial stability and good health, our 50s can be a time of experimentation with ways to redesign the youthful mosaic that once defined us—or to add a whole new color to the pattern of our life.

Eva comes from a small town in Switzerland and had initially envisioned a life working for the government. Yet her love of learning and adventure, led her to make some unconventional choices. The first choice was to satisfy her curiosity by grabbing an opportunity to work in Bolivia. In spite of seeing herself as cautious, she then started to work for a major consulting firm, when there were few other women working there. It was becoming a consultant that changed everything. She suddenly realized how different life could be. She loved the challenge and the problem-solving and eventually learned how to stand up for herself.

Since then, she has made major changes in her life. Her international career in consulting started in New York and continued in Paris and London, where she married and had two children. Her career flourished, although her marriage did not.

As the children matured, she started thinking about 'what next?' She knew that she had a portfolio of skills and knowledge, but she did not know what her next developmental step should be. She took advantage of an offer to teach, even though it meant commuting and creating a whole new curriculum for the course. What might have seemed rather an unconventional choice evolved into a wonderful opportunity to expand her repertoire and develop a reputation as a leader in her field.

And yet, in spite of appearances, Eva says she really does not like change. From the outside, she seems to be an expert in personal and professional change, as well as an expert in organizational change. She also says that she is not by nature a risk-taker, but has to admit that she has taken many risks.

After getting a divorce, Eva describes her return to Switzerland after the end of her marriage: 'Re-entry – and nobody knew me. I had to build my way back. I had to earn money. I had no family around. I could see the risk of being too rootless and lonely. I needed to invest for the next five to ten years.'

She continues: 'A pivotal moment came when I had the opportunity to write a column. I knew that I could do this until I was 80. I like it. I am more confident now, and I have a real feeling for it. It has helped me build a base and be known in the Swiss business community. I focus on living with my choices. I am planting the seeds for feeling at home in my later life.'

A key aspect of making this new chapter work for Eva is making a name for herself in Switzerland. Writing, her renown as a result of her teaching and research, and her work on various boards have all contributed to her feeling at home once again. She has established herself with her business column and her local board membership. Creating a home with a man she loves has contributed significantly to her sense of well-being. She is enjoying bringing her Global Cosmopolitan Mindset home.

As she continues to teach and work on boards outside of Switzerland, she has found a balance she is enjoying. As the opportunities multiply, she tells me that her biggest challenge has been learning how to say no.

Keiko, conversely, is a woman with a mission. She is determined to bring some of her global lessons home to Japan.

With over 30 years of experience working and studying in Europe and the United States, Keiko thought long and hard about leaving her 'big golden cage' in investment banking. She was bored and tried other options, including commuting to advise an international organization, but soon realized that she wanted something else – and that was to go back to Japan and make a difference. It would mean lengthy separations from her husband, Hiro, which she knew would be painful. It was a self-made mission, and she was willing to sacrifice a few years to make it happen. The timing seemed right, her mother was aging and she wanted to be near her.

She says: 'Given that I had spent most of my adult life away from Japan, I had many ideas about bringing change to Japan. I have developed what you call a Global Cosmopolitan Mindset and I want to share that in a constructive way. I wanted to help women in business, I wanted to help create student exchanges with other countries, and I really felt that I was well placed to help Japan become more global. When I first came back, I wanted to have an impact on many things, starting with the amount of time people spend in the office. Japan did not have flexible hours. People were judged more on being at their desk rather than on their performance.'

Keiko landed in Tokyo without a job to go to, which worried her greatly, but she knew that she had transferable skills and an attitude of not giving up. In addition, she had to learn new skills and, hardest of all, she had to face her own insecurities about reading the social codes among her peers. In spite of being Japanese, she had to re-learn what home was all about. Even while she was still adjusting to being back after all these years, she took risks, first by starting to write a column for a newspaper, and then by moving to another city and becoming a professor. 'It was a terrific opportunity that has given me a lot of visibility and flexibility,' she says. 'I am also working on a government project and on a corporate board. I hope to continue writing.'

In the beginning, teaching was frightening, but she found that the students were much more appreciative than she expected. She found she could be successful by being different. Her students liked her young attitude and open mind.

'There are more changes on the horizon,' she says today. 'My teaching allows me to expand what I am doing. I can work until I am 65 at the university, so I can have five to six good years here.' Keiko has established herself as a teacher and a writer in Japan. She is involved in a number of exciting projects that she hopes will model some of the changes she would like to see in Japan. And another big change is about to happen. Hiro will be moving to Japan. He has already planned his re-entry.

As we saw with Eva, Keiko's Global Cosmopolitan Mindset and Skillset have been acquired and were her greatest assets in creating this new chapter of her life. She puts a particular emphasis on giving herself time to adapt:

One of the biggest challenges has been learning how to manage transitions. In my experience, changing career has involved living in different countries and learning new languages. Beginning is always difficult – the first three to six months is always hard. Will we stay this time? It is hard to say now. I would love to split my time between Japan and Europe. In many ways, I am very comfortable in Europe. When I was younger, I was more impatient, but look at me – I am still talking about what next!

The decisions made in midlife are often family decisions. This was the case for João, whose story is very different from that of Eva or Keiko. Leaving Silicon Valley was difficult for an entrepreneur like him, but he was highly motivated to return to Brazil with his family.

João was born in San Francisco to a Portuguese father and Brazilian mother. He lived in California for seven years before moving to Brazil, where he went to a British school. He wanted to be independent, so he moved to New York at 18 and joined the US military, which he believes was great luck. It was a much more significant choice than he had recognized at the time. He got out with an engineering degree, which helped him get the job of his dreams. His career started in the US before he decided to get his MBA. He then worked as a consultant in Asia for five years where he met his Brazilian wife. They moved back to Brazil for a while and later to California.

People often describe João as a serial entrepreneur, although he describes himself as an 'accidental entrepreneur' and 'risk-taker'. He has had, as he puts it, 'a storied career' in both large organizations and startups. He and his wife have both been moving around since childhood. Yet they are aware of the importance of having a home and 'deep-rooted connections to family and friends'. 'Like most Brazilians,' he says, they want to go home.

At 56, João says he is in 'a strange situation, with startups I thought that I had abandoned taking off.' At the same time, he adds, 'I have other projects that might have legs with banks and tech firms. I do like creating. I have a great imagination, but getting traction is hard. Once [my projects] have traction, I can create again.'

Now back in Brazil, he explains: 'I have kept the business in California, which works, although eventually we'll have to deal with the time zone difference. I have people starting to work in both places. Luckily, the younger generation is a global generation. They can work from anywhere. They take it for granted that they can work from home or in Bali.'

He continues: 'Brazil is a great place to live. It is so different. I am very happy to be back. Professionally it is challenging. Silicon Valley was special. I learned a lot. There, everyone is uber-effective with time. Here, everything takes time. On the positive side, I was competing with the best in Silicon Valley. Coming here, I have a competitive edge. But I miss my cohort group. And it was so easy to meet people from different countries and different backgrounds. I am starting to see more foreigners in São Paulo.'

As for the family, they are doing fine: 'My younger son thought it was traumatic to leave the US yet he is flourishing here. For a while, the older one was at university in Colorado. It took him two weeks to say, "Get me out of here." It was culture shock. He had gone to school in Silicon Valley, with very global kids. He is now in a graduate business degree program, and the students, like him, have already lived in other countries. I know he will soon be traveling on his own, but at least I know that it will not be out of rebellion, but out of choice. My wife is very happy. She is three blocks away from her family and close to her friends.'

João concludes: As my business evolves, I will probably have to travel more. I have a lot of really good friends in Latin America. We can get together easily, which is incredibly reassuring. I feel Brazilian. I like my projects. Let's see where they go. Being an outsider is the role that I enjoy. When you learn how to play that game, it can be quite powerful.'

Living the Change

What lessons can we learn from the stories of Eva, Keiko and João?

They—like all the seasoned travelers I talked to who were moving home—already know that with every move, there is a certain level of unpredictability. All three have an experiential understanding that changes do not always play out the way that they expect. And they all know from experience how important goals—and the motivation for those goals—need to be if they are to cope with the inevitable unpredictability.

João experienced this when a business that he thought he had laid to rest suddenly came back to life and needed his full attention. He also recounted how his concerns about his sons' resistance to the move—and giving them the space to find their own way—allowed him to discover his own motivation for life in Brazil.

Eva's story highlights her concern about creating a new reputation that will open doors, allow professional possibilities to emerge, and ensure that her opinions will have influence. This does not just happen; it comes with hard work plus stretching and expanding personal strengths.

Keiko returned to Japan with a mission. She decided that she really wanted a meaningful life at this stage, which would integrate her sense of responsibility to share what she has learned on her global journey for the betterment of Japan.

For all three, part of the process of re-entry is clarifying what the sense of belonging and feeling rooted means to them at this stage in their lives. Fears can build up over the years about the ability to belong and maintain a sense of self that has developed over decades. Will I fit in and find people who reinforce my vision of the world? The three stories show that the transition is a lot easier if you are confident about finding a new balance between your global mentality and local engagement.

These three people have made their choice from a position of strength: They have all felt successful in the previous chapters of their lives. Each one has faced difficult challenges along the way. None of them talks about having a perfect existence, but they all have the confidence that comes with having navigated other transitions successfully and having created a reputation for excellence in their professional spheres. They recognize that living the change is a fluid process that requires openness to more change and necessitates small or even large acts of creativity. Above all, they know that this takes time.

Even if a change is voluntary, there can still be a process of letting go and acknowledging loss. Feelings of loss for what you had in an earlier chapter can return unexpectedly and must be acknowledged, so that you can regain your 'I can make it' attitude. While Eva, Keiko, and João all operated with different levels of planning, they all have one thing in common: They had to *decide* to make their plans work. They all realized that there would probably be further significant chapters to come, but were prepared to take responsibility for the chapter they were currently creating.

While they knew who they were and what they could do from their previous life chapters, this was an opportunity to learn about what might be possible. This awareness of personal growth and new possibilities helped them through the difficult challenges associated with multiple beginnings—and reaffirmed their Global Cosmopolitan Mindsets.

As Keiko says, 'Try things: you have nothing to lose, but you cannot win if you do not try.' Even in the phase of adjusting to Japan, where she had not lived since she was 17, she was aware that she did not know the rules of appropriate behavior that were so crucial in that society. Nevertheless, she took risks, first to write a column for a newspaper and then to move to another city and become a professor. Both she and Eva started writing newspaper columns, something neither had done before, to cement a professional reputation. Eva continued to take advantage of learning opportunities. Similarly, João knew his next entrepreneurial projects would be difficult, but why not try? Taking creative risks was normal for him, but this time he had to commit to creating two projects at once—and finding people to help him in Brazil and in California.

For all three, their previous experiences of moving and realizing that not knowing is a part of life, helped them to persist. They had done this before and had the confidence that they could do it again. While they know that there are trade-offs—and that they cannot have everything—they also know that it is possible to have something beyond what they ever expected.

Self Awareness: Knowing What Your Reality Is Now

Attunement to our internal register of thoughts and feelings is a crucial aspect of the process of integrating change and self-knowledge and the ability to recognize and articulate personal changes are particularly relevant skills. Whatever the rationale for making a choice, living its reality can focus your attention on your feelings as you try to set a course for change.

Re-entry for Keiko meant facing the reality that she had not lived in Japan since she was a teenager. She quickly realized how insecure she felt socially, and was concerned about being accepted. She also acknowledged that in spite of all her experience, transitions were emotionally challenging for her. Eva knew that networking would be key to her successful integration, but while she was extremely skillful with people, telling her story and raising controversial points of view, she also recognized that she was an introvert who needed a lot of time to herself.

João was particularly attuned to the 'relational and contextual register.' Along with his feelings of responsibility for kick-starting his professional life in Spain, he felt a major responsibility to make it work for his family.

His goal had been for his sons to go to university in Brazil, make friends, and feel at home there. Although he was delighted to get in touch with his friends and family in Brazil and his many Latin Americans contacts, he missed the professional climate in Silicon Valley and sought out other Global Cosmopolitans to help him make the transition.

It's Never Too Late to Learn

With all of the skills that Global Cosmopolitans have developed on their voyage, there is plenty of room for the development of new abilities through a major change chapter later in life.

Keiko had never taught until her move back to Japan. She had already become bored of reusing her old skills, so she found this phase of developing new skills exciting, as well as a little frightening. Teaching also marked a new beginning for Eva. Developing herself as a star teacher gave her the confidence to expand her skillsets at home. She then became a successful columnist and learned how to be an active board member. While it is important to benefit from the skills acquired from a global life, it is important not to stop there. There is a danger of overusing skills that block you from developing.

All three stories also emphasize the importance of learning what it takes to integrate into a context that should be easy—after all, it is home. But if you have been away for many years, you no longer really know the rules of social interactions. The ideal is to turn that to your advantage. As João put it, 'I can be more effective in Brazil being the American and more effective in Silicon Valley being the Brazilian.'

Important Relationships Make a Difference

Help comes from different parts of the relational fabric, including the next generation, as they mature. Global Cosmopolitans have seen the nature of their important relationships ebb and flow over time. Many have felt the need to carefully manage their relationships given their global mobility. They have learned that relationships cannot be taken for granted and they need to pay attention to evolving needs and opportunities.

Networks evolve and so do the people in them. Taking the time to nurture these relationships is an important skill and takes time. Moving back to Brazil gave Jáao easy access to his Latin American network, while he still was still able to consult his colleagues in Silicon Valley for help. As he mentioned, he is also starting to nurture relationships with the growing population of Global Cosmopolitans in São Paulo.

As people enter their 50s, their relationships tend to evolve. Some shift their positions on the concentric circles of connections in life. Some friends and family drift away, some reunite, and new people arrive.

A partner can be particularly stressful—yet also exhilarating—for a couple. Often, a partner is the only person who has shared the journey with you, so the stress of possibly wanting different things can bring you closer together. Or it can drive you apart—if only temporarily.

As for the next generation, a move at this stage can be unsettling—even for grown-up children. They can be happy for you and at the same time as being concerned about where is home for them now. They might even feel a bit abandoned.

The connections and nature of relationships vary as much as individuals do. People invest in their relationships in very different ways. Each of the people I described here mentioned the importance of communication skills with people they encounter in their new chapters and attunement to the evolving needs of the different people in their lives.

The Global Adventure Continues

Eva, Keiko, and João all took the step to 'go home' (like the people on an 'Odyssey' in Chapter 11). But many of the 50-something Global Cosmopolitans I talked to were starting new chapters in a 'new home'—the place they had chosen to stay… or to go to next.

As people lead even longer lives, the notion of retirement is becoming moot for many, either out of economic necessity or choice. The expression itself is losing meaning and certainly does not represent the situation that many people today face as they enter their 60s and 70s or even 80s.

However, people do tend to took at their finances differently at this stage in life and for a variety of reasons feel that their next chapters are shaped by their financial constraints. Others are limited in their choices by their health and health care or by that of other members of their families.

Some of the Global Cosmopolitans I interviewed talked about the death of a husband or wife and how painfully it has impacted their choices. Yet, for the most part, they were finding pathways through the transition. Their Global Cosmopolitan Mindset had helped each of them, albeit in very different ways.

Finding what meets their changing needs or dealing with certain realities in their life when 'retirement' (or something like it) looms is seen by Global Cosmopolitans as an opportunity to continue the process of creating a life story that is consistent with their identity. Hence, they often describe their 60s as heralding opportunities to explore new possibilities and options.

Amy's husband George, who had spent his childhood in Spain with his British parents, took early retirement and they expected to start a new chapter in the UK. They had lived in Mexico, Argentina, Chile, France and Malaysia. They invested in a property and spent their vacations in England for over 30 years, but had hardly lived there. Nevertheless, they planned to call it home.

They loved their life of adventure. Wherever they had moved during George's career, Amy had been able to find work. Her credentials helped. Amy started her professional life as a computer analyst, when very few women did this. She continually upgraded her skills and rarely had trouble finding work. She knew how to create work possibilities that allowed her to grow, develop, and contribute as a professional.

After George's, 'retirement', which took place in his early 60s, they moved home. At first he said that he would play the piano and take a few on-line courses. That did not last long, and he went back to work as an interim manager, traveling throughout the UK to do so. Amy found a part-time job educating the children of immigrants, teaching them computer skills. Their own children were scattered, having decided to pursue global careers, their daughter in Mexico and their son in Malaysia.

But while Amy was happy, her husband realized that he did not have what it took to work as an interim manager and he missed the excitement of living in another culture.

Healthy and active, Amy and George realized that retirement was a concept that should be retired. At the same time, they did not want to work full time or feel burdened by too much administrative work. After all, they were now grandparents and wanted to have blocks of time to spend with their children and grandchildren.

Now another chapter is unfolding. George has had an offer to help get a company get started in Malaysia, which would mean living close to their son. While Amy enjoys her work and was starting to feel rooted in her community, as always, she is open to change. However, she has to consider what she can do in Kuala Lumpur. If she could continue teaching for a community service organization, she would be happy. Like George, she is working on the assumption that they will be there for one to two years, but they both admit that they are open to what the future might bring.

This story focuses attention on the realities of retirement. When we retire, we often say: 'We'll do this or do that—but it's too early now.' Barring issues of health and financial concerns, people who have worked for organizations that retire people at a specific age often find they are a loss at what to do at this stage. Having had exciting and demanding careers, which have structured their lives, many Global Cosmopolitans talk about the surprises they face when they suddenly have the freedom of retirement.

Even if they are happily living in the place that they call home, their attitudes toward the lack of structure and involvement can leave many unanswered questions, and they find they have to call on their creative thinking to find opportunities that will give their lives meaning. Those who come from fairly traditional backgrounds sometimes hold on to their old life scripts and retire to a place they call 'home.' But their children are almost always Global Cosmopolitans themselves and may well be living in the four corners of the globe rather than round the corner from their retired parents. Thus, it usually proves impossible to shake off the Global Cosmopolitan Mindset entirely.

Rosa was born in Buenos Aires, but moved to London with her parents and siblings at the age of eight. She still has strong roots in London, as she does in Spain, where she and her husband, Fernando, have a house, but she currently calls Miami her home.

Rosa is creating the next chapter in her life after an intriguing career that has taken her to Argentina, Spain, the UK, and the US. Now, she says, she's nearly ready to 'stop', but doesn't see that as an ending. Instead, she's looking forward to taking another chance to move her life and career in a new direction, having spent her global experience moving and growing whenever the opportunity arose.

Educated in the UK, she decided to start her career in Argentina, working for a large multinational. After four years, Rosa acknowledged that she wanted to move back to London, where her parents were, but decided to get her MBA in Boston. After graduating, she moved to Spain, with her Spanish boyfriend, and worked at another multinational. She remained working in Spain, until she took the plunge and founded her own marketing company. By this time, she was married to her Spanish boyfriend, Fernando and pregnant with her first child.

Within ten years, she had a successful business and three children. But the temptation to make another move and open another new chapter was strong. She was offered an exciting opportunity in London and Fernando easily transferred to the London office of his consulting company. Before they left, they bought a summer home in Spain. Her parents were thrilled and the children were happy to try something different.

Four years later, Fernando wanted a change and a very interesting offer came his way in Miami. Rosa was not thrilled about this move, but knew that she could easily be transferred there. Since boredom had set in at work, she decided to take advantage of the move to start another business. They bought a huge apartment so that their parents could come and visit. It took some work, but the children adjusted to new schools and a new culture. Always looking to the future, Rosa continued her education first by studying sustainable development and then coaching.

What she expected to be the last step in her career has taken her in a new direction, and now she is focusing on executive coaching and women's leadership. Having spent her early career years believing that women could progress in their careers based simply on their qualifications, she is now working on three boards, actively promoting women's leadership.

Rosa has continued to create new chapters throughout her life, using new positions and postings to expand her own knowledge and experience on her exciting Global Cosmopolitan journey. At each turning point, she has taken stock of what she already knows, and what she feels she needs to learn next. And she recognizes that the journey does not end with what is still called 'retirement' but now means so many different things to different people. Even Fernando, who talked about retiring for years, has decided to become an advisor for small business development and is teaching English to immigrant children. Rosa has multiple homes: one in the USA, another in Spain, and her parents' home in England that she shares with her siblings. She admits that she spends too much time traveling, keeping in touch with the people that make England and Spain her homes as well as Miami, but she has a lot of energy, and all of the people and the places are important to her. Each place allows her to enjoy different aspects of who she is.

While she may remain in the USA and not make another permanent move, she will continue to be a Global Cosmopolitan. In addition to traveling and reconnecting with her past experiences, she is determined to mentor and encourage younger women to pursue their careers, create their own chapters, and embark on global voyages.

The Elixir of Youth?

Discussions with Global Cosmopolitans in their 60s and 70s reflect some of the same questions that people raise at other times in their lives. Although possibly haunted by health scares and the reality of death, most of them are working as hard as ever, doing what they know best and enjoying the impact that they are having on others.

For some exercising professional know-how is more of an identity issue than a financial need; for others, the pleasure of making money and providing for their families contributes to the enjoyment of a long life. Situation permitting, however, many have started giving more attention to other aspects of life—whether spending more time with family and friends, taking special vacations, enjoying cultural activities, or dedicating more time to philanthropic interests.

It is encouraging that so many seem to have the same energy levels for trying new things: learning something totally different, tutoring refugees, or engaging in other community activities. Others simply relish having more time to enjoy the homes and relationships they have established in two or more countries. Ultimately, it is as if the Global Cosmopolitan Mindset is keeping them young.

Epilogue

Learning from Stories

While I have tried to capture in this book a number of key concepts that characterize Global Cosmopolitans, their mindsets, skillsets and the experiences that develop these qualities; I hope you have also experienced the power of life stories to convey these messages. These stories give a richer texture of the unique complexity and choices that compose their lives. Each story contributes to a deeper understanding of the experience of creating a Global Cosmopolitan life. The cumulative contribution of these stories provides an insight into the unique experience as well as the shared qualities of this group who by their very nature and growing numbers are creating a new global reality.

While their stories illustrate the challenges and complexities of composing a life that crosses significant distances and boundaries of geography and culture, they also provide a more visible view of the issues facing individuals and families who have constructed a life in a single location or have encountered issues in a single country or career.

A Guided Conversation About Personal Development

This book was designed to describe the character of Global Cosmopolitan lives and conceptualize some shared qualities that cut across the unique experiences of these individuals and their families. Yet, this format can also

© The Editor(s) (if applicable) and The Author(s) 2018
L. Brimm, *The Global Cosmopolitan Mindset*,
https://doi.org/10.1057/978-1-349-95345-5

serve as a guidebook for self-reflection in composing a life whether or not one identifies as a Global Cosmopolitan. Each chapter can serve as a guide for self-assessment, coaching or simply building supportive relationships for dealing with life concerns and choices.

Knowing your 'story' and being able to articulate your story is an essential skill for composing a life that can be developed by simply writing these reflections. It is even more powerful when expressed to a friend or colleague in a reciprocal conversation where the listener's role is to seek understanding through asking questions rather than expressing judgment of the 'goodness' of the experience. Each chapter raises issues that provide important perspectives for reflecting on one's life.

Some chapters allow reflection on the nature of past choices. Others, such as the Seven C's provide a basics for analyzing change and future choices. These concepts have proved useful not only with Global Cosmopolitans but for anyone facing life choices.

Giving people the chance to tell their stories, or part of their stories, is both a gift to them and a gift to yourself. Taking the time and the opportunity to listen to individuals' stories is an opportunity to learn. Learning about people through the stories they tell can provide depth to how you understand the world and the people in it. Learning how people create their stories can truly be fascinating. Our minds work differently, and one can see how each individual puts the pieces together in a pattern that creates a unique life story.

Creating New Chapters

Lifetime employment is increasingly a thing of the past for many people in different societies. The young Japanese student who joined a company for a lifetime of employment is becoming less the model. Large western companies like GE and Shell no longer make a commitment to anything other than a "lifetime of opportunities" some of which may be in other companies. A increasing number of people recognize that their lives and their circumstances will change over time, requiring the skills and motivations to create 'new life chapters' more than simply adjusting to minor changes. Reading or listening to stories of Global Cosmopolitans who have experienced the dilemmas and difficulties of significant changes does not give answers but offers perspectives and pictures of possibilities from their own personal experiences. Learning how to re-create oneself is increasingly a skill that people will need to develop over a lifetime. While for many people, this will not involve changing cultural contexts; but these changes will require the resilience and knowhow to create new chapters that contribute to life satisfaction.

A New World Reality

While putting the final touches to this book, I have realized that the forces for change have continued if not accelerated the rate of disruption and impact on lives of individuals. Yet periods of intense change also open up new possibilities. This is where what I have labeled the Global Cosmopolitan Mindset can play a constructive role to help people. Men and women who have experienced complex change—and see beyond the immediate difficulty of what is to a more positive identification of what can be—are the people the world needs to lead new global initiatives.

But the composing of new life chapters is facilitated in a context that promotes problem solving and choices by individuals. Key institutions have important roles to play in assisting individuals through these difficult transitions.

First, large businesses need to develop the capacity to identify and recognize the positive competence and contribution of their Global Cosmopolitans. These individuals represent models for operating in the new, ever-changing world and need to be recognized as such. This is not to argue that all people should become Global Cosmopolitans but rather to recognize the unique contribution provided by this subset of the population. As businesses talk about re-training those whose work has disappeared because of technology, there needs to be attention to the other aspects of change and transition well understood by the Global Cosmopolitans in the organization. The unique experience and skills of the Global Cosmopolitans need to be captured and integrated into the human resource information systems in order to retain these unique resources and use them wisely, not just as another "worker."

Similarly, investors and private equity groups need to recognize the unique capability for entrepreneurship exhibited by many of the Global Cosmopolitans in the stories in this book. Seeing these individuals as "uniquely experienced" rather than "itinerant," "opportunistic careers" rather than "unplanned" ones should allow more positive views of the "start up" mentality that they have exhibited in their lives.

Finally, starting much earlier in the educational systems of each country, a celebration of the contribution of diversity as opposed to a singular focus on adaptation and integration allows an early background for those who choose (or are cast into) global careers.

While nationalism emerges in some locations as a resistance to globalization, it is clear that some issues of trade, immigration and climate transcend any one country and its ability to resolve these problems alone. The Global Cosmopolitans who have obtained experience in moving skillfully across borders are a major source of energy and expertise to build the coalitions that can address such cross national, cross cultural issues.

Every New Generation Brings New Possibilities

Labels such as Millennials, Gen X and Gen Y have tried to capture the differences in age groups entering this changing world of career and family. The notion of generations has long been a way of capturing generalizations about age groups and their response to major world events. While not precise distinctions, generations capture a sense of the orientations of age groups responding to global trends or a significant event (e.g. war, new technology, etc.) Most significantly, the accelerating pace of change has shortened significantly the time span of what one would call a generation, creating the iconic "generation gaps" at shorter intervals with smaller sub groups. Whatever their age or generation, they are a force to be reckoned with. The name I choose to give that force is the Global Cosmopolitan Mindset.

What Next?

Ending this book is particularly challenging for me as I know that there are so many more stories out there that would provide further insights into the creation of new life chapters. I am struck by the skill of Global Cosmopolitans as they move from one opportunity to another often crossing borders of culture and geography.

End Notes

Chapter 1: Introduction

1. To ensure anonymity, I have used pseudonyms for all participants in my research study. In addition, some details of their lives, such as nationality or where they have lived or worked, have been altered or not included.

2. Linda Brimm, *Global Cosmopolitans: The Creative Edge of Difference* (London: Palgrave Macmillan, 2010). This book gives an introduction to Global Cosmopolitanism from the perspective of a younger population, mainly those undertaking MBA programs—complemented by chapters from the next decade of their life stories. Many Global Cosmopolitans have found the naming of this phenomenon extremely powerful, as it provides a way to frame their experience and potential for leading change in organizations.

3. The young professionals currently considering global lives are from the generation often referred to as Millennials or Generation Y. From Wikipedia on November 1, 2017: 'Millennials are the demographic cohort following Generation X. There are no precise dates for when this cohort starts or ends; demographers and researchers typically use the early 1980s as starting birth years and the mid-1990s to early 2000s as ending birth years.' My colleague, Henrik Bresman, from INSEAD has written about Millennials from an international perspective: https://hbr.org/2015/02/what-millennials-want-from-work-charted-across-the-world.

4. While people have different perspectives on the future of work, I have found this recent report on talent mobility from PwC quite helpful: https://www.pwc.com/gx/en/managing-tomorrows-people/future-of-work/pdf/pwc-talent-mobility-2020.pdf. While the challenges of global mobility

© The Editor(s) (if applicable) and The Author(s) 2018
L. Brimm, *The Global Cosmopolitan Mindset*,
https://doi.org/10.1057/978-1-349-95345-5

are constantly evolving with changes in the political and economic climate, there are some challenges that remain more or less the same.

5. The narrative approach to understanding identity is the basis of my research. Stories that begin to capture the richness of how people experience and understand their lives will be used throughout this book. The stories used for this book are far from complete, but they are illustrative examples. A good introduction to the narrative approach is: Dan McAdams, 'Personality, Modernity, and the Storied Self: A Contemporary Framework for Studying Persons', *Psychological Inquiry 7,* no. 4 (1996): 295–321.

6. Robert Coles, *The Call of Stories: Teaching and the Moral Imagination* (Boston, MA: Houghton, Mifflin Company, 1989). Long before he wrote this book, I had the opportunity to have Robert Coles supervise my attempts to help a group of returning veterans from the Vietnam War, when I was in my early 20s. I was overwhelmed with the difference of their life experience, and lacking the knowledge we now have about trauma, but his advice to me was simple and powerful: 'Listen, let them tell their stories.' His belief that listening to stories promotes learning and discovery had a major impact on me.

7. Historically, there have been many accounts of people living in very different cultures, and in that sense, Global Cosmopolitans are not a new phenomenon. Accounts of people living in different parts of the globe have helped us understand history and the impact of context on people over time. There are many memoirs or works of fiction that I have also read to put into a historical perspective the recent experiences of Global Cosmopolitans that I have interviewed.

Part I: Learning from a Global Life

Chapter 2: The Global Cosmopolitan Mindset

1. Learning and The Growth Mindset: Carol Dweck, *Mindset: The New Psychology of Success* (New York: Ballantine Books, 2016). Dweck's book was written with education in mind, yet it captures the importance that Global Cosmopolitans place on having a life that allows learning and growth.

2. There is a chapter by Noel Tichy, Michael Brimm, Ram Charan, and Hirotaka Takeuchi that describes a global mindset in Vladimir Pucik, Noel M. Tichy, and Carole K. Barnett (Editors), *Globalizing Management: Creating and Leading the Competitive Organization* (New York: John Wiley & Sons, Inc., 1992). There is an elaborate

description of a global mindset in Paul Evans, Vladimir Pucik, and Ingmar Björkman, *The Global Challenge: International Human Resource Management,* 3rd Edition (Chicago: Chicago Business Press, 2010).

3. Ed Schein wrote about the important group dynamic in the fourth edition of *Organizational Culture and Leadership* (San Francisco: Jossey Bass, 1992). He particularly describes collective attempts to address two sets of group issues: external threats and internal integration.

4. Mihaly Csikszentmihalyi has written extensively on connecting complexity to creativity in, for example, *Flow and the Psychology of Discovery and Invention* (New York: Harper Perennial Modern Classics, 2008).

5. Warren Bennis's original studies of leadership emphasized the importance of learning and how learning is based on experience. See his classic book, *On Becoming a Leader,* 4th Edition (New York: Basic Books, 2009).

6. *Financial Times Lexicon.* http://lexicon.ft.com/Term?term=global-mindset (accessed November 12, 2017).

7. Howard Gardner has written a number of books about how our minds work, including, *Changing Minds: The Art and Science of Changing Our Own and Other People's Minds* (Cambridge, MA: Harvard Business School, 2004).

Chapter 3: The Global Cosmopolitan Skillset

1. Neuroscience has contributed to considerably to our understanding of the different ways our minds work. Two books that I have found informative and helpful on the topic of neuroplasticity and cognitive complexity are: Norman Doidge, *The Brain that Changes Itself* (London: Penguin Books, 2007); and Daniel J. Siegal, *The Developing Mind, Second Edition: How Relationships and the Brain Interact to Shape Who We Are* (New York: The Guilford Press, 2012).

2. In Linda Brimm, *Global Cosmopolitans: The Creative Edge of Difference* (London: Palgrave Macmillan, 2010), I named skills that I noticed in this population. I have returned to certain skills here, either because they have been particularly useful for people over time or because they are skills that particularly evolve over time. They include peripheral vision, which I based on the work of Mary Catherine Bateson, *Peripheral Visions: Learning Along the Way* (New York: HarperCollins Publishers, 1994). I also went into depth about the two-edged swords of mobility in my previous book.

3. IGI Global attempts to define cognitive flexibility as 'the ability to spontaneously restructure one's knowledge, in many ways, in adaptive response to radically changing situational demands.' See IGI Global Disseminator of Knowledge: https://www.igi-global.com/dictionary/cognitive-flexibility/4215 (accessed November 12, 2017).

4. In this book, I have not gone into depth about knowledge of culture and understanding how to navigate across cultural differences. Two books that I would recommend include: Erin Meyer, *The Culture Map: Breaking Through the Invisible Boundaries of Global Business* (New York: Public Affairs, 2014); and Andy Molinsky, *Global Dexterity, How to Adapt Your Behavior across Cultures without Losing Yourself in the Process* (Boston: Harvard Business Review Press, 2013). There is a growing library of books and articles on this area, including many by my colleagues at INSEAD.

Part II: Composing a Global Life: Navigating the Challenges and Benefits Along the Way

Chapter 4: Who Am I? Identity and the Global Cosmopolitan

1. Erik Erikson's classic on developmental theory, originally published in 1959, is *Identity and the Life Cycle* (New York: W.W. Norton and Co., 1994).

2. Parents have found this well-worth reading: David C. Pollock, and Ruth E. Van Reken, *Third Culture Kids: Growing Up Among Worlds* (Cambridge, MA: Nicholas Brealey Publishing, 2009).

3. There are a number of classics that I have found useful over the years when looking at the issue of identity development.

   - Carl Rogers, *On Becoming a Person: A Therapist's View of Psychotherapy* (New York: Houghton Mifflin Company, 1961).
   - Viktor Frankl, *Man's Search for Meaning* (Boston: Beacon Press, 2006).
   - Maslow's hierarchy of needs is described in Abraham H. Maslow, 'A Theory of Human Motivation', *Psychological Review* 50, no. 4 (1943).
   - Hazel Markus, and Paula Nurius, 'Possible Selves', *American Psychologist* 41, no. 9 (1986): 954–969.

In addition, Dan McAdams and Ruthellen Josselson have written extensively on development of identity and the narrative study of lives. See in particular: Dan P. McAdams, *The Art and Science of Personality Development* (New York: The Guilford Press, 2015); and Dan P. McAdams, Ruthellen Josselson, and Amia Lieblich (Editors), *Identity and Story: Creating Self in Narrative* ('Narrative Study of Lives' series) (Washington, DC: American Psychological Association, 2006).

Finally, the following handbooks are useful source material on Identity:

- Kate C. McLean, and Moin Syed, *The Oxford Handbook of Identity Development* (Oxford: Oxford University Press, 2016).
- Veronica Benet-Martinez, Veronica, and Ying Yi Hong, *The Oxford Handbook of Multicultural Identity* (Oxford: Oxford University Press, 2014).
- Shinobu Kitayama, and Dov Cohen, *Handbook of Cultural Psychology* (New York: The Guilford Press, 2010).

Chapter 5: The Professional Me

I have written a number of short articles about the professional identity of Global Cosmopolitans. For example, INSEAD Knowledge (https://knowledge.insead.edu) has published a number of my articles and blogs over the years. See also a brief online article on hbr.org, 'What the Best Cross-Cultural Managers Have in Common by Linda Brimm' (https://hbr.org/2016/06/what-the-best-cross-cultural-managers-have-in-common).

I have often shared Ed Schein's work with people looking at their professional identity including a book that he published with John Van Maanen, *Career Anchors* (San Francisco: John Wiley and sons, 2013). Ed Schein continues to contribute excellent work, including his latest, *Humble Consulting: How to Provide Real Help Faster* (Oakland, CA: Berrett-Koehler Publishers, Inc., 2016). His classic work, *Process Consultation* (Reading, MA: Addison-Wesley, 1969), is still a valuable resource for me.

Two other useful books on professional identity are Herminia Ibarra's *Working Identity* (Boston: Harvard Business Review Publishing, 2004) and *Act Like A Leader, Think Like A Leader* (Boston: Harvard Business Review Publishing, 2015).

Chapter 6: The Relational Me

I have found two books on a relational perspective of identity development particularly useful. This book highlights the importance of relationships in the development of identity: Christina Robb, *This Changes Everything: The Relational Revolution in Psychology* (New York: Farrar, Straus & Giroux, 2006).

This book explores the history, theory, and practice of a relationship-centered, culturally oriented form of therapy, with a strong emphasis on the impact of isolation: Judith Jordan, *Relational-Cultural Therapy* (Washington, DC: American Psychological Association, 2010).

There are also many books on attachment theory. The classic is John Bowlby's *Attachment*, which is itself the subject of a more recent book by Jeremy Holmes: *John Bowlby and Attachment Theory* (London: Routledge, 1993).

Chapter 7: Making It Work as a Global Cosmopolitan Couple

While books are helpful, psychological support for creating a relationship that can withstand the challenges of living in different cultures is often crucial. Many large organizations actively propose support services to ease transitions.

While there are many theories and books out there, I have found this one particularly useful: Douglas Stone and Bruce Patton, *Difficult Conversations: How to Discuss What Matters Most* (New York: Viking Penguin, 1999).

1. I have used the term 'becoming an ex' to describe multiple aspects of this phenomena. It is based on Helen Fuchs Ebaugh's *Becoming an Ex: The Process of Role Exit* (Chicago: University of Chicago Press, 1988).

Chapter 8: Raising the Next Generation

As previously mentioned (in the notes to Chapter 2), this book is a classic and well-worth reading: David C. Pollock & Ruth E. Van Reken, *Third Culture Kids: Growing Up Among Worlds* (Cambridge, MA: Nicholas Brealey Publishing, 2009). Another classic on building resilience is: Michael and Marjorie Rutter, *Developing Minds: Challenge and Continuity Across The Life Span* (New York: Penguin Books, 1993).

Chapter 10: Embracing Complex Change

In this book, I have built on what I wrote previously about change in *Global Cosmopolitans: The Creative Edge of Difference.* I have also written a number of short articles since the publication of that book in 2010. These include:

'Embracing Complex Change' in *Harvard Business Review,* September 2015 (https://hbr.org/2015/09/how-to-embrace-complex-change).

An earlier version of Amy and Jeff's story was published in INSEAD Knowledge in May 2016 (http://knowledge.insead.edu/career/embracing-the-complexity-of-global-mobility-4670).

1. First published in 1980, this book is a classic whose framework continues to be helpful: William Bridges, *Transitions, Making Sense of Life's Changes* (Cambridge, MA: Da Capo Press, 2004). A very useful book when you are stuck is Robert Kegan and Lisa Laskow Lahey's, *Immunity to Change* (Boston: Harvard Business School Press, 2009).

Part III: Creating New Chapters in an Already Interesting Life

1. Robert Frost, 'The Road Not Taken', https://www.poetryfoundation.org/poems/44272/the-road-not-taken.

Chapter 11: The Global Cosmopolitan Odyssey

This is a great example of information on aging and the new reality that people are experiencing: Lynda Gratton and Andrew Scott, *The 100-Year Life: Living and Working in an Age of Longevity* (London: Bloomsbury, 2016).

1. Daniel Mendelsohn's translation of *Complete Poems by C.P. Cavafy* (New York: Alfred A. Knopf, 2012).

Epilogue

For the first version of these ideas, see my letter in: Thinkers50, *Dear CEO 50 Personal Letters from the World's Leading Business Thinkers* (London: Bloomsbury, 2017).

Acknowledgements

Writing a book is an opportunity to learn, and there have been so many people who have helped me to do just that. This book is my opportunity to share what I have learned. I owe a tremendous debt of gratitude to each person who helped me.

Global Cosmopolitans have such thought-provoking stories to tell, so gathering their stories was a pleasure and a fascinating way to learn. I want to thank all of the men and women who participated in my study of Global Cosmopolitans and contributed to the development of this book *Global Cosmopolitan Mindset: Lessons from the New Global Leaders*. Their insights and stories have been invaluable and I appreciate their openness and their trust in me.

I also want to thank my ex-students and the people whom I interviewed for my first book, *Global Cosmopolitans: The Creative Edge of Difference*. Many of them have kept me up to date on their Global Cosmopolitan lives and have shared with me precious information about the development of people's lives and careers and what it means to have a global lifestyle.

In addition, I want to thank *all* the wonderful students I have taught over the years. Learning about people from all over the world has contributed to a broad and deep perspective on what it means to be a Global Cosmopolitan. By sharing their stories, their ideas and their questions, they have taught me so much about how people develop over time and, in particular, what it means to have a Global Cosmopolitan Mindset.

Continual motivation to share my research comes from new classes of students at INSEAD, as they question whether they should embark on global lives. They ask very astute questions that often go to the heart of the reality

© The Editor(s) (if applicable) and The Author(s) 2018
L. Brimm, *The Global Cosmopolitan Mindset*,
https://doi.org/10.1057/978-1-349-95345-5

of global living—and leaving home, losing friends, raising children, and evolving as people as a result of the Global Cosmopolitan experience.

Similarly, each time I had an opportunity to share my ideas about the Global Cosmopolitan Mindset, wherever I was in the world, I found people who were happy to share their personal stories, questions, and encouraging comments with me. My thanks go out to all of them.

I used pseudonyms for all of the people who participated in this research study to guarantee anonymity. In addition, I changed certain details in their lives, such as where they have lived and live now. You will notice that I have also left out details of their career history or where they are currently working.

At each step along the way, many other people have gone out of their way to make this journey of researching and writing this book easier.

The alumni relations team at INSEAD helped me expand the circle of successful Global Cosmopolitans in my study and was particularly helpful in putting me in touch with people who are making a difference and creating interesting lives within the alumni community. Chris Howells, editor of INSEAD Knowledge (knowledge.insead.edu), has encouraged and helped me to communicate to a larger circle as well. The online interest has been so inspiring.

Thank you to Stuart Crainer and Des Dearlove from Thinkers50, who encouraged me to write this book and helped with my initial proposal. Your incredible ability to listen, to hear, and then to express my ideas better than I could at the time was quite remarkable.

Thank you, Alison Beard, for contacting me and helping me communicate my ideas about embracing complex change and Global Cosmopolitans in the Harvard Business Review. Encouraging comments from people who read the articles contributed to my motivation to share my thoughts with an even larger circle of people.

Stephen Partridge from Palgrave Macmillan, thank you for encouraging my book proposal and all of your support. Knowing you were there, with encouraging comments along the way, was extremely useful.

I cannot thank Elin Williams, the writer and editor, enough. She came to my rescue and helped me give a final edit for this book. While she would have loved more time to improve my book even further, I think that she did a marvelous job. She helped me communicate my author's voice and at the same time was sensitive to the tone of the stories shared. Her own life experience and her work with people at INSEAD have certainly given her a perspective on the subject. The sense of trust I had in her understanding and communication of my material was essential.

I am lucky to have a very supportive and encouraging family. Observing my children and grandchildren has motivated me to be articulate about what I have learned about Global Cosmopolitans. It is always hard to have a perspective on your own family, yet I do believe that Tracy and Benjamin have benefited from their global experiences, see the world with Global Cosmopolitan Mindsets, and navigate their lives with the skills and knowledge they have developed along the way. It is magical watching them raise their own children and exciting to see how they transmit their attitudes, knowledge, and skills. Exhausting as it can be to raise young families, they are ever careful to communicate their values, which gives me a great sense of pride. And Flavia, Benjamin's wife, has added a Peruvian flavor to our lives and to our food. She has joined us in sharing the basic values, attitudes, and skills from her global journey and background.

Michael Brimm, my husband, has been my biggest supporter, particularly at the times when I got distracted by other projects, reminding me that this book was worth writing. He has a deep understanding of what it means to be a Global Cosmopolitan, so I can rely on him to be my biggest enthusiast, but also my biggest critic. If my thinking is not clear, he is the first one to let me know with thoughtful, honest, and constructive feedback.

Index

© The Editor(s) (if applicable) and The Author(s) 2018
L. Brimm, *The Global Cosmopolitan Mindset*,
https://doi.org/10.1057/978-1-349-95345-5

Printed by Printforce, the Netherlands